Introduction to Supply Chain Management

Robert B. Handfield

Associate Professor of Purchasing and Operations Management
Department of Marketing and Supply Chain Management
The Eli Broad Graduate School of Management, Michigan State University

Ernest L. Nichols, Jr.

Associate Professor of Operations Management, Decision Sciences Area, and
Director of FedEx Center for Cycle Time Research
Fogelman College of Business and Economics
The University of Memphis

PRENTICE HALL, Upper Saddle River, New Jersey 07458

Acquisitions Editor: Tom Tucker
Editorial Assistant: Melissa Back
Editor-in-Chief: Natalie Anderson
Marketing Manager: Debbie Clare
Production Coordinator: Maureen Wilson
Managing Editor: Dee Josephson
Manufacturing Buyer: Diane Peirano
Manufacturing Supervisor: Arnold Vila
Manufacturing Manager: Vincent Scelta
Design Manager: Patricia Smythe
Cover Design: Bruce Kenselaar
Composition: Omegatype Typography, Inc.

Copyright © 1999 by Prentice-Hall, Inc.
A Simon & Schuster Company
Upper Saddle River, New Jersey 07458

Library of Congress Cataloging-In-Publication Data
Handfield, Robert B.
    Introduction to supply chain management / Robert B. Handfield,
    Ernest L. Nichols.
        p.   cm.
    Includes bibliographical references and index.
    ISBN 0-13-621616-1
    1. Business logistics.   2. Delivery of goods—Management.
I. Nichols, Ernest L.   II. Title.
HD38.5.H36   1999
658.7—dc21   98-14603
                                                    CIP

Prentice-Hall International (UK) Limited, London
Prentice-Hall of Australia Pty. Limited, Sydney
Prentice-Hall Canada, Inc., Toronto
Prentice-Hall Hispanoamericana, S.A., Mexico
Prentice-Hall of India Private Limited, New Delhi
Prentice-Hall of Japan, Inc., Tokyo
Simon & Schuster Asia Pte. Ltd., Singapore
Éditora Prentice-Hall do Brasil, Ltda., Rio de Janeiro

Printed in the United States of America

10 9 8 7

To Sandi
RBH

To Christine, John, Megan, and Katie
ELN

Contents

Preface   vii

CHAPTER 1:   Introduction to Supply Chain Management   1

Information Systems and Supply Chain Management   6
Inventory Management across the Supply Chain   7
Supply Chain Relationships   9
Challenges Facing Supply Chain Managers   12
Purpose of the Book   13

**CHAPTER 2:   The Role of Information Systems and Technology
in Supply Chain Management**   14

Introduction   14
The Importance of Information in an Integrated Supply Chain
     Management Environment   15
Interorganizational Information Systems   19
Information Requirements Determination for a Supply Chain IOIS   21
Information and Technology Applications for Supply
     Chain Management   28
Summary   38

**CHAPTER 3:   Managing the Flow of Materials
across the Supply Chain**   40

Introduction   40
Understanding Supply Chains   41
Reengineering Supply Chain Logistics   46
The Importance of Time   53
Performance Measurement   61
Summary   65

**CHAPTER 4: Developing and Maintaining Supply
            Chain Relationships**   67

A Conceptual Model of Alliance Development   69

Developing a Trusting Relationship with Partners
    in the Supply Chain   83

Resolving Conflicts in a Supply Chain Relationship   89

Summary   93

CHAPTER 5: Cases in Supply Chain Management   94

Case One Consumable Computer Supplies   94

Case Two Computer Hardware and Software   100

Case Three Upscale Men's Shoes   106

Case Four Biochemicals   123

Case Five Solectron   138

CHAPTER 6: Future Challenges in Supply Chain Management   153

Sharing Risks in Interorganizational Relationships   154

Managing the Global Supply Chain   156

The "Greening" of the Supply Chain   159

Design for Supply Chain Management   166

Intelligent Information Systems   171

When Things Go Wrong   173

Index   177

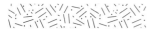

Preface

Integrated supply chain management is becoming recognized as a core competitive strategy. As organizations continuously seek to provide their products and services to customers faster, cheaper, and better than the competition, managers have come to realize that they cannot do it alone; rather, they must work on a cooperative basis with the best organizations in their supply chains in order to succeed.

This book shares insights gained from our research, which has brought us in contact with managers in engineering, purchasing, operations, logistics, information systems, and sales functions across a range of industries. These experiences have been synthesized to create a managerial perspective of the core tasks and challenges required to effectively manage supply chains. This text is unique in that it describes a phenomenon that has been rapidly evolving. Although other books have dealt with the individual processes associated with developing new products, buying materials, transforming them, and shipping them to customers, none has specifically dealt with the integration of information and material flows across multiple organizations in the supply chain.

Because supply chain management involves all functions within organizations, this book has been written for a general audience and provides insights into the conceptual foundations of supply chain management. It also presents a topical discussion of what a supply chain is, why it is important, and what types of challenges are implicit in managing supply chains. Because the text is relatively short, it can be employed as an "add-in" to undergraduate or M.B.A. classes in strategy, management, or marketing. The text is also well suited to educational programs for practitioners.

In sum, this book will enable readers to better understand:

- The impact of supply chain management on the success and profitability of the modern organization;
- The influence of integrated supply chain management on major functional activities, including product design, information systems, manufacturing planning and control, inventory management, human resource development, financial planning, forecasting, sales, quality management, and many other areas; and
- The major challenges faced in implementing an integrated supply chain management strategy, as well as approaches for meeting these challenges.

Acknowledgments

The authors wish to acknowledge Christian Bechtel, Yongbiao Chang, Mark Frolick, Terrence Gable, Amy Morgan, and Donna Retzlaff-Roberts for their contributions to the development of this book. We also wish to thank Mohammad Amini, Mark Gillenson, Brian Janz, and Christine Nichols for reviewing the manuscript and their valuable suggestions. Support provided by Jim Wetherbe and the FedEx Center for Cycle Time Research at The University of Memphis and by Robert Monczka and the Global Procurement and Supply Chain Benchmarking Initiative at Michigan State University is also appreciated. Finally, we are both very grateful for the ongoing support of our families.

Robert B. Handfield
Ernest L. Nichols, Jr.

About the Authors

Robert B. Handfield is Associate Professor of Purchasing and Operations Management at Michigan State University. He received a Ph.D. in operations management from the University of North Carolina at Chapel Hill. His research combines qualitative and structural modeling approaches to the study of time-based competition, quality and environmental management, and strategic sourcing. He is associate editor of the *Journal of Operations Management* and serves on the editorial review board of *Decision Sciences*. He has co-authored two NSF grants, and is Co-Director of the MSU Annual Executive Purchasing Seminar.

Ernest L. Nichols, Jr. is Associate Professor of Operations Management and Director of the FedEx Center for Cycle Time Research in the Fogelman College of Business and Economics at The University of Memphis. He received a Ph.D. in purchasing and operations management from Michigan State University. His research interests include a range of integrated supply chain management issues. He is senior associate editor of *Cycle Time Research*.

CHAPTER 1

Introduction to Supply Chain Management

Managers in the last two decades have witnessed a period of change unparalleled in the history of the world, in terms of advances in technology, globalization of markets, and stabilization of political economies. With the increasing number of "world-class" competitors both domestically and abroad, organizations have had to improve their internal processes rapidly in order to stay competitive. In the 1960s–1970s, companies began to develop detailed market strategies, which focused on creating and capturing customer loyalty. Organizations also realized that strong engineering, design, and manufacturing functions were necessary in order to support these market requirements. Design engineers had to be able to translate customer needs into product and service specifications, which then had to be produced at a high level of quality and at a reasonable cost. As the demand for new products escalated in the 1980s, manufacturing organizations were required to become increasingly flexible and responsive to modify existing products and processes or to develop new ones in order to meet ever-changing customer needs. As manufacturing capabilities improved in the 1990s, managers realized that material and service inputs from suppliers had a major impact on their organizations' ability to meet customer needs. This led to an increased focus on the supply base and the organization's sourcing strategy. Managers also realized that producing a quality product was not enough. Getting the products to customers when, where, how, and in the quantity that they want, in a cost-effective manner, constituted an entirely new type of challenge. More recently, the era of the "Logistics Renaissance" was also born, spawning a whole set of time-reducing information technologies and logistics networks aimed at meeting these challenges.[1]

As a result of these changes, organizations now find that it is no longer enough to manage their organizations. They must also be involved in the management of the network of all upstream firms that provide inputs (directly or indirectly), as well as the network of downstream firms responsible for delivery and after-market service of

---

[1] *World Class Logistics: The Challenge of Managing Continuous Change,* prepared by The Global Logistics Research Team, Michigan State University (Oak Brook, IL: Council of Logistics Management, 1995).

the product to the end customer. From this realization emerged the concept of the "supply chain." For purposes of this book, we define the terms *supply chain* and *supply chain management* as follows:

> The *supply chain* encompasses all activities associated with the flow and transformation of goods from the raw materials stage (extraction), through to the end user, as well as the associated information flows. Material and information flow both up and down the supply chain.
>
> *Supply chain management* (SCM) is the integration of these activities through improved supply chain relationships, to achieve a sustainable competitive advantage.

If we consider an individual firm within the context of this definition, we must include both its upstream supplier network and its downstream distribution channel (see Figure 1-1). In this definition, the supply chain includes the management of information systems, sourcing and procurement, production scheduling, order processing, inventory management, warehousing, customer service, and after-market disposition of packaging and materials. The supplier network consists of all organizations that provide inputs, either directly or indirectly, to the focal firm. For example, an automotive company's supplier network includes the thousands of firms that provide items ranging from raw materials such as steel and plastics, to complex assemblies and subassemblies such as transmissions and brakes. As shown in Figure 1-1, the supplier network may include both internal divisions of the company as well as external suppliers. A given material may pass through multiple processes within multiple suppliers and divisions before being assembled into a vehicle. A supplier for this company has its own set of suppliers that provide inputs (called second-tier suppliers) that are also part of this supply chain. The beginning of a supply chain inevitably can be traced back to "Mother Earth"; that is, the ultimate original source of all materials that flow through the chain (e.g., iron ore, coal, petroleum, wood, etc.). Supply chains are essentially a series of linked suppliers and customers; every customer is in turn a supplier to the next downstream organization until a finished product reaches the ultimate end user.

It is important to note that from the focal firm's perspective, the supply chain includes internal functions, upstream suppliers, and downstream customers. A firm's *internal functions* include the different processes used in transforming the inputs provided by the supplier network. In the case of an automotive company, this includes all of its parts manufacturing (e.g., stamping, power train, and components), which are eventually brought together in their final assembly operations into actual automobiles. The coordination and scheduling of these internal flows is very challenging, particularly in a large organization such as an automotive company (see Figure 1-1). For example, order-processing managers are responsible for translating customer requirements into actual orders, which are input into the system. In the case of an automotive company, these individuals work primarily with the extensive dealer network to ensure that the right mix of automobiles, spare parts, and service parts are available so that dealers can meet the needs of their customers. Order processing may also involve extensive customer interaction, including quoting prices, possible delivery dates, delivery arrangements, and after-market service. Another important internal function is production scheduling, which translates orders into actual production tasks. This may involve working with materials

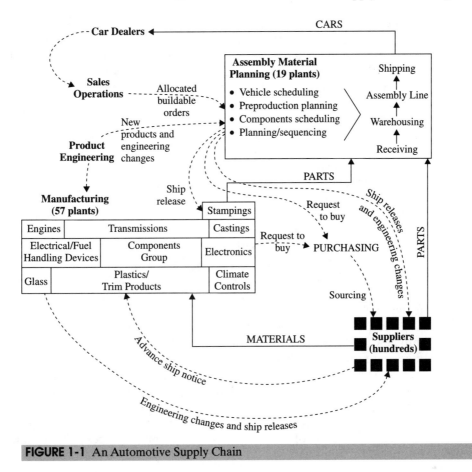

FIGURE 1-1 An Automotive Supply Chain

requirements planning (MRP) systems, scheduling work centers, employees, and maintenance on machines.

The second major part of supply chain management involves the management of *upstream external* supply chain members. In order to manage the flow of materials between all of the upstream organizations in a supply chain, firms employ an array of managers who ensure that the right materials arrive at the right locations, at the right time. Purchasing managers are responsible for ensuring that (1) the right suppliers are selected, (2) they are meeting performance expectations, (3) appropriate contractual mechanisms are employed, and (4) a good relationship is maintained with these suppliers. They may also be responsible for driving improvement in the supply base and acting as a liaison between suppliers and other internal members (engineering, accounting, etc.). Materials managers are responsible for planning, forecasting, and scheduling material flows between suppliers in the chain. Materials managers work closely with production schedulers to ensure that suppliers are able to deliver the materials on time to the required locations, and that they have some advance warning regarding upcoming requirements so that they can plan ahead of actual production and delivery dates.

Finally, a firm's *external downstream* supply chain encompasses all of the downstream distribution channels, processes, and functions that the product passes through on its way to the end customer. In the case of an automotive company's distribution network, this includes its finished goods and pipeline inventory, warehouses, dealer network, and sales operations (see Figure 1-1). This particular distribution channel is relatively short. Other types of supply chains may have relatively small internal supply chains but fairly long downstream distribution channels. For instance, Figure 1-2 shows the supply chain for a cereal manufacturer, and the extensive distribution network involved in getting the packaged cereal to the final customer. Within the downstream portion of the supply chain, logistics managers are responsible for the actual movement of materials between locations. One major part of logistics is transportation management, involving the selection and management of external carriers (trucking companies, airlines, railroads, shipping companies) or internal private fleets of carriers. Distribution management involves the management of packaging, storing, and handling of materials at receiving docks, warehouses, and retail outlets.

An important new trend in supply chain management is the recovery, recycling, or reuse of products from the end user after they have reached the end of their useful life. Organizations are now extending their distribution channels beyond the end customer to include the acceptance and "disassembly" of final products for reuse in new products. Organizations are seeking to "close the loop" and eventually transform used products into new products and/or materials that can be returned to the earth without harming the environment. In other cases, organizations have developed extensive repair networks to handle warranty and quality problems that occur with products returned by customers. This function may include after-sales service functions, maintenance services, and other types of activities related to continually satisfying the customer. Here again, organizations are actively working to improve their "reverse logistics" functions, to manage the flow of products and services moving backward through the supply chain.

FIGURE 1-2 A Cereal Manufacturer's Supply Chain

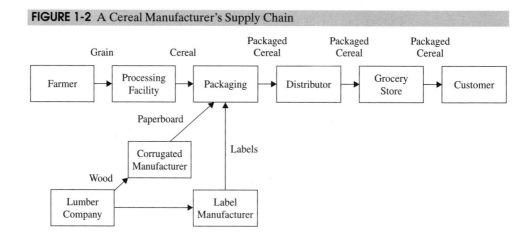

All organizations are part of one or more supply chains. Whether a company sells directly to the end customer, provides a service, manufactures a product, or extracts material from the earth, it can be characterized within the context of its supply chain. Until recently, however, organizations focused primarily on their direct customers and internal functions, and placed relatively little emphasis on other organizations within their supply chain network. However, three major developments in global markets and technologies have brought supply chain management to the forefront of management's attention:

1. The information revolution.
2. Customer demands in areas of product and service cost, quality, delivery, technology, and cycle time brought about by increased global competition.
3. The emergence of new forms of interorganizational relationships.

Each of these developments has fostered the emergence of an integrated supply chain approach. The model presented in Figure 1-3 illustrates the nature of supply chain management and integrates all three developments mentioned above. The model also provides a framework for this text, where a chapter is devoted to each of the three evolutionary developments. Before moving on, it is worthwhile to provide a brief overview of the model and its components first.

FIGURE 1-3 Integrated Supply Chain Model

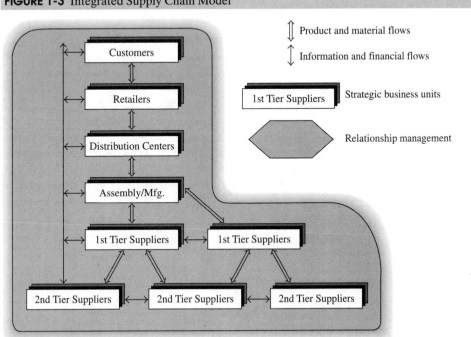

Bidirectional arrows reflect the accommodation of reverse materials and information feedback flows.

Information Systems and Supply Chain Management

In the early 1960s when computers were first developed, a mainframe computer filled an entire room with vacuum tubes and wires. With the development of the integrated circuit, the cost of the computer decreased radically while at the same time the speed of computer power increased exponentially. Today, a laptop computer weighing 5 pounds exceeds all of the power of an old mainframe by several orders of magnitude.

With the emergence of the personal computer, optical fiber networks, the explosion of the Internet and the World Wide Web, the cost and availability of information resources allows easy linkages and eliminates information-related time delays in any supply chain network. This means that organizations are moving toward a concept known as *Electronic Commerce,* where transactions are completed via a variety of electronic media, including electronic data interchange (EDI), electronic funds transfer (EFT), bar codes, fax, automated voice mail, CD-ROM catalogs, and a variety of others. This means that the old "paper"-type transactions are becoming increasingly obsolete. Leading-edge organizations no longer require paper purchase requisitions, purchase orders, invoices, receiving forms, and a manual accounts payable "matching" process. All required information is recorded electronically, and associated transactions are performed with a minimum amount of human intervention. Recent developments in database structures allow part numbers to be accumulated, coded, and stored in databases, and electronically ordered. This means that with the application of the appropriate information systems, the need to constantly monitor inventory levels, place orders, and expedite orders will soon become a thing of the past.

The proliferation of new telecommunications and computer technology has also made real-time, on-line communications throughout the entire supply chain a reality. These systems are now being linked between suppliers, manufacturers, distributors, retail outlets, and ultimately, customers, regardless of location. These technologies are supply chain "enablers," in that they can substantially reduce paperwork, improve communication, and reduce lead time and non-value-added activities if properly implemented.

Managers developing information systems should not visualize information as a set of repetitive transactions between entities such as buyers and suppliers, or distributors and retailers. Rather, an ideal system should span all functions and organizations throughout the entire supply chain. With the explosion of the Internet, the World Wide Web, and company "Intranets," future systems will possess the following set of characteristics:[2]

- Centralized coordination of information flows.
- Total logistics management—integrating all transportation, ordering, and manufacturing systems.
- Order-change notices that trigger a cascading series of modifications to production schedules, logistics plans, and warehouse operations.
- Global visibility into transportation resources across business units and national boundaries.
- Global inventory management—ability to locate and track the movement of every item.

---

[2] F. L. Dubois and E. Carmel, "Information Technology and Leadtime Management in International Manufacturing Operations," in *Global Information Systems and Technology: Focus on the Organization and Its Functional Areas,* ed. P. Candace Deans and Kirk R. Karwan (London: Idea Group Publishing, 1994), pp. 279–293.

- Global sourcing—consolidation of the purchasing function across organizational lines, facilitating purchasing leverage and component standardization across business units.
- Intercompany information access—clarity of production and demand information residing in organizations both upstream and downstream throughout the value chain.
- Data interchange—between affiliates and nonaffiliates through standard telecommunications channels.
- Data capture—ability to acquire data about an order at the point of origin, and to track products during movement and as their characteristics change.
- Transformation of the business from within—managers who can see the "big picture" and accept the new forms of business processes and systems.
- Improvements in supplier-customer relationships—to justify investments in technology linkages.

The ideal supply chain information system is shown in Figure 1-3 (information flows between organizations are indicated by the bold arrows). Note that information is available to any party within the chain, as well as the number of feedback loops defining a totally integrated system. These linkages are critical, as they allow just-in-time (JIT) deliveries to occur between every linkage in the chain, inventories to be minimized, and entities to respond to fluctuations in a timely and effective manner. Point-of-sale data is transferred immediately throughout the supply chain, allowing managers to spot trends, plan capacity requirements, allocate materials, and notify suppliers throughout the entire chain. The information flows also permit interorganization payments for goods and services through electronic funds transfers between banks, which ensures quick payment for supply chain members. With all of these elements in place, total information freedom permits accessibility, improved decision making, and quicker action. These critical information systems issues are discussed in chapter 2.

Inventory Management across the Supply Chain

The second major trend facing organizations today is the demand for ever-greater levels of responsiveness and shorter defined cycle times for deliveries of high-quality goods and services. A variety of changes occurring throughout global markets have resulted in an increasingly competitive environment. The rate of change in markets, products, technology, and competitors occurs at an increasingly rapid pace, leading to a condition in which managers must make decisions on shorter notice, with less information, and with higher penalty costs. At the same time, customers are demanding quicker delivery responsiveness. These same customers require products that incorporate state-of-the-art technology and features. Products are becoming less standardized, and customers are demanding options that are tailored to their unique requirements. In many segments of the marketplace, only those firms that have the ability to "mass-customize" are successful.[3] Computers are assessed based on their speed and cost, automobiles on their safety and reliability, and long-distance telephone carriers on price competitiveness. This means

---

[3] B. J. Pine, *Mass Customization: The New Frontier in Business Competition* (Boston: Harvard Business School Press, 1993).

that such products are becoming more complex, have a greater variety of options, and must be tailored to a greater number of shrinking market "niches." In some industries, product life cycles are shrinking from years to a matter of 2 or 3 months. This has led one popular management author to compare many current global markets to the fashion industry, in which products go in and out of style with the season.[4]

Managers throughout the supply chain are feeling the full effect of these changes. Cutbacks in staffing are forcing managers to handle a greater number of channels with fewer people, while cost pressures require that they do so with less inventory. Because of the ever-increasing levels of competition found in many markets, supply chain–related mistakes leading to lost sales cannot be easily dismissed and written off. Furthermore, both customers and suppliers are becoming better at measuring performance, so that these mistakes are more easily detected. "Perfect orders" are being demanded, requiring a supply chain that is quick, precise, and provides a top-quality product every time.

Despite the imposing challenges of today's competitive environment, some organizations are thriving. These firms have embraced these changes and have integrated quick response and flexibility into their day-to-day culture. They are managing by paying attention to *time*. For example, the reduction of delivery times both in the marketplace and throughout the supply chain has earned such firms as Hewlett-Packard, Northern Telecom, Toyota, and Xerox a reputation as "time-based competitors."[5] Entire industries have changed to reflect time-based capabilities. For instance, Johnson Controls can now receive a seat order release from Ford and deliver the order 4 hours later, starting from the raw materials stage. Another auto supplier producing stamped metal parts has reduced its finished goods inventory to 2 hours' worth of goods, yet is faced with a penalty of $10,000 per minute if it delivers late to its customer's assembly line. A number of "buzzwords" have emerged to describe time-based capabilities: *throughput time reduction, delivery speed, fast cycle capability, quick response or resupply time, lead-time reduction,* and *time compression.*[6] Unlike many management fads, however, time-based competition is a phenomenon that is here to stay because of its direct linkage to profits. The advantages achieved by time-based competitors enable them to grow faster and earn higher profits relative to other firms in their industry; increase market share through early introduction of new products; control overhead and inventory costs; and move to positions of industry leadership.[7]

A number of firms, including Wal-Mart, Thomasville, Northern Telecom, Xerox, and Motorola, have experienced a significant improvement in corporate performance, whether measured using return on assets, return on net assets, or return on sales as a result of their focus on cycle time. All of these firms were able to link corporate performance to several market factors.[8] First, they were able to translate time into profits

---

[4] Tom Peters, *Liberation Management* (New York: Alfred A. Knopf, 1992).

[5] Roy Merrills, "How Northern Telecom Competes on Time," *Harvard Business Review* 67 (July–August 1989), 108–114; George Stalk Jr. and Thomas M. Hout, *Competing Against Time: How Time-Based Competition Is Reshaping Global Markets* (New York: The Free Press, 1990); Joseph D. Blackburn, "The Time Factor," in *Time-Based Competition: The Next Battleground in American Manufacturing,* ed. Joseph Blackburn (Homewood, IL: Business One Irwin, 1991), pp. 3–23.

[6] Roger W. Schmenner, "The Merit of Making Things Fast," *Sloan Management Review,* Fall 1988, pp. 11–17.

[7] Robert Handfield and Ronald Pannesi, "An Empirical Study of Delivery Speed and Reliability," *International Journal of Operations and Production Management* 12 (1992), 60–74; Stalk and Hout, *Competing.*

[8] Steven Melnyk, Phillip Carter, and Robert Handfield, "Identifying the Basic Strategies for Time-Based Competition," *Production and Inventory Management,* First Quarter 1995, pp. 65–70.

by satisfying their "impatient" customers. These customers are willing to pay a premium if they can get their goods and services very quickly. Customers will award their business to time-based competitors because it means that they too can reduce their inventory levels while saving time and money. In a well-managed integrated supply chain, the amount of inventory held throughout the chain decreases, such that inventory is now "flowing" between parties in the chain with only minor delays (as shown in Figure 1-3). Organizations such as Bose, Black and Decker, Ford, and others have developed "dock to stock" delivery systems. Supplier deliveries of component parts that are made directly to the plant floor end up in finished products by the end of the day!

There is a secondary effect for companies that achieve time-based capabilities: Reductions in delivery lead time translate into not only less inventory but also less rework, higher product quality, and less overhead throughout every element of the supply chain. Each of these improvements has a direct impact on the organization's bottom line. In many cases, these benefits are jointly shared by all of the parties within a given supply chain.

There are both internal and external benefits associated with being a time-based competitor. The external effects refer to benefits enjoyed by time-based organizations in the marketplace relative to their competitors (such as higher quality, quicker customer response, technologically advanced products). The internal benefits are found within and between the different functional areas in the firm (including simplified organizations, shorter planning loops, increased responsiveness, better communication, coordination, and cooperation between functions).

These capabilities become even more important when considered on a global scale. To survive, organizations today must increase market share on a global basis, in order to sustain growth objectives and be on the "ground floor" of rapid global economic expansion. Simultaneously, these same organizations must vigorously defend their domestic market share from a host of "world-class" international competitors. To meet this challenge, managers are seeking ways to rapidly expand their global logistics and distribution networks, in order to ship products to the customers who demand them, in a dynamic and rapidly changing set of market channels. This requires the strategic positioning of inventories, so that products are available when customers (regardless of location) want them, in the right quantity, and for the right price. This level of performance is a continuous challenge facing organizations and can occur only when all parties in a supply chain are "on the same wavelength." The management of inventory in a supply chain is discussed in chapter 3.

Supply Chain Relationships

This leads us to the final, and perhaps most difficult and important component of effective supply chain management shown in Figure 1-3: supply chain relationships. The prior two components (information systems and supply chain cycle-time reduction) are both relatively well understood. Information technology is constantly changing, but the primary *technical* elements required to achieve the linkages shown in Figure 1-3 are currently available. Inventory strategies are also relatively well understood, and the processes associated with cycle-time reduction have been successfully implemented in many different organizations and continue to evolve. However, without a foundation of effective supply chain organizational relationships, any efforts to manage the flow of information or materials across the supply chain are likely to be unsuccessful.

Of the three primary activities associated with supply chain management, relationship management is perhaps the most fragile and tenuous, and is therefore the most susceptible to breaking down. A poor relationship with any link in the supply chain can have disastrous consequences for all other supply chain members. For example, an undependable source of parts can virtually cripple a plant, leading to inflated lead times and resulting in problems across the chain, all the way to the final customer.

To avoid such problems, organizations must develop a better understanding of their processes, as well as their suppliers' quality and delivery performance, in order to find better ways to serve their customers. To ensure that this occurs, communication links with customers and suppliers must be established and utilized on a regular basis. In short, supply chain relationships are probably one of the most important management interfaces within the entire supply chain and are the subject of chapter 4.

Nevertheless, many organizations continue to view suppliers (and even customers!) as adversaries who are not to be trusted and with whom long-term relationships should be avoided. This model is reflected in the typical procurement and logistics function found in many organizations. These departments often have no strategic role and are viewed as merely "buying" or "shipping" functions. In many cases, materials management is considered a separate "silo" activity, and personnel have little or no process communication with other internal functions, suppliers, or customers. Many of these individuals want to maintain the status quo, are protective of their "turf," and focus on individual transactions rather than on establishing and maintaining an ongoing set of supply relationships. Performance measures are very often "efficiency-based" and rely on metrics such as "purchase orders processed per buyer" or "$ purchased per buyer," rather than time-based or cost-based measures of overall supply chain effectiveness. Finally, most purchasing and logistics departments have a manufacturing and supply orientation, with almost no input into critical new-product design, pipeline inventory reduction, quality improvement, information systems, or process reengineering initiatives. Buyers and distribution managers in many purchasing organizations choose suppliers and carriers on the basis of one criterion only—price. (Note that this criterion does not include other factors that account for the "total cost," but rather reflects only the bottom-line price, which includes both the supplier's/carrier's cost and profit.) As such, suppliers/carriers are often played off against one another, are dropped on a moment's notice, and are chosen from a large pool on an order-by-order basis. (Unless otherwise noted, carriers will also be referred to as "suppliers" from here on in).

An increasing number of organizations are attempting to develop closer relationships with their major suppliers, and even their suppliers' suppliers. Given the dependency of firms on supplier performance, some organizations are adopting strategies that can help foster improvement, including greater information sharing between parties and the visible presence of "co-destiny" relationships. The latter refers to the commitment of the focal firm to using a single or dual source of supply over an extended period of time. In such cases, the focal firm makes a set of long-term strategic decisions focusing on improved supplier/carrier relationships. As the degree of trust between the purchasing firm and its suppliers becomes firmly entrenched, a smoother flow of both materials and information between the organizations within the supply chain occurs.

The contrary scenario, observed in many situations, is one in which the focal firm generally distrusts its suppliers, provides "shaky" schedules, and maintains high levels of inventory to safeguard against the possibility of being crossed. Such adversarial supply chain strategies do not consider the long term. It is surprising that given the benefits observed from establishing closer buyer-supplier relationships, many supply chain managers continue to adopt an adversarial, open-market view of suppliers.

A key element of improved supplier relationships is the presence of an objective performance measurement system, which is used to ensure that both parties are operating according to expectations and are meeting stated objectives. In addition, parties must emphasize clear objectives, expectations, and potential sources of conflict up front in order to facilitate communication and joint problem solving. As a result of this communication, trust between buyers and suppliers begins to grow, leading to further improvements.

At the other end of the spectrum, power in a broad array of channels has shifted downstream toward the customer or user. As the customer calls the shots in the marketplace, the manufacturer and the intermediaries must be nimble and quick or face the prospect of losing market share. To effectively implement integrated supply chain management, however, a relationship based on mutual benefits and trust must exist. This means that downstream buyers must also be *good "customers."* Major customers must provide supply partners with the information they need to be responsive, deliver on time, and meet performance expectations. The improvement of supply chain relationships occurs through a great deal of communication and problem-solving activities between organizations, including joint improvement projects, training seminars and workshops on sharing corporate philosophies, and meetings between the respective organizations' top management. Organizations are also beginning to hold supply chain councils, which include representatives from all major suppliers and customers in a supply chain, that meet on a regular basis. Such councils can provide top materials management executives with directives and insights regarding changes in policies, information systems and standards, and other suggestions that can effectively remove costs from the supply chain and eliminate non-value-added processes.

As the level of communication between customers and suppliers increases, parties often witness greater informal information sharing. Managers and engineers from supplying organizations may be invited to customer facilities to encourage a dialogue leading to improvements in the supplying process. Firms may share different types of production and forecasting data, including product-level and part-level material requirements planning schedules. Companies may even begin to share cost data in order to identify non-value-added drivers (such as rework, scrap, excess inventory, etc.), which could be reduced through joint efforts.

In many American industries, true "supply chain networks" like those found in Japan may not develop as readily. Firms are often geographically distant, and there are not as many small, family-owned suppliers as in Japan. In the case of high-tech firms, many components may be sole-sourced to overseas suppliers who are proprietary owners of the required technology. In these environments, it becomes more important to choose a few select suppliers with whom to work, thereby paving the way for informal interaction and information sharing that can foster time-based improvements. The topic of developing supply chain relationships is discussed extensively in chapter 4.

Challenges Facing Supply Chain Managers

Although the topic of integrated supply chains holds great appeal to many academics, consultants, and practitioners alike, the difficulty involved in implementing this strategy is evident. The integrated management of information and materials across the supply chain offers the benefits of increasing the value-added by supply chain members, reducing waste, reducing cost, and improving customer satisfaction. However, deploying and managing this strategy is a challenging and significant task.

The process of implementing an integrated supply chain has been shown to be very difficult. In many cases, problems occur in the implementation of information systems, such that the appropriate information is not available to the people who need it. In other cases, the information is available, but supply chain members are reluctant to share it, due to a lack of trust and a fear that the information will be revealed to competitors.

Inventory management is no less difficult. Although inventory systems are continuously improving, the need for expediting late shipments never seems to disappear entirely. There are always delays in shipments for a variety of reasons: Slowdowns resulting from customs crossing international borders, adverse weather patterns, poor communication, and, of course, simple human error, are inevitable. With the double-edged sword of lower inventory levels and increasing demand for improvements in fill rates and on-time delivery, the management of inventory throughout a supply chain becomes an increasingly complex and demanding task. Finally, establishing trust between parties in a supply chain is perhaps the greatest challenge. Legal experts may produce reams of contractual agreements that fail to work when parties inevitably have a conflict. Conflict management in interorganizational relationships is becoming increasingly difficult to manage. Having broken the fragile bond of trust, it becomes more difficult to repair, and some supply chain relationships eventually buckle under the strain.

Both of the authors have experience in working with companies that have attempted to implement supply chains. Many organizations struggle to complete even one link in the chain. The challenge of integrating information requirements and inventory flows across multiple tiers of suppliers and customers is proving to be immense. To provide additional insights about how these strategies are being deployed, chapter 5 presents several case examples of supply chain management in action. The cases were developed through in-depth interviews with selected leading-edge firms currently implementing integrated supply chain management. In some of the cases the names of the firms are "disguised" to avoid confidentiality problems. These cases are instrumental in illustrating the concepts described in the earlier chapters and provide a template to guide managers and students. Based on our discussions with managers at these organizations (as well as others not explicitly discussed in the book), we also provide a short overview in the final chapter of what the future holds in store for supply chain management. Chapter 6 focuses on emerging trends in supply chain management, including such topics as the evolution of "reverse logistics" systems, "design for supply chain" processes in new product development, the globalization of supply chains, and the future for information technology and supply chain management worldwide.

Purpose of the Book

The purpose of this book is to provide the reader with a framework for understanding supply chains and supply chain management and to show examples of what firms are actually doing to better manage their supply chains. This book is intended to provide readers with a topical discussion of what a supply chain is, why it is important, and the types of challenges implicit in managing supply chains. The authors plan to periodically update the book with the latest developments in supply chain management. In order to facilitate this process, readers are invited to provide their insights and case examples to the authors. We hope that you will benefit from the insights provided in this book and that we can learn from you as well.

CHAPTER 2

The Role of Information Systems and Technology in Supply Chain Management

Introduction

As discussed in chapter 1, supply chain management is concerned with the flow of products and *information* between the supply chain member organizations. At the limit, it encompasses all of those organizations (i.e., suppliers, customers, producers, and service providers) that link together to acquire, purchase, convert/manufacture, assemble, and distribute goods and services, from suppliers to the ultimate end users. These flows are bidirectional.[1] This chapter addresses the information required for effective supply chain management and introduces a number of technologies that organizations are using to make this information readily available across the supply chain. (see Figure 2-1).

Recent developments in technology have brought information to the forefront of resources from which forward-thinking firms can cultivate genuine competitive advantage. These technologies provide the means for multiple organizations to coordinate their activities in an effort to truly manage a supply chain. As the rate of these technological advances increases, the cost associated with this information has decreased. Simultaneously, the speed with which this vital information can be made useful and applicable in a variety of business situations continues to increase.

By 1980, the information revolution was in full swing in the world's advanced economies. During this period, many standard business processes and functions such as customer order processing, inventory management, and purchasing were altered through the use of computer technology. However, only as the variety of available information

---

[1] Lisa Harrington, "Logistics, Agent for Change: Shaping the Integrated Supply Chain," *Transportation & Distribution* 36, no. 1 (January 1995), pp. 30–34.

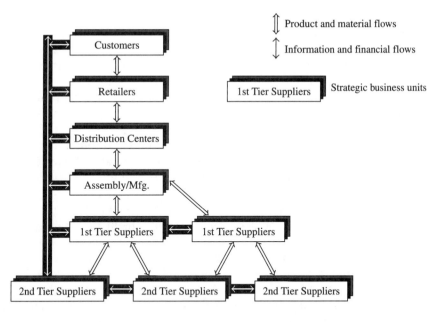

Bidirectional arrows reflect the accommodation of reverse materials and
information feedback flows.

FIGURE 2-1 Integrated Supply Chain Model

technologies and capabilities began to grow exponentially mid-decade, did a more expanded *information technology* (IT) paradigm begin to emerge.

Industry observers writing at that time suggested, ". . . managers need to understand that information technology is more than just computers. Today, information technology must be conceived of broadly to encompass the information that businesses create and use as well as a wide spectrum of increasingly convergent and linked technologies that process the information. In addition to computers, then, data recognition equipment, communications technologies, factory automation, and other hardware and services are included."[2] We utilize this paradigm in this chapter describing the role of information and information technology in the supply chain.

The Importance of Information in an Integrated Supply Chain Management Environment

Prior to the 1980s, a significant portion of the information flows between functional areas within an organization, and between supply chain member organizations, were paper-based. In many instances, these paper-based transactions and communications were slow,

---

[2] Michael E. Porter and Victor E. Millar, "How Information Gives You Competitive Advantage," *Harvard Business Review,* July–August 1985, pp. 149–161.

unreliable, and error prone. Conducting business in this manner was costly because it decreased firms' effectiveness in being able to design, develop, procure, manufacture, and distribute their products. This approach also impeded efforts to develop and capitalize on successful interorganizational ventures. During this period, information was often overlooked as a critical competitive resource because its value to supply chain members was not clearly understood. However, firms that are embarking upon supply chain management initiatives now recognize the vital importance of information and the technologies that make this information available.

IT infrastructures today may be quite complex and comprehensive, supporting the firm's communication networks, databases, and operating systems. In fact, "IT infrastructure capabilities underpin the competitive positioning of business initiatives such as cycle time reduction, implementing redesigned cross-functional processes, utilizing cross-selling opportunities and capturing the channel to the customer."[3] These infrastructures also support the development, management, and maintenance of interorganizational supply chains.

In a sense, the information systems and the technologies utilized in these systems represent one of the fundamental elements that "link" the organizations of a supply chain into a unified and coordinated system. In the current competitive climate, little doubt remains about the importance of information and information technology to the ultimate success, and perhaps even the survival, of any supply chain management initiative.

Several well-known firms involved in supply chain–type relationships owe much of their success to the notion of information and the systems utilized to share this information with one another. Among the most notable examples are Procter & Gamble (P&G) and Wal-Mart. Through a series of agreements with giant retail customers, P&G has made a major commitment to the development of dedicated customer teams to handle these major accounts. A primary objective of these teams is to facilitate the sharing of information between the firms and will typically address a full range of logistics, finance, accounting, MIS, and supply issues.

According to Bowersox and Closs (1996), timely and accurate information is more critical now than at any time in the history of American business. Three factors have strongly impacted this change in the importance of information. First, satisfying, in fact pleasing, customers has become something of a corporate obsession. Serving the customer in the best, most efficient, and effective manner has become critical, and information about issues such as order status, product availability, delivery schedules, and invoices has become a necessary part of the total customer service experience. Second, information is a crucial factor in the managers' abilities to reduce inventory and human resources requirements to a competitive level. Finally, information flows play an essential role in the strategic planning for and deployment of resources.

A key notion in the essential nature of information systems in the development and maintenance of successful supply chains is the need for virtually seamless bonds within and between organizations. This means creating intraorganizational processes and links to facilitate delivery of seamless information between marketing, sales, purchasing, finance, manufacturing, distribution and transportation internally, as well as

---

[3] Marianne Broadbent and Peter Weill, "Management by Maxim: How Business and IT Managers Can Create Infrastructures," *Sloan Management Review,* Spring 1997, p. 77.

interorganizationally, to customers, suppliers, carriers, and retailers across the supply chain. Perhaps more importantly, it means alteration of perspective at the firm's highest levels. Changes in thinking that become necessary include aligning corporate strategies to the IT paradigm, providing incentives for functions to achieve common goals through the sharing of information, and implementing the technologies to redesign the movement of goods to maximize channel value and lower cost.[4] Several examples that demonstrate the benefits associated with information sharing are presented in the following paragraphs.

Through the 1992 acquisition of GTE's Sylvania lighting division, Osram, Inc. launched an ambitious and mutually beneficial supply chain integration program. Six months into the new venture, fill rates of the customer service unit were at 95 percent and rising; SKU forecast accuracy had improved by 16 percent; slow moving or obsolete inventory as a percentage of total inventory was down 10 percent; and the company had saved more than $300,000 on transportation costs.

AVOIDING THE STING OF THE "BULLWHIP"

Clearly, the need to share information across the supply chain is of paramount importance. Less frequently addressed but equally as important is the need to make certain that this information is accurate. In fact, "distorted information from one end of a supply chain to the other can lead to tremendous inefficiencies: excessive inventory investment, poor customer service, lost revenues, misguided capacity plans, ineffective transportation, and missed production schedules."[5] Are these deliberate attempts to sabotage the performance of fellow supply chain members? No, they are not. Rather, distorted information throughout the supply chain is a common result from what logistics executives at P&G and other organizations have termed the *bullwhip effect.*

P&G began to explore this phenomenon after a series of particularly erratic shifts in ordering up and down the supply chain for one of its most popular products, Pampers disposable diapers. After determining that it was highly unlikely that the infants and toddlers at the ultimate user level for Pampers were creating extreme swings in demand for the product, the examination began to work back through the supply chain. It was found that distributors' orders showed far more variability than the level of demand represented at retail stores themselves. Continuing through the supply chain, P&G's orders to its supplier, 3M, indicated the most variability of all.[6] Four causes of this phenomenon were identified:

1. Demand forecast updating,
2. Order batching,
3. Price fluctuations, and
4. Rationing within the supply chain.[7]

---

[4] Donald J. Bowersox and David J. Closs, *Logistical Management: The Integrated Supply Chain Process* (New York: McGraw Hill, 1996).

[5] Lee L. Hau, V. Padmanabhan, and Seungjin Whang, "The Bullwhip Effect in Supply Chains," *Sloan Management Review,* Spring 1997, pp. 93–102.

[6] Ibid.

[7] Ibid.

This so-called bullwhip effect is certainly not unique to P&G or even to the consumer packaged-goods industry. Firms from Hewlett-Packard in the computer industry to Bristol-Myers Squibb in the pharmaceutical field have experienced a similar phenomenon. Basically, even slight to moderate demand uncertainties and variabilities become magnified when viewed through the eyes of managers at each link in the supply chain. If each distinct entity makes ordering and inventory decisions with an eye to its own interest above those of the change, stockpiling may be simultaneously occurring at as many as seven or eight places across the supply chain, leading to, in some cases, as many as 100 days of inventory—waiting "just in case."[8] A recent industry study projected $30 billion in savings could result from a streamlining of the order information-sharing process in the grocery industry supply chains alone.[9]

SUPPLY CHAIN ORGANIZATIONAL DYNAMICS

Several interorganizational dynamics come into play when addressing information sharing across the supply chain. Two issues in particular are risk and power. All enterprises participating in a supply chain management initiative accept a specific role to perform. They also share the joint belief that they and all the other supply chain participants will be better off because of this collaborative effort. Each member specializes in the function or area that best aligns with its distinctive competencies. Risk occurs in that rather than prospering or failing on the basis of its own efforts, each firm must now rely on other supply chain members as well as its own efforts in determining the success of the supply chain. Some supply chain members are more dependent on the supply chain success than others. Thus, members with the most at stake may take more active roles and assume greater responsibility for fostering cooperation, including the information-sharing efforts, throughout the supply chain.

Power within the supply chain is a central issue, one that in today's marketplace centers on information sharing. Although not universal to all industries, there has been a general shift of power from manufacturers to retailers over the last two decades, which has resulted from a combination of factors. One is the trend toward consolidation at the retail level within the supply chain. Gone are the days of "Mom and Pop" grocery stores in every neighborhood. In the interest of capitalizing on the benefits of economies of scale, giant retail conglomerates operate as part of nationwide supply chains. In fact, relatively few of the thousands of retailers operating in the United States control the majority of dollars in this industry. Clearly, this consolidation impacts the entire supply chain. Fewer and fewer firms control access to consumer trading areas.

Perhaps more importantly, retailers sit in a very important position in terms of information access for the supply chain. For several reasons, major retailers have risen to this position of prominence through (1) technologies such as bar codes and scanners, (2) their sheer size and sales volume, and most importantly, (3) their position within the

---

[8] Ibid.
[9] Ibid.

supply chain right next to the final consumer. This combination of factors has put re-tailers in a very powerful position within the supply chain.

The Wal-Mart and P&G experiences demonstrate how information sharing can be utilized for mutual advantage. Through state-of-the-art information systems, Wal-Mart shares point-of-sale information from its many retail outlets directly with P&G and other major suppliers. Rather than causing Wal-Mart to lose power within these part-nerships, this willingness to share information provides the retailer with a competitive advantage by freeing its resources from management of the supplier's products. The product suppliers themselves become responsible for the sales and marketing of their products in the Wal-Mart stores through easy access to information on consumer buy-ing patterns and transactions.[10]

Interorganizational Information Systems

Recognizing the critical importance of information in an integrated supply chain envi-ronment, many organizations are implementing some form of an *interorganizational information system* (IOIS). IOISs are "systems based on information technologies that cross organizational boundaries."[11] In fact, at "the ultimate level of integration, all mem-ber links in the supply chain are continuously supplied with information in real time."[12] The foundation of this ability to share information is the effective use of IT within the supply chain. Appropriate application of these technologies provides decision makers with timely access to all required information from any location within the supply chain.

Barrett describes an IOIS as an integrated data-processing/data-communication system utilized by two or more separate organizations. These organizations may (buyer-supplier) or may not (credit clearinghouse) have a preexisting business relationship. What must exist is a computer-based electronic link between the two organizations that automates some element of work, such as order processing, order-status checking, inventory-level review, shipment tracking information or, minimally, transaction trans-fer, which would previously have been performed manually or through other media, such as the mail.[13]

Among the earliest forms of IOISs were those developed by time-sharing services and on-line database vendors. The potential impact of such systems on the way business is conducted was recognized as early as the 1960s. Since that time, new technologies have been integrated to produce systems of increasing capability.

Examples of such implementations include electronic funds transfer (EFT) sys-tems, the Treasury Department's decision support system, a variety of buyer-supplier order-processing systems, and on-line professional tool support systems. Existing im-plementations serve the grocery industry, the drug wholesaling industry, the insurance

---

[10] Ira Lewis and Alexander Talalayevsky, "Logistics and Information Technology: A Coordination Perspec-tive," *Journal of Business Logistics* 18, no. 1, (1997), 141–157.

[11] Yannis Bakos, "Information Links and Electronic Marketplaces: The Role of Interorganizational Informa-tion Systems in Vertical Markets," *Journal of Management Information Systems,* Fall 1991, pp. 15–34.

[12] Phillip W. Balsmeier and Wendell J. Voisin, "Supply Chain Management: A Time-Based Strategy," *Industrial Management,* September–October 1996, pp. 24–27.

industry, and the transportation industry, with more systems coming into existence each year.

The development of an IOIS for the supply chain has three distinct advantages: cost reductions, productivity improvements, and product/market strategy.[14] Five basic levels of participation for individual firms within the interorganizational system have been identified by Barrett and Konsynski:

1. *Remote I/O node,* in which the member participates from a remote location within the application system supported by one or more higher-level participants;
2. *Application processing node,* in which the member develops and shares a single application such as an inventory-query or order-processing system;
3. *Multiparticipant exchange node,* in which the member develops and shares a network interlinking itself and any number of lower-level participants with whom it has an established business relationship;
4. *Network control node,* in which the member develops and shares a network with diverse applications that may be used by many different types of lower-level participants; and, finally
5. *Integrating network node,* in which the member literally becomes a data-communications/data-processing utility that integrates any number of lower-level participants and applications in real time.[15]

A sixth level of participation also appears within the context of the supply chain in which the participant shares a network of diverse applications with any number of participants with whom it has an established business relationship. This level is similar to Barrett and Konsynski's network control node but does not restrict the IOIS participants to a specific level. Therefore, IOIS participants may, in fact, be at a level lower, higher, or equal to the IOIS sharing organizations. We will describe this level of participation as the *supply chain partner node.* The various IOIS configuration types are presented in Figure 2-2.

As organizations explore development of IOISs to support their supply chain management efforts, they will be faced with several challenges. One impediment undoubtedly lies in developing a common language in terms of planning, format, and priority across several vastly different constituencies. Information-sharing requirements are well beyond those of a manufacturer, and its distributor's need to process orders in a consistent way. All relevant information ultimately must circulate to and among all organizations between the supply chain's point of origin and its point of consumption, such as ordering (i.e., orders for component parts, services, and finished products), inbound transportation, manufacturing, warehousing, inventory management, outbound transportation, sales, marketing, forecasts, and customer-service information.[16] Although organizations recognize the importance of an IOIS for effective supply chain management, no one standard approach is being utilized in terms of technology or information. The next section presents insights on system development to help ensure that the correct information is included in the IOIS.

---

[13] Stephanie S. Barrett, "Strategic Alternatives and Inter-organizational System Implementations: An Overview," *Journal of Management Information Systems* III, no. 3 (Winter 1986–1987), 5–16.
[14] Stephanie Barrett and Benn Konsynski, "Inter-Organization Information Sharing Systems," *MIS Quarterly,* 1982, pp. 74–92.
[15] Ibid.
[16] Ibid.

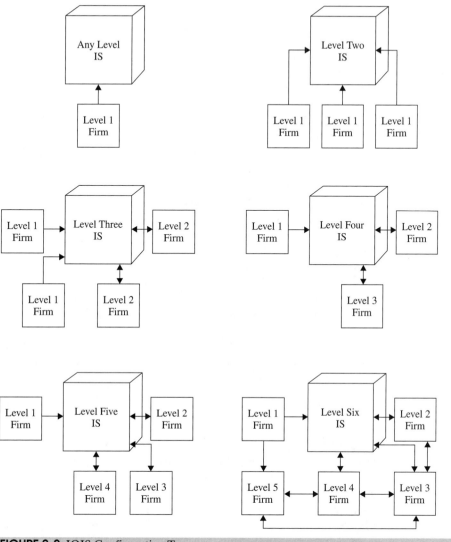

FIGURE 2-2 IOIS Configuration Types

Information Requirements Determination for a Supply Chain IOIS[17]

BACKGROUND INFORMATION

Given the importance of an IOIS organization's efforts to manage supply chains, it is critical that the system captures the "right" information—that information required by decision makers in the member organizations to effectively and efficiently perform their

---

[17] Adapted from Ernest L. Nichols Jr., Mark N. Frolick, and James C. Wetherbe, "Cycle Time Reduction: An Interorganizational Supply Chain Perspective," *Cycle Time Research* 1, no. 1 (1995), 63–84.

roles within the supply chain. A portfolio approach to information requirements determination focused on ensuring that the "right" information is in fact captured in the IOIS is presented here. This section also details insights gained by one of the authors while participating in a research project that included the design of a supply chain management IOIS.

This study addressed a "typical" supply chain in the computer electronics industry that extended from raw materials supplier to finished products available on the shelf at the retail supply chain member's stores. Representatives from five supply chain member organizations participated in this project.

A recurring theme in the cycle-time problems discussed by the participating organizations was a critical lack of information. The specific problems discussed varied by organization and situation, but, repeatedly, it was a matter of "the right hand not knowing what the left hand was doing," or in some cases "the right hand discovers what the left hand is doing, but not in adequate time to act in a cost-effective manner." Situations of this type were found both within organizations and between supply chain members.

The participants indicated that current approaches used to share information internally, and with suppliers and customers, are in themselves deterrents to improving cycle-time performance. Furthermore, they stated that they could improve performance in a number of areas, including cycle time, if they had access to information held by other supply chain members. Therefore, what was required was a means of making this information that exists within the various supply chain organizations available to all supply chain members.

Clearly, the main point of leverage for improving cycle-time performance across the supply chain was "informating"[18] (i.e., information sharing). To facilitate the informating process, the research team decided to explore the development of an IOIS. In the following section, techniques used to identify the information required for the supply chain IOIS are presented.

INFORMATION REQUIREMENTS DETERMINATION OVERVIEW

On several levels, free sharing of accurate and timely information across the supply chain is a key factor for success. In addressing the hurdles to be faced in the development and cultivation of successful supply chain management arrangements, Mike Aghajanian, a consultant and director of Pittilio Rabin Todd and McGrath (PRTM), noted that "By far the largest single element in impeding progress is lack of a common language to describe, analyze, measure, and improve."[19] In other words, the basic tools of communication are essential to the development of successful supply chain relationships. The sharing of information between and among several diverse constituents requires a great deal of care and sophistication. Information coordination requirements are numerous, including strategic objectives, capacity constraints, as well as logistics, manufacturing, and procurement requirements for all of the supply chain members.[20]

Determining information requirements for an information system can, at best, be described as a difficult process. Historically, systems analysts simply asked managers what information they needed. This assumes, of course, that the managers are able to

---

[18] For a discussion on "informating" and other proven techniques for cycle-time reduction, see James C. Wetherbe, "Principles of Cycle Time Reduction: You Can Have Your Cake and Eat It Too," *Cycle Time Research* 1, no. 1 (1995), 1–24.

[19] Robert Bowman, "The State of the Supply Chain," *Distribution,* January 1997, pp. 28–36.

[20] Bowersox and Closs, *Logistical Management.*

express their information needs in a way that will allow the analyst to design information systems. Often, this assumption is not valid. Managers don't know what information they actually need. They make their best attempt to specify their information needs assuming that analysts can fill in the gaps. Analysts, alternatively, may not know that actual information requirements are likely to differ from what managers say they want. This leads to an information "no man's land."[21] The result is that some information requirements are certain to be unidentified.[22] When the information system is implemented, one of the first things that managers do is ask for changes.

Information requirements determination becomes even more problematic when one attempts to determine requirements across organizations.[23,24] This is especially true when designing information systems to support an integrated supply chain.

Information requirements determination is indeed one of the most critical issues to be considered when developing IOISs to support a supply chain. In a study of 12 large IOISs, it was found that no organization had a formal structure in place to manage the IOIS, but all felt that such a mechanism should be in place to ensure the balanced and widespread exchange of information.[25] It was suggested that a steering committee with representatives from each organization be formed to identify the information to share across the IOIS. This group also needs to dictate standards and facilitate implementation of IOISs. [26] One of the tasks of this steering committee is to determine the information requirements of the IOIS in question, a task not to be taken lightly. Unfortunately, many information requirements are often overlooked. For this reason, the steering committee should be aware of the most common mistakes associated with the information requirements determination process.

The four fundamental mistakes made when determining information requirements are:

- Viewing systems as functional instead of cross-functional.
- Interviewing managers individually instead of jointly.
- Not allowing for trial and error in the detail design process.
- Asking the wrong questions during the interview.[27]

Viewing systems as functional instead of cross-functional is a very narrow and inappropriate perspective to take in the information requirements determination process. Much of the information needed to make decisions within a given function will come from sources outside the function. Therefore, it is necessary to include all of the functions involved in an information system in order to facilitate the development of a system that

---

[21] Surya B. Yadav, "Determining an Organization's Information Requirements: A State of the Art Survey," *Data Base,* Spring 1983, pp. 3–20.

[22] John R. Valusek and Dennis G. Fryback, "Information Requirements Determination: Obstacles Within, Among and Between Participants," *Proceedings of the End User Computing Conference,* Minneapolis, MN, 1985.

[23] Erik K. Clemons and Paul R. Kleindorfer, "An Economic Analysis of Interorganizational Information Technology," *Decision Support Systems* 8, no. 5 (September 1992), 431–446.

[24] Nanette S. Levinson, "IOISs: New Approaches to Global Economic Development," *Information & Management* 26, no. 5 (May 1994), 257–263.

[25] Ibid.

[26] Nanette S. Levinson and R. Meier, "Toward the 1990s: Information Management Trends," Xerox Corporation, 1988.

[27] Adapted from James C. Wetherbe and Nicholas P. Vitalari, *Systems Analysis and Design: Best Practices,* 4th ed. (St Paul, MN: West Publishing, 1994).

allows information to flow cross-functionally. When developing information systems to support an integrated supply chain, this cross-functional perspective needs to be extended to be cross-functional and *interorganizational,* because the information required to make decisions within one organization may come from another supply chain member.

Interviewing managers individually, although it has been the historical standard approach for conducting information requirements determination, has several problems. It places stress on managers, thereby limiting their ability to respond to questions. The most popular method for overcoming the problems associated with individual interviews is to undertake a group interview process known as *joint application design* (JAD). This allows the group to pool their memories concerning their information requirements by having all of the affected functions represented in the same room at the same time. This overall information requirements perspective is difficult to achieve if each manager is interviewed individually. Building an effective IOIS would be virtually impossible without taking a JAD approach to determining information requirements.

Analysts often ask managers the wrong questions. For example, an analyst might ask a manager, "What information do you need from your new system?" Although this might appear to be an obvious question, it is not helpful to managers in determining what information they need. This approach often leads directly to the information "no man's land" discussed earlier. To avoid asking the wrong questions, three different information requirements determination methodologies were developed: business systems planning, critical success factors, and ends/means analysis.

DETERMINING THE INFORMATION REQUIREMENTS FOR THE SUPPLY CHAIN MANAGEMENT IOIS

To properly determine information requirements across organizations, it is important to use a portfolio of information requirements determination methods rather than relying on one method.[28] Although this may result in some duplication of requirements identification, it will help to ensure that all information requirements are identified. Therefore, to properly determine the information requirements for the IOIS, a cross-organizational JAD session using several structured interviewing techniques, including business systems planning, critical success factors, and ends/means analysis, is suggested.

Business systems planning (BSP) is a structured interview technique developed by IBM. It focuses on the identification of problems and decisions associated with an organizational process and determines what information is needed to address them. For a supply chain management IOIS, analysts must identify supply chain management problems and decisions for the member organizations. The result of this process is a set of tables listing the problems that must be addressed, the decisions that must be made across the supply chain, and the information required to address them. Tables 2-1 and 2-2 present BSP examples.

Critical success factors (CSF) focus on key performance areas that must function effectively for the organization to be successful and associated information requirements. For the supply chain IOIS, CSFs have to be identified for each of the member organizations. As one might imagine, most of the organizations have common CSFs. Once

---

[28] Hugh J. Watson and Mark N. Frolick, "A Field Study of Methods for Determining Information Requirements for an EIS," *MIS Quarterly* 17, no. 3 (September 1993), 255–269.

TABLE 2-1 BSP—Problems/Solutions/Information		
Problems	*Solutions*	*Information*
• Reduce order-fulfillment cycle times between supply chain member organizations while maintaining or reducing total supply chain logistics cost	• Need to understand current order-fulfillment performance between supply chain members and logistics cost/performance trade-offs across the supply chain	• Order-fulfillment performance for each organization • Total supply chain logistics cost • Order history between supply chain members • Inventory carrying cost per item for each organization • Transportation cost and lead times by mode and carrier

TABLE 2-2 BSP—Decisions/Information	
Decisions	*Information*
• How to transport Product X	• Carrier and mode used by competition • Transportation cost and performance by mode and carriers

the CSFs are determined, the information needed to address the CSFs is then identified. An example is presented in Table 2-3.

Ends/means (E/M) *analysis* focuses on what it takes for an organization to be both effective (doing the "right" things) and efficient (doing these things well) and on the information needed to manage it.[29] This interview technique consists of two phases. First, the analyst identifies the ends that the supply chain members consider important, the effectiveness issues associated with the ends, and the information needed to address them (see Table 2-4). The second phase deals with means, their associated efficiency issues, and the information needed to address them (see Table 2-5).

The result of each of the structured interview techniques is a set of tables that identifies areas of concern across the organizations and the associated information needed to address these concerns. There will be some redundancy in the information requirements

TABLE 2-3 CSF—CSF/Information	
CSF	*Information*
• Integrated supply chain performance measurement system	• Performance measures for integrated supply chain • Performance measures for individual member organizations • Actual performance for supply chain and organizational measures • Targets/goals for measures • Historical performance for measures

---

[29] James C. Wetherbe, "Executive Information Requirements: Getting it Right," *MIS Quarterly* 15, no. 1 (March 1991), 51–65.

TABLE 2-4   Ends/Means Analysis—Ends/Effectiveness/Information

Ends	Effectiveness	Information
• Reduce order-fulfillment cycle times across the supply chain in a way that decreases costs and increases customer satisfaction	• Minimize total supply chain logistics costs • Maximize profit	• Activity-based cost accounting information • Customer preferences (features, cost, time) • Profit by supply chain member organization • Supply chain performance (order-fulfillment cycle time, inventory levels, capacity, customer satisfaction)

TABLE 2-5   Ends/Means Analysis—Means/Efficiency/Information

Means	Efficiency	Information
• Monitor inventory performance: - total supply chain inventory levels (days, dollars) - organization inventory levels (days, dollars) - turns - service levels - costs	• Minimize cost required to measure inventory performance	• Actual cost for measuring each factor

identified when using multiple structured interview techniques. This helps to ensure that the analyst has a comprehensive and accurate set of information requirements.

Traditional systems development also does not allow for trial and error when designing information systems. The outcome of this approach to systems development has resulted in systems that need to be changed the day they are implemented and, in a worst-case scenario, systems that are totally unusable. Prototyping was introduced as a way to overcome these problems by validating systems requirements through experimenting, refining, and testing the system until the development team and users are satisfied that they have identified all of the information requirements for the system being developed. A discussion of prototype development is presented in the following section.

TRANSLATION TO AN INFORMATION SYSTEMS PROTOTYPE

Upon completion of the information requirements determination process, the analyst translates the requirements into a prototype to help refine the information requirements further. As discussed earlier, one of the mistakes of the historical approach to information requirements determination has been that it does not allow for trial and error in the detail design process. To overcome this problem, it is important to consider building a prototype that allows for change. The first step in the prototype process is to take the information requirements elicited using the cross-organizational, cross-functional JAD structured interview session and organize them into major information categories. This process is based on *entity-attribute analysis*. Entities are things, such as customers, products, and orders, about which you want to store information. Attributes are the characteristics of these entities. For example, an attribute of customers is customer name. Using the information requirements tables that were built during the structured interviews, an analyst can build a comprehensive data model by identifying entities and their related attributes. The result of this process is an overall profile of the information needed to develop the prototype for the supply chain IOIS.

Prototype development continues with the creation of a series of reports that presents the information requirements identified during the structured interview process. A key to facilitating this task is to give each information field (attribute) in the data model a unique identifier. This helps the development team ensure that each field from the data model is addressed in the report as well as facilitates easy information field reference. Through trial-and-error development using the prototype design method, the developers are able to go through several iterations of design review to ensure that all information requirements were properly addressed. A final version of the prototype consists of a series of reports related to each of the entities identified in the data model.

The next phase of prototype development involves the computer-based operationalization of the entities. This allows for the presentation of the prototype to the interorganizational supply chain team in a manner that shows how the system will actually look when it is implemented.

PROTOTYPE REVIEW

The next step in the development process is to review the prototype with the supply chain team. Reactions to the prototype are likely to vary across organizations. As might be expected, some supply chain organizations will find that the IOIS duplicated information already available within their organization's internal systems. Other representatives will find that their organization's current systems capture little of the information presented in the supply chain IOIS. This situation illustrates one of the challenges of developing an IOIS that satisfies multiple users across the supply chain, given the information systems differences that are likely to exist between organizations. Clearly, the appropriateness of specific information entities for the IOIS is a matter of organizational and functional perspective. However, if all of the information contained in the IOIS could be "mapped" to the information requirements determination interview, it was considered necessary. The interview technique does not, however, address whether or not this information was available within an organization's current information systems. Also, the interview technique does not require that all organizations and functional areas represented "need" a specific type of information before it can be included in the IOIS. To the contrary, if only one individual indicated a need for the information, it was included in the design. However, reactions of this nature provide validation for the need to determine the information requirements for an IOIS with a cross-functional, cross-organizational approach.

The specific information identified for the supply chain IOIS consists of 10 primary categories. These categories and examples of information contained within them are in Table 2-6.[30]

---

[30] Sample information is present for each category to provide a sample of the information content in each category.

TABLE 2-6 Supply Chain IOIS Information Categories

Information Categories	*Examples of Information Contained in Category*
Product information	Product specifications, price/cost, product sales history
Customer information	Customer forecasts, customer sales history, management team
Supplier information	Product line, product lead times, sales terms and conditions
Production process information	Capacities, commitments, production plans
Transportation information	Carriers, lead times, cost
Inventory information	Inventory levels, inventory carrying costs, inventory locations
Supply chain alliance information	Key contacts for each organization, partner roles and responsibilities, meeting schedules
Competitive information	Benchmarking information, competitive product offering, market share information
Sales and marketing information	Point-of-sale information, promotional plans
Supply chain process and performance information	Process descriptions, performance measures, cost, quality, delivery, time, customer satisfaction, etc.

Information and Technology Applications for Supply Chain Management

Exciting technology-based approaches emerge almost daily. Many of these innovations are well suited to the enhancement of supply chain management, including Just In Time, Quick Response, Efficient Consumer Response, and Continuous Replenishment. Regardless of the technology-based approach, all are attempts by businesses to manage activities across company boundaries in a coordinated, integrated fashion.[31] Similarly, all rely heavily on the information made available through the latest technological advances.

Although the importance of information, and the supporting technology, to supply chain management is evident, determining which specific systems and applications can provide a specific supply chain with the greatest benefit is not at all clear. Venkatraman (1997) suggests that "How to best extract value from information technology resources is a major challenge facing both business and IT managers, particularly as they turn their focus to searching for competitive benefits of strategic information systems and striving for benefits beyond process reengineering."[32] This search becomes increasingly complex for those organizations attempting to operate in supply chains with multiple participants.

In the development and maintenance of the supply chain's information systems, both hardware and software must be addressed. Hardware includes computers, input/output devices, and storage media. Software includes all of the system and application programs used for processing transactions, management control, decision making, and strategic planning.

The development of software applications pertinent to supply chain management is currently a hotbed of activity, promising continued growth into the future. A recent

---

[31] Harrington, "Logistics, Agent for Change."

[32] N. Venkatraman, "Beyond Outsourcing: Managing IT Resources as a Value Center," *Sloan Management Review,* Spring 1997, pp. 51–64.

article in *Distribution* magazine described several of the most current developments in supply chain management, including:

- *Base Rate, Carrier Select, and Match Pay* (version 2.0), developed by Distribution Sciences, Inc., with which users can compute freight costs, compare transportation mode rates, analyze cost and service effectiveness of carriers, and audit and pay freight bills;
- A new software program developed by Ross Systems, Inc. called *Supply Chain Planning* is an integrated suite of constraint-based planning tools that provide demand, replenishment, and manufacturing tools for accurate planning and scheduling of those activities. This software provides an end-to-end enterprise-resource planning solution incorporating the most advanced supply chain planning capabilities available;
- A technology partnership between Procter & Gamble Distributing Co. and Sabre Decision Technologies resulted in a software system called *Transportation Network Optimization,* which allows shippers to give bidding carriers preanalyzed information, in turn streamlining the bidding and award process; and
- Finally, *Logitility Planning Solutions* was recently introduced to provide a program capable of managing the entire supply chain from demand to supply by synchronizing customer demand and supply constraints through the provision of Internet-enabled communications about forecasts, inventory, and replenishments for all members of the chain.[33]

These are just a few examples of hundreds of software titles that address some aspect of supply chain management.

Several technologies have gained popularity recently, due to their ability to facilitate the flow of information across the supply chain. Many of the technologies fall, in today's language, under the heading of electronic communication. Other relevant technologies include bar coding/scanning, data warehouses, and decision support systems (DSS). It is interesting to note that several of these technologies have been available for a number of years; however, the application to interorganizational supply chains is a relatively recent phenomenon.

ELECTRONIC COMMERCE

Electronic commerce is the term used to describe the wide range of tools and techniques utilized to conduct business in a paperless environment. Electronic commerce therefore includes electronic data interchange (EDI), e-mail, electronic funds transfers, electronic publishing, image processing, electronic bulletin boards, shared databases, and magnetic/optical data capture (such as bar coding), the Internet, and Web sites.[34] Electronic commerce is having a significant effect on how organizations conduct business. Companies are able to automate the process of moving documents electronically between suppliers and customers in such a manner that the entire process is handled electronically; no paperwork is involved. With the rise of the Internet and the ability to transfer information cheaply and effectively over the whole world, electronic commerce is becoming

---

[33] Adapted from "Software + Systems = Solutions," *Distribution,* June 1997, pp. 42–44.

[34] "The IT Committees' Top 10 List," *Journal of Accountancy* 183, no. 2 (February 1997), 12–13.

a major focus for many organizations and represents a significant opportunity for integrated supply chain management efforts.[35]

Several examples of how electronic commerce can be utilized to conduct business more effectively and efficiently can be seen at General Electric (GE).

GE, the world's largest diversified manufacturer, has an electronic commerce strategy with the goal of making the World Wide Web a central feature of its business activities with both its suppliers and its customers. GE's electronic commerce applications include a Web-based automated procurement system and a Web-based ordering and order-tracking service at GE's electrical products distribution unit. GE will also release software to meld traditional EDI with the Internet.

GE does more business on the Internet than any noncomputer manufacturer. GE is now the most profitable U.S. company, reporting 1996 earnings of $7.28 billion on sales of $79.2 billion. The company believes the combination is no coincidence. GE attributes much of its bottom-line success to IT and electronic commerce initiatives that have made the organization more efficient in purchasing, manufacturing, bringing products to market, and designing services.

Cutting costs is another primary objective of GE's electronic commerce initiatives. A prime example is the GE Trading Process Network, a secure Web site that automates purchasing by GE's Lighting unit. Since joining the network in mid-1996, the GE Lighting unit has cut its average purchasing cycle time from 14 to 7 days. It has also reduced prices paid for materials by 10 to 15 percent. The reason provided for this reduction is the "openness of the Web" as "suppliers aren't sure who else is out there bidding." This procurement Web site is linked directly to GE Lighting's manufacturing resource planning software that allows GE's purchasing agents to provide up-to-date product blueprints directly from the factory floor, thereby providing "full end-to-end automation, from the factory to the buyer to the supplier."

Suppliers like the GE Web-based system as well. GE Lighting used to receive bids from its suppliers via EDI on the GE Information Services network, but that required suppliers to use proprietary EDI software, and the process was much less flexible than the current approach. Suppliers indicated that the new system has made it significantly easier to conduct business with GE.

In another Internet application, GE Supply, its electrical products distribution unit, will roll out GE SupplyNet, a Web-based ordering and order-tracking service. This system will serve as an on-line front end to GE Supply's order-entry system, part of the unit's just-in-time inventory and distribution system for overnight delivery.

GE is improving not only its own processes but is also selling its expertise in products and services outside of the company. For example, Actra Business Systems, a joint venture formed by GE Information Services and Netscape Communications, will soon release its first product, Business Document Gateway. This software will convert conventional EDI software into Internet formats, letting EDI users do business on the Internet.

In addition, GE Information Services recently released the second generation of GE TradeWeb, a service that lets companies that don't have conventional EDI soft-

---

[35] Dennis Keeling, "A Buyer's Guide: High-End Accounting Software," *Journal of Accountancy* 182, no. 6 (June 1996), 43–52.

ware use Web browsers to link to companies that do. On the services side, GE plans to turn the trading network into a revenue generator by offering the service to other manufacturers that want to buy goods from their suppliers over the Internet.[36]

ELECTRONIC DATA INTERCHANGE

EDI refers to a computer-to-computer exchange of business documents in a standard format. EDI describes both the capability and practice of communicating information between two organizations electronically instead of the traditional forms of mail, courier, or fax. Capability refers to the ability of the various members of the supply chain to use their computer systems to communicate effectively, whereas the practice refers to the ability of the members of the supply chain to willingly share and effectively utilize the information exchanged.[37] EDI is being utilized to link supply chain members together in terms of order processing, production, inventory, accounting, and transportation. "It allows members of the supply chain to reduce paperwork and share information on invoices, orders, payments, inquiries, and scheduling among all channel members."[38] The benefits of EDI are numerous, including:

- Quick access to information,
- Better customer service,
- Reduced paperwork,
- Better communications,
- Increased productivity,
- Improved tracing and expediting,
- Cost efficiency,
- Competitive advantage, and
- Improved billing.[39]

EDI improves productivity through faster information transmission as well as reduced information entry redundancy. Accuracy is improved by reducing the number of times an individual is involved in data entry. The use of EDI results in reduced costs on several levels, including:

- Reduced labor and material cost associated with printing, mailing, and handling paper-based transactions;
- Reduced telephone and fax transmissions; and
- Reduced clerical costs.[40]

EDI is also tremendously beneficial in counteracting the bullwhip effect described earlier in this chapter. Through the use of EDI, supply chain partners can overcome the distortions and exaggerations in supply and demand information by using technology to facilitate real-time sharing of actual demand and supply information. Although about 20

---

[36] Adapted from Clinton Wilder and Marianne Kolbasuk McGee, "GE: The Net Pays Off," *Informationweek* 615 (February 1997), 14–16.

[37] Bowersox and Closs, *Logistical Management.*

[38] William M. Pride and O. C. Ferrell, *Marketing,* 10th ed. (Boston: Houghton Mifflin, 1995).

[39] Paul R. Murphy and J. Daley, "International Freight Forwarder Perspectives on Electronic Data Interchange and Information Management Issue," *Journal of Business Logistics* 17, no. 1 (1996), 63–84.

[40] Bowersox and Closs, *Logistical Management.*

percent of all retailer orders for consumer products were placed via EDI in 1990, that percentage had grown to well over 60 percent by the end of 1995.[41] Clearly, firms are realizing that the use of EDI to facilitate information sharing throughout the supply chain is beneficial.

The use of EDI technologies has numerous applications throughout the supply chain. For example, several consumer products manufacturers such as Campbell's Soup, Nabisco, and Quaker Oats have implemented EDI to support their *continuous replenishment program* (CRP) with many of their customers. In these programs, also referred to as *vendor-managed inventory* (VMI) systems, the downstream members of the supply chain, in this case the retailers, become essentially passive in the information-sharing process. Through the CRP, the manufacturers gain access to demand and inventory information for each downstream supply chain site and make necessary modifications and forecasts for them. Estimates indicate that implementation of these types of applications have resulted in inventory reductions of up to 25 percent.[42]

EDI also represents clear cost savings for many of its users. Several firms, including Nabisco, GE, and P&G, have relied on EDI to implement various types of paperless transactions with their supply chain partners. At GE, the savings from implementing EDI have been documented at as much as $45 per order.[43]

BAR CODING AND SCANNING

At its most basic level, bar coding refers to the placement of computer readable codes on items, cartons, containers, and even railcars. This particular technology application drastically influenced the flows of product and information within the supply chain. As noted throughout the chapter, information exchange is critical to the success of supply chain management. In the past, this exchange was conducted manually, with error-prone and time-consuming paper-based procedures. Bar coding and electronic scanning are identification technologies that facilitate information collection and exchange, allowing supply chain members to track and communicate movement details quickly with a greatly reduced probability of error. The critical point-of-sale data that organizations such as Wal-Mart provide to their supply chain partners is made possible through the use of bar coding and scanning technology. This same technology is critical to transportation companies, such as FedEx, by enabling them to provide their customers with detailed tracking information in a matter of seconds.

Bar code scanners are most visible in the checkout counters of the supermarket. They scan the black-and-white bars of the Universal Product Code (UPC). This code specifies the name of the product and its manufacturer. Bar codes are used in hundreds of situations, ranging from airline stickers on luggage to blood samples in laboratories. They are especially useful in high-volume tracking where keyboard entry is too slow and/or inaccurate. Other applications are the tracking of moving items, such as components in PC assembly operations, railroad cars at various locations, and automobiles in assembly plants.[44]

---

[41] Lee et al., "The Bullwhip Effect."

[42] Ibid.

[43] Ibid.

[44] Efraim Turban, Ephraim McLean, and James Wetherbe, *Information Technology for Management: Improving Quality and Productivity* (New York: John Wiley, 1996), p. 233.

DATA WAREHOUSE

Although definitions vary, a data warehouse is generally thought of as a decision support tool for collecting information from multiple sources and making that information available to end users in a consolidated, consistent manner. The concept originated in the 1970s, when corporations realized they had many isolated information systems "islands" that could neither share information nor provide an enterprise-wide picture of corporate activities. Recently, there has been a renewed interest in this concept, as organizations adopt distributed computing architectures while they leverage their isolated legacy systems. Rather than trying to develop one unified system or linking all systems in terms of processing, a data warehouse provides a means to combine the data in one place and make it available to all of the systems.

In most cases, a data warehouse is a consolidated database maintained separately from an organization's production system databases. It is significantly different from a design standpoint. Production databases are organized around business functions or processes such as payroll and order processing. Many organizations have multiple databases, often containing duplicate data. A data warehouse, in contrast, is organized around informational subjects rather than specific business processes. The data warehouse, then, is used to store data fed to it from multiple production databases in a format that is readily accessible by end users. Data held in data warehouses are time-dependent, historical data and may also be aggregated.

For example, separate production systems may track sales and coupon mailings. Combining data from these different systems may yield insights into the effectiveness of coupon sales promotions that would not be immediately evident from the output data of either system alone. Integrated within a data warehouse, however, such information could be easily extracted.

One immediate benefit of data warehousing is the one previously described in the example about sales and marketing data. Providing a consolidated view of corporate data is better than many smaller (and differently formatted) views. Another benefit, however, is that data warehousing allows information processing to be off-loaded from individual (legacy) systems onto lower-cost servers. Once done, a significant number of end-user information requests can be handled by the end users themselves, using graphical interfaces and easy-to-use query and analysis tools. Accessing data from an updated information warehouse should be much easier than doing the same thing with older, separate systems. Furthermore, some production system reporting requirements can be moved to decision support systems—thus freeing up production processing.[45]

INTERNET

In terms of advancement in technology and communications capabilities, perhaps the most influential development over the past decade has been the adaptation of the Internet from strictly government and research applications into the areas of commerce and mass communications. At the most basic level, a network of networks, the Internet provides instant and global access to an amazing number of organizations, individuals, and information sources. Through systems like the popular World Wide Web (the Web), Internet users are able to conduct organized searches on specific topics as well as browse various Web sites to discover the vast resources available to them through their computer.

---

[45] Adapted from Turban, McLean, and Wetherbe, *Information Technology for Management*, pp. 358–359.

Originally, the Internet was an initiative sponsored by the U.S. Department of Defense to link its labs with American universities in an ingenious and robust way. Instead of connecting computers in a hierarchical, trunk-and-branch fashion (such as with a city's electric or water supply network), the Internet ties computers together in a decentralized system, analogous to a grid pattern of streets crisscrossing a city. As a message leaves a computer in, say Portland, Maine, bound for another one in Memphis, Tennessee, it is broken into a series of small "packets" of several characters each. Each packet is sent along the route of interconnected computers that is at the instant of its dispatch less crowded than any other path. At the receiving end, the packets, which may have come by completely different paths, are reassembled into a complete message.

During the Cold War, the great advantage of this approach was that it made the Internet virtually indestructible, even by an atomic blast. An electric network can be knocked out if you destroy its central station, but in principle the Internet simply could send messages along new paths if some of its nodes were destroyed. The same design concept now makes the Internet surprisingly scalable; that is, able to absorb dramatically increasing traffic without becoming frozen by the "information superhighway's" version of gridlock.

The Internet offers tremendous potential for supply chain members to share information in a timely and cost-effective manner, with relative ease. Many organizations are now exploring the numerous opportunities provided by the Internet. For example, the Internet provides opportunities for the development of EDI systems.[46] It also provides an incredible source of information about potential suppliers of products and services. A few examples of the type of information available on the Internet are provided in the section on the World Wide Web presented later in this chapter.

Although the potential benefits of supply chain applications on the Internet are substantial, as with any emergent technology, certain issues must be resolved. A key Internet concern is the issue of privacy, the level of security for sensitive information. Privacy of information transmitted on the Internet is an issue for all users, particularly in the use of credit-card numbers and other sensitive information. For supply chain members already struggling with the challenge of freely sharing information, these issues only add to their concerns.

These issues may soon be resolved. Currently, Web software called "merchant server" is in advanced stages of development.[47] Although present applications are being developed to assist with consumer transactions, such as providing secure conduits for payment information and transactions, other applications are not far behind. One approach for such security problems is the development of the supply chain's own Intranet.

INTRANET/EXTRANET

Intranets are networks internal to an organization that use the same technology that is the foundation of the global Internet. Many industry analysts expect such corporate networks to provide most of the revenue for computer hardware and software vendors over the next few years as an increasing number of businesses expand their internal networks to improve efficiency.

---

[46] Pride and Ferrell, *Marketing.*

[47] Rod Newing, "Secure Internet Transactions at Last!" *Logistics Management,* May 1997, pp. 15–17.

By using Web browsers and server software with their own internal systems, organizations can improve internal information systems and link otherwise incompatible groups of computers. Internal networks often start out as ways to link employees to company information, such as lists, product prices, or benefits. Because internal networks use the same language and seamlessly connect to the public Internet, they can easily be extended to include customers and suppliers, forming a supply chain "Extranet" at far less cost than a proprietary network.

WORLD WIDE WEB

The World Wide Web is the Internet system for hypertext linking of multimedia documents, allowing users to move from one Internet site to another and to inspect the information available without having to use complicated commands and protocols.

The implications of the Web for business applications are obvious and far-reaching. Web-based technology and tools have been developed in virtually every industry and form of commerce supply chain organizations are no exception. For instance, *Enterprise Transportation Management* was recently launched by Metasys Inc. Through the Oracle Web Applications Server, this system deploys a variety of critical information about transportation and distribution applications throughout the supply chain. Further, the system can be accessed with any Java-enabled browser. Access may be controlled through a corporate network, via the Internet or an Intranet Web site.[48]

The number of Web sites relevant to supply chain management is growing at a rapid pace. From specific sites providing information about the capabilities and fees of potential supply chain partners to educational sites developed primarily as reference tools, the number of sites and variety of information available on the Web is impressive. Examples of the Web sites available include the following:

WWW.con-waynow.com provides information about the expedited motor-carrier arm of Con-Way Transportation Services, providing information about the company's services, market coverage, and truck fleets, as well as direct e-mail links to Con-Way NOW's sales, operations, and human resources departments;

WWW.fedex.com provides a wide range of information including services offered, shipment tracking, billing information, shipping software, press releases, and drop-box locations;

WWW.gebn.bus.msu.edu provides access to Global Procurement and Supply Chain Benchmarking Initiative home page. The Global Procurement and Supply Chain Benchmarking Initiative is a third-party procurement and supply chain benchmarking effort housed in The Eli Broad Graduate School of Management at Michigan State University. The primary mission of this group is to collect and disseminate information concerning the best procurement and supply chain strategies, practices, and processes being employed by companies across a wide range of industries worldwide;

WWW.nitl.org is a site developed by and partially reserved for members of the National Industrial Transportation League. Other parts of the site are available to the general public, including information on the organization itself, a list of its member

---

[48] "Software + Systems = Solutions," pp. 42–44.

firms, and various other pieces of information about the organization and other transportation-related sites;

WWW.supply-chain.com developed by the Supply-Chain Council provides a valuable reference source introducing shippers to the council's mission and *Supply-Chain Reference Model,* a leading-edge benchmarking tool being developed for specific supply chain applications;

WWW.transportlink.com is a searchable site developed by Southern Motor Carrier, a leading data software and information service provider, crafted specifically for the motor-carrier industry to help locate information related to freight transport. The site links home pages of motor carriers, shippers, third-party logistics companies, and industry provider organizations; and

WWW.transportlaw.com developed by the Transportation Consumer Protection Council contains information on the council's educational programs and news on transportation law with the goal of providing a clearinghouse for information on legal issues in the transportation industry.[49]

Most of the supply chain–related professional societies have highly informative home pages. These Web sites typically provide information about the organization's objectives, educational and training opportunities, educational products, reference libraries, job placement services, discussion forums, conferences, and membership requirements. Examples of professional societies include:

- American Production and Inventory Control Society (APICS): **WWW.apics.org**
- Council of Logistics Management (CLM): **WWW.clm1.org**
- National Association of Purchasing Management (NAPM): **WWW.napm.org**

DECISION SUPPORT SYSTEMS

By the early 1970s, the demand for all types of IS started to accelerate. The increased capabilities and reduced costs justified computerized support for an increased number of nonroutine applications. At that time, the discipline of decision support systems (DSS) was initiated. The basic objective of a DSS is to provide computerized support to complex nonroutine and partially structured decisions.

At first, the cost of building a DSS prohibited its widespread use. However, the availability of low-cost personal computers around 1980 changed this situation. Desktop PCs, which are easily programmable, made it possible for a person with limited programming ability to build useful DSS applications (e.g., spreadsheets with built-in macros). This was the beginning of the era of end-user computing. Analysts, managers, many other professionals, and secretaries began building their own systems.[50]

Given the complexity of supply chains, development of DSS to assist decision makers in terms of both the design and operation of integrated supply chains is likely to increase. These DSS will help decision makers identify opportunities for improvements across the supply chain, far beyond what even the most experienced manager could provide through intuitive insight. Supply chain–wide DSS will allow management to look at the

---

[49] Adapted from "Logistics on the Web," *Logistics Management,* March 1997, pp. 33, 35.

[50] Turban, McLean, and Wetherbe, *Information Technology for Management,* pp. 41–42.

relationships across the supply chain, including suppliers, manufacturing plants, distribution centers, transportation options, product demand, relationships among product families, and a host of other factors to optimize supply chain performance at a strategic level.

Supply chain DSS require large amounts of both static and dynamic information from the member organizations. The static information includes production rates and capabilities for all supply chain entities, bills of material, routings, and facility preference. The dynamic information includes forecasts, orders, and current deliveries. Using all of this information to solve, for example, a quick-response scheduling problem across the supply chain is virtually impossible with a single technology. However, all the data can be readily obtained from existing information systems through structured query language (SQL) calls to various relational databases or to the "supply chain data warehouse" if one exists.

Specific technologies that may be utilized for an effective supply chain management DSS include the following:

1. **SQL interface.** Efficient relational databases are required to handle the vast amount of forecast, order, inventory, process, and product information. The DSS must serve as a data concentrator and have an SQL interface for direct links to common relational databases.

2. **Expert system rules.** Once the data have been gathered and a schedule produced, the scheduler interprets the schedule and determines its validity. Expert systems technology can capture some of the scheduler's expertise. The expert system can apply and test the validity of production rules of thumb, analyze the schedule, and recommend policy changes that yield cost savings.

3. **Scheduling algorithms.** The scheduling tool should be able to develop a schedule based on the information in its database. The process of generating the schedule involves determining what should be made, when, how much, and on what production units. The scheduling tool should contain algorithms based in traditional operations research algorithms, including capacity balancing, materials explosion, sequencing, lot sizing, just-in-time scheduling, and material flow adjustment.

4. **Linear programming capabilities.** The software tool should have the capability to formulate any linear, nonlinear, or mixed-integer model. Direct links should be available to the best commercially available optimizers. Special algorithms and approaches are needed for large-scale nonlinear problems and decision making under risk and uncertainty.

5. **Blocked scheduling.** Blocked operations defy most algorithmic approaches, especially when transitions involve significant sequence-dependent setup costs and losses. Examples of blocked operations that are particularly difficult include chemical reactors, plastics extruders, paper machines, continuous blenders, packaging lines, printing presses, and some flexible manufacturing processes. A combination of linear programming and expert system rules is particularly effective.

6. **Multisite/multistage scheduling.** Multiplant and multistage processes are encountered routinely. Linear programming can allocate production across plants and optimally distribute products to warehouses and demand centers. The information required includes raw material availability and costs, transportation costs, inventory storage costs, and plant capacity and capabilities for all supply chain entities. Multistage processes can be handled within the bill-of-material structure, which

provides for different recipes and routings for making a product at each distinct stage of production.

7. **Graphical user interface.** A powerful graphical user interface (GUI) is needed to provide facilities for the on-line creation of custom windows and dialog boxes, pull-down menus, presentation graphics, and hypertext help. These capabilities enable new applications to be built in just a few days and user interfaces to be constructed quickly and easily.

8. **User definable database.** Every scheduling application has unique attributes that need to be defined in the form of large matrices, bills of materials, product flows, and so on. The database should be user definable and utilize an object-oriented approach. Extensive data manipulation capabilities should be provided via set and matrix algebra, a macro language, and an integrated expert system shell that operates directly on the database.

9. **Available-to-promise.** In today's customer-driven business environment, customers want a quicker response to their inquiries as to whether a product or capacity is available-to-promise. Soon customers will want response time to shrink to near zero. As global competition increases, more companies will move to such scheduling practices and bring their customers into their production processes.

10. **Demand management.** Demand management is the operational management of demand information for planning purposes. In every supply chain there are operations that need to be planned based on predicted demand. The specific operations, including production of intermediates, purchase of raw materials, and production of finished goods are a function of asset flexibility and market lead times. The issue is not just forecasts but how to generate forecasts, manage them, reconcile new information with the forecasts, and constantly keep them up-to-date.[51]

Summary

The sharing of information among supply chain members is a fundamental requirement for effective supply chain management. At the ultimate level of integration, decision makers at all levels within the supply chain member organizations are provided with the information they need, in the desired format, when they need it, regardless of where within the supply chain this information originates. Providing decision makers within the supply chain with the "right" information, in the necessary format, and in a timely manner is a major challenge. In an effort to meet this challenge, many organizations will need to implement some type of IOIS. These IOISs must then contain the information required for the key decision makers in all relevant functional areas, in all supply member organizations. The information requirements determination approaches presented in this chapter have been shown to be effective in ensuring that these information requirements are met.

The information systems and the technologies utilized in these systems represent one of the fundamental elements that "link" the organizations of a supply chain. The range of technologies available to support supply chain management efforts is vast and ever changing. Unfortunately, there is not a single "right" IT solution to supply chain management. Organizations need to explore various options to arrive at a solution that

---

[51] Adapted from Bernd H. Flickinger and Thomas E. Baker, "Supply Chain Management in the 1990s," *APICS—The Performance Advantage,* February 1995, pp. 24–28.

provides the functionality required for their specific supply chain management initiative. Toward this end, benchmarking other organizations involved in integrated supply chain efforts to identify "best practices" is essential.

Supply chain management initiatives are unlikely to succeed without the appropriate information systems and the technology required to support them. Given this situation, information systems and technology decisions can not be taken lightly. These important decisions should be made by a cross-functional, interorganizational management group that has been afforded the time and resources required to develop a supply chain information systems strategy, implement the strategy, and oversee its ongoing performance.

Managing the Flow of Materials across the Supply Chain

Introduction

The critical importance of effectively managing the flow of materials across the supply chain (see Figure 3-1) has in recent years been realized by corporate executives and academicians alike. The cost associated with this flow of materials has been a matter of particular interest to these executives. Industry experts estimate not only that total supply chain costs represent the majority share of operating expenses for most organizations but also that, in some industries, these costs approach 75 percent of the total operating budget.[1] "According to the U.S. Department of Commerce, companies are spending more than $600 billion annually on logistics-related services and activities."[2] One of the main promises that supply chain management holds is the opportunity to improve this flow of materials across the supply chain from the perspective of the end user, while reducing supply chain costs at the same time.

Establishing integrated supply chains that provide end customers and supply chain member organizations with the materials required, in the proper quantities, in the desired form, with the appropriate documentation, at the desired location, at the right time, and at the lowest possible cost lies at the very heart of supply chain management. As organizations attempt to create and manage these integrated supply chains, several key issues need to be addressed, including:

- Understanding of existing supply chains,
- Reengineering supply chain logistics,

---

[1] Francis J. Quinn, "What's the Buzz? Supply Chain Management; Part 1," *Logistics Management* 36 (February 1997), 43; and *Business Wire,* "Supply Chain Management Becoming Leading Strategic Concern in Chemical Industry, New A. T. Kearney Study Shows," June 1997, p. 30

[2] H. Donald Ratliff, "Logistics Management: Integrate Your Way to an Improved Bottom Line," *IIE Solutions* 27, no. 10 (October 1995), 31.

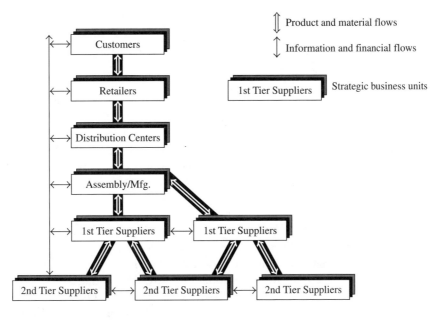

Bidirectional arrows reflect the accommodation of reverse materials and
information feedback flows.

FIGURE 3-1 Integrated Supply Chain Model

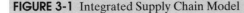

- Recognizing the importance of time, and
- Establishing a performance measurement system for the supply chain.

Each of these issues is addressed in this chapter.

Understanding Supply Chains

In recent years, few topics have generated more interest than SCM. The notion of your
organization, its suppliers, their suppliers, your customers, and their customers, all working together to meet the needs of the ultimate end customer for the mutual benefit of all
parties concerned is a very appealing proposition. However, adopting and implementing
an SCM strategy requires considerable effort and represents a quantum change in
direction for many organizations. Prior to embarking into the promising, but largely "un-
charted" world of SCM, it is critically important that organizations have a detailed understanding of current supply chains and associated processes. This understanding will serve
the organization well in its efforts to determine the relative importance of its various
supply chains and to identify those processes most in need of improvement. In this section, we describe several tools and techniques employed by managers to help them fully
understand their organizations' supply chains.

SUPPLY CHAIN BASICS

Most organizations are simultaneously members of multiple supply chains. An organization in each chain typically offers a number of products and services, purchases materials from a wide range of suppliers, and sells to multiple customers. From the perspective of a typical organization, each of its supply chains will have both internal and external "linkages." However, it is unlikely that all of the organization's supply chains will be part of formal interorganizational SCM initiatives. An organization must, therefore, focus its SCM efforts on those supply chains most critical to the organization's success. By critical, we mean those supply chains, related processes, suppliers, and customers that offer the greatest potential for achieving a competitive advantage, and that, therefore, hold the greatest promise for the ongoing success of the organization. In discussing supply chains, we will first differentiate between internal and external supply chains.

INTERNAL SUPPLY CHAINS

The internal supply chain is that portion of a given supply chain that occurs within an individual organization. Internal supply chains can be quite complex. Given the multi-divisional, international organizational structures found in many businesses, it is not uncommon for the internal part of a supply chain to have multiple "links" that span the globe. Developing an understanding of the organization's internal supply chain is often an appropriate starting point for firms considering an SCM initiative. It is interesting to note that in these multidivisional structures, the employees of one division often view the "other" divisions in much the same manner as they would external suppliers or customers. In some cases, the "turf wars" that exist between divisions make it very difficult to integrate cross-divisional functions and processes.

Development of supply chain process maps (flowcharts) for major supply chains and their related processes is a useful technique for establishing an understanding of the internal supply chain. Process map development is best accomplished through the use of cross-functional teams comprised of personnel from all parts of the organization included in the supply chain under review. Team members must be knowledgeable regarding their part of the supply chain and must also have an understanding of how their part interfaces with the other supply chain members.

To facilitate the process mapping activity, each team member should be provided with instructions about the mapping convention to be utilized and other information requirements. The objective of this exercise is to develop supply chain maps that present all supply chain entities along with key processes. Examples of key processes and associated entities include order transmittal (sales), order entry (materials planning), order preparation (purchasing, manufacturing, warehousing), and order shipment (distribution and transportation). Each team member documents the steps in its portion of the supply chain along with current performance information.

Once the team members have completed the process maps for their part of the supply chain, the entire cross-functional team meets to develop the overall internal supply chain map. This step should be conducted in a workshop session because there is often considerable "learning" that takes place when the team members present their portion of the supply chain. It is interesting to note during the workshops the different (and in some cases limited) levels of understanding that individuals exhibit regarding "what happens" outside of their part of the process. (Examples of internal supply chain process maps are presented in the chapter 5 cases.)

EXTERNAL SUPPLY CHAINS

Once an understanding of the internal supply chain is gained, it is necessary to extend the analysis to the external portion of the supply chain (i.e., key suppliers and customers). This is an important step as significant opportunities for improvement often lie at the interfaces between the various supply chain member organizations. This step also adds a greater level of complexity, given that multiple organizations and their representatives are now participating in the analysis. At this point in the analysis, the organization needs to focus its efforts on those supply chains that are most important to the organization's success.

Once the key supply chains have been identified, it is also necessary to identify the supply chain member organizations (suppliers and customers) that are considered most critical to the organization's supply chain management efforts. These key suppliers and customers are likely to provide the greatest benefits to the SCM initiative. Organizations must be important members of the supply chain because the time and effort required for a significant SCM program is not warranted for "minor players."

In selecting external members, several issues should be addressed. First, consideration should be taken to identify the competitive situation that exists between prospective SCM members. SCM endeavors are likely to be more productive if participating organizations are not direct competitors. There may be limits to collaborative supply chain efforts when both buyer-supplier and competitor relationships exist between participating organizations (i.e., company A is supplier to company B in one market, but A and B are direct competitors in several other markets). Second, all organizations and their representatives must be pursuing similar goals. This does not mean that each organization should have identical goals, but their respective goals must be compatible with the overall SCM initiative. Third, SCM efforts have limited potential for success unless all organizations feel their involvement is beneficial. In an internal setting, participants may be able to survive situations where individual business units or functional areas may feel like "losers" (in terms of loss of planning authority, responsibility, resources, etc.) as a result of decisions considered optimal for the overall organization. An external SCM initiative is unlikely to be successful unless all members from each organization involved feel they are benefiting from participation.

Once the external participants have been identified, the development of the external supply chain process map is conducted in the same manner as discussed earlier for the internal supply chain. However, the team is now both cross-functional and interorganizational in its composition. This team should include representatives from all functional areas and all member organizations in the supply chain under consideration. Here again, the interorganizational workshop sessions have been found to be an effective means to complete the development of the external supply chain process maps. As with the internal supply chain workshops, significant learning takes place during these sessions.

BENEFITS OF INTERORGANIZATIONAL
SUPPLY CHAIN COLLABORATION

External supply workshop participants indicate that a number of benefits are associated with these sessions in addition to documenting existing supply chain processes. Specific benefits include (1) establishing valuable contacts across the supply chain, (2) gaining insights into current organizational practices, and (3) identifying opportunities for joint projects between supply chain members. This phenomenon is consistent with other research findings in the area of interorganizational collaboration.[3]

Establishing Contacts across the Supply Chain   Participants became acquainted with key personnel from other supply chain member organizations. Establishing this network within the supply chain provides organizations with "real person" contacts within the other organizations. These contacts can be extremely valuable when organizations are presented with future supply chain problems ("opportunities"). Supply chains, where an established network exists, will be better positioned to respond to these situations than their counterparts where these contacts do not exist.

Gaining Insights into Current Organizational Practices   Simply giving organizations a forum to discuss their current practices with the entire supply chain membership is a very productive activity. These sessions often lead to the discovery of problems as well as identify potential remedies to correct these problems. For example, in a workshop facilitated by the authors, one organization discovered it was ordering a key component from its supplier considerably later than necessary. The organization knew its order requirements for the component after the completion of an intermediate stage in the production process. However, the organization was not communicating this requirement to its supplier until the production process was completed, *approximately two weeks later!* In another example, one supplying organization's performance measurement system for customer order fulfillment was based on the time period from placement of the customer's order through order shipment. According to this measure, the organization believed it was doing a "good" job. However, the organization's customer did not share this view. The customer measured order-fulfillment performance from its order placement through order receipt. On the basis of this measure, the supplying organization was late approximately 75 percent of the time. Further investigation revealed that 60 percent of the time that orders were late the problems were shipping-related. Prior to discussing this situation with its customer, the supplying organization was not even aware that there was a problem.

Joint Projects between Supply Chain Members   Oftentimes opportunities for joint projects between "subgroups" of the supply chain organizations are identified and projects initiated during sessions. Although these projects do not focus on the entire supply chain, they often address issues that improve overall supply chain performance. For example, in one project in which the authors participated, an internal consulting group of one organization conducted detailed studies of the linkages between its organization and the organizations adjacent to it in the supply chain, that is, its supplier and its customer. This approach helped identify the level of process variability and its causes. Once the sources of variability were identified, efforts were made to remove the root causes of variability or to determine the appropriate location and quantity of inventory required to protect against this uncertainty. In another project, the two organizations that discovered the order-fulfillment problem, discussed in the preceding section, established a joint project team to address this problem. Now an interorganizational cross-functional team from these organizations holds weekly conference calls and meets on a monthly basis. The group's objective is to improve the processes between the two organizations on an ongoing basis.

---

[3] Benjamin Gomes-Casseres, "Group Versus Group: How Alliance Networks Compete," *Harvard Business Review* 72, no. 4 (July–August 1994), 62–74; Rosabeth Moss Kantner, "Collaborative Advantage: The Art of Alliances," *Harvard Business Review* 72, no. 4 (July–August 1994), 96–108.

SUPPLY CHAIN PERFORMANCE

In order to assess the performance of an existing supply chain and its related processes accurately, it is necessary to have objective performance information. Ideally, this information should cover the full range of performance areas, including, but not limited to:

Products and services offered	Delivery
Sales	Cycle times
Market share	Assets utilized
Cost	Responsiveness
Quality	Customer service

Gathering this information for internal supply chain activities represents a significant undertaking. Obtaining and sharing information of this nature with other supply chain members represents one of the more significant challenges faced in SCM initiatives. However, if supply chains are to be improved, decisions need to be based on objective performance information and will require sharing of this type of information with key supply chain members. Organizational willingness to share information with other supply chain members is a critical selection criterion for SCM membership. An organization that is willing to receive information from other supply chain members but is reluctant to share information is a poor candidate for inclusion in an SCM initiative.

ROLE OF BENCHMARKING

In developing an understanding of existing supply chains and their associated processes, benchmarking analysis has been shown to be an effective means to determine the supply chain's performance relative to those of other organizations. Cook (1995) defines benchmarking as "the process of identifying, understanding, and adapting outstanding practices from within the same organization or from other businesses to help improve performance. This involves a process of comparing practices and procedures to those of the 'best' to identify ways in which an organization (or organizations) can make improvements. Thus new standards and goals can be set which, in turn, will help better satisfy the customer's requirements for quality, cost, product and service."[4]

The steps typically found in the benchmarking process include:[5]

1. Identify and understand current processes.
2. Form benchmarking team.
3. Determine what to benchmark.
4. Identify benchmarking partners.
5. Collect data.
6. Analyze data and identify performance gaps.
7. Take actions to improve.
8. Review results.

Benchmarking provides a means to focus the supply chain management efforts on those areas most in need of improvement. Identification of these high-priority areas is

---

[4] Sarah Cook, *Practical Benchmarking: A Manager's Guide to Creating a Competitive Advantage* (London: Kogan Page Limited, 1995), p. 13.

[5] Adapted from Ibid, p. 17

also useful prior to undertaking initiatives focused on reengineering the supply chain, which are discussed in the next section.

Reengineering Supply Chain Logistics

LOGISTICS AS A SOURCE OF COMPETITIVE ADVANTAGE
FOR THE SUPPLY CHAIN

Logistics is defined by the Council of Logistics Management (CLM) as ". . . the process of planning, implementing and controlling the efficient, effective flow and storage of goods, services and related information from the point of origin to the point of consumption for the purpose of conforming to customer requirements." Another author defines logistics as "the design and operation of the physical, managerial, and informational systems needed to allow goods to overcome time and space."[6] Logistics entails the planning and control of all factors that will have an impact on getting the correct product to where it is needed, on time and at the optimum cost. Superior logistical performance is one of the primary opportunity areas where organizations participating in an integrated SCM initiative can make significant improvements. Logistical management is vital not only to manufacturing and assembly industries, which are goods-oriented, but also to retailing, transport, and other distribution or service-oriented industries. Due to intensive competition in global markets, logistical management is considered an important source of competitive advantage. David Gertz, the author of *Grow to Be Great: Breaking the Downsizing Cycle,* says, "Supply chain and logistics are critical components of any successful growth strategy."[7] A study done by CLM found "world-class firms are more apt to exploit logistics as a core competency than their less advanced competitors."[8] This logic can certainly be extended to interorganizational supply chains. The CLM study identified what the "best-of-the-best" logistics firms do to achieve world-class status. The key focus areas include:

1. Positioning concerning the selection of strategic and structural approaches to guide logistics operations;
2. Integration of internal achievement of logistical operating excellence and boundary-spanning development of solid supply chain relationships;
3. Agility in terms of the firm's competency with respect to relevancy, accommodation, and flexibility; and
4. Measurement of internal and external performance.

In this section, we describe the types of changes being made by organizations to improve their logistics capabilities across the entire supply chain.

---

[6] Huan Neng Chiu, "The Integrated Logistics Management System: A Framework and Case Study," *International Journal of Physical Distribution & Logistics Management* 25, no. 6 (1995), 4–22. As quoted from M. S. Daskin, "Logistics: An Overview of the State of the Art and Perspectives on Future Research," *Transportation Research* 19A, no. 5/6 (1985), 383–398.

[7] Helen Richardson, Sarah Bergin, Perry Trunick, and Lisa Harrington, "New Life Through Logistics," *Transportation & Distribution* 37, no. 12 (December 1996), 46.

[8] Helen Richardson and Perry A. Trunick, "Breakthrough Thinking in Logistics," *Transportation & Distribution* 36, no. 12 (December 1995), 34.

SCM AND LOGISTICS

Integrated SCM will only increase the importance of logistics activities. SCM provides supply chain members with the opportunity to optimize logistical performance at the interorganizational level. At the limit, this means integrated management of the movement of materials from initial raw materials supplier across the chain to the ultimate end customer. This represents a major departure from current logistics practices that are often characterized by independent efforts with limited coordination between organizations.

Logistics professionals will continue to be challenged to manage the movement of products across the supply chain in a timely and cost-effective manner that meets customers' required service levels. In order to meet this challenge, a supply chain–wide logistics strategy is required, which will be the primary driver for the specific logistics strategy within each of the supply chain member organizations. Distribution networks, transportation modes, carrier management, inventory management, warehousing, order processing, and all other related activities will still have to be addressed. The scope of the logistics strategy is now the entire supply chain (not just each individual unit in the chain). It will no longer be necessary or desirable for each supply chain member organization to manage its logistics activities on an independent basis.

ROLE OF THIRD-PARTY LOGISTICS SERVICE PROVIDERS

Partnership is defined as a tailored business relationship featuring mutual trust, openness, and shared risk and reward that yields strategic competitive advantage. Often the formula for success in logistics is the one that leads to partnership. According to a 1996 CLM study into the market positioning and development of the third-party logistics industry, partnerships with third parties add value for a growing number of companies. Fully 72 percent of respondents used third-party logistics providers with outbound transportation as their most frequently outsourced service, followed by warehousing at just under 60 percent. In the future, freight consolidation and distribution were the logistics activities thought most likely to be outsourced (by 22.1 percent of respondents), followed by warehousing and inbound transportation and/or freight bill auditing/payments (18.2 percent and 16.6 percent of respondents, respectively). Outsourcing of logistics activities was considered to be extremely successful for the customers of 38 percent of respondents. Another 52 percent of respondents' customers considered outsourcing somewhat successful.[9]

Many firms engaged in international business also use external logistics service providers to handle most of their logistics needs. This clearly shows the need for these companies to establish a close relationship with their service providers. These partnerships reduce uncertainty and complexity in an everchanging global environment and minimize the risk while maintaining flexibility. Research by Daugherty et al. on international third-party service providers shows that partnerships are extremely important to help minimize some of the problems associated with information flow that can easily damage the supplier-customer relationship.[10]

Third-party partnership provides the advantages of ownership without the associated burden and allows organizations to take advantage of "best-in-class" expertise, achieve

---

[9] Richardson et al., "New Life Through Logistics," p. 46.

[10] Patricia J. Daugherty, Theodore P. Stank, and Dale S. Rogers, "Third-Party Logistics Service Providers: Purchasers' Perceptions," *International Journal of Purchasing & Materials Management* 32, no. 2 (Spring 1996), 23–29.

customer service improvement, respond to competition, and eliminate assets. "However, partnerships are not the way to go in all cases. They may not always be feasible or appropriate. Partnerships are complex relationships demanding corporate cultural compatibility, a strong perspective of mutuality, and symmetry between the two sides. To succeed, partnerships must include components that management controls and can put in place, like planning, joint operating controls, risk/reward sharing, trust/commitment, contract style, expanded scope, and financial investment."[11] As organizations adopt integrated SCM approaches, the role of third-party logistics services providers is likely to expand. This will be the case particularly for those third-party service providers that function effectively as part of the overall supply chain team. Third-party service providers may even be sought out for their SCM expertise.

INTERNATIONAL CONSIDERATIONS

Relative to domestic supply chains, international supply chains often entail (1) greater geographic distances and time differences, (2) multiple national markets, (3) multiple national operations locations, and (4) greater opportunities because of diversity of supply and demand conditions.[12] There are also additional costs associated with global supply chains. Major costs categories for a global supply chain include:

1. Manufacturing costs—purchased materials, labor, equipment charge, and supplier's margin;
2. Movement costs—transportation cost, inventory in pipeline and safety stock cost, and duty;
3. Incentive costs and subsidies—taxes and subsidies;
4. Intangible costs—quality costs, product adaptation or performance costs, and coordination;
5. Overhead costs—total current landed costs;
6. Sensitivity to long-term costs—productivity and wage changes, exchange rate changes, product design, and core competence.[13]

The current round of supply chain performance improvement by leading organizations has involved (1) rationalizing supply chains by changing locations and transportation modes, (2) reducing the buffers of inventory and time between successive steps in the supply chain, (3) increasing the geographic and international scope of the supply chains, and (4) increasing the sophistication of the goods and services accessed through supply chains.

Changes in foreign government regulations and policies may also create the need for changes in supply chain strategy. In Europe, for example, the deregulation of European Community (EC) economic, financial, and operational barriers have resulted in companies having to rethink their logistics strategy.[14] The single market environment has allowed greater flexibility in supplier sourcing and customer deliveries. Many companies are reengineering and rationalizing their logistical networks to take advantage of the reduction in, or elimination of, numerous artificial barriers that have previously affected all logistics decisions.

---

[11] Ibid., p. 52.

[12] M. Therese Flaherty, *Global Operations Management* (New York: McGraw-Hill, 1996), p. 286.

[13] Ibid., p. 288.

[14] Jack Berry, Herve Mathe, and Cynthia Perras, "Planning for the Long Haul: The Single Market Reroutes Logistics Management," *Journal of European Business* 4, no. 1 (September/October 1992), 32–36.

In addition to regulations, organizations must recognize the cultural differences found in many countries where they do business. "Seemingly small cultural differences among Asian countries are only an indication of the complexity of the task of managing logistics within the region."[15] Performance standards may vary from region to region or by organization. Therefore, a detailed understanding of foreign supply chain partners' capabilities as well as regional performance standards and regional infrastructure is required in global supply chains. Managers attempting to create global supply chains must be sensitive to specific local conditions and modify their strategies accordingly.

REENGINEERING CHALLENGES AND OPPORTUNITIES

As organizations embark on various initiatives to manage supply chains, they need to recognize that these efforts provide an opportunity to do much more than merely align their current logistical processes with those of their supply chain partners. SCM provides a platform to make significant improvements in logistical performance across the supply chain. These improvements may be the result of significant changes in roles of the supply chain member organizations. Organizations that ignore this reengineering opportunity may make improvements, but they are apt to be incremental in nature.

DeRoulet and Kallock[16] suggest the need for logistics to reengineer. They argue that "new approaches to business partnerships, dramatic innovations in technology, and reinvented supply chain strategies all result in new logistical expectations, none of which are attainable through mild-mannered, incremental tweaks to an existing process."[17] Whirlpool and Hewlett-Packard are among those companies that have successfully reengineered their logistics functions. At Whirlpool the reengineering process relies on computer systems and third-party partners that enable the company to fill orders within 24 hours. The Hewlett-Packard reengineering process takes the form of an improved delivery strategy, which was formulated and prototyped to meet the needs of the company.

The Council of Logistics Management suggests the following issues should be considered when making efforts to improve the supply chain:[18]

1. Help customers become more knowledgeable about logistics.
2. Unless an activity in logistics adds customer value, it should be eliminated.
3. Remove the barriers among the members of the supply chain to improve customer focus, make better and faster decisions, improve supply chain efficiency, and achieve sustainability.
4. Manage partnerships with third parties.

Organizations must recognize that their current logistical processes and practices may not be the best approach within the context of an interorganizational supply chain. Although organizations recognize the danger of suboptimization on a functional or departmental basis within the context of a single organization, this logic must now be applied to the supply chain to avoid "suboptimizing" performance at the organizational level. This means that the level of analysis for the reengineering effort is the entire supply chain, and it is this larger system that the member organizations must attempt to optimize.

---
[15] Richardson et al., "New Life Through Logistics," p. 43.

[16] David G. DeRoulet and Roger W. Kallock, "Logistics Drives Dramatic Innovations," *Transportation & Distribution* 33, no. 11 (November 1992), 40–44.

[17] Ibid., p. 40.

[18] Richardson et al., "New Life Through Logistics," pp. 44–53.

Although internal corporate process improvements can lead to significant performance gains, managers and academicians alike have realized that reengineering must extend beyond the organization to include other members of the supply chain. This outward-focused approach to reengineering is not only needed to align corporate actions with customer desires in terms of the timely provision of goods and services, but in most cases can also significantly improve profitability. One study, for example, found that supply chain reengineering can boost profits by 150 percent to 250 percent and can reduce order cycle time by up to 70 percent.[19] Process improvements in the supply chain may also significantly reduce the cost of doing business for supply chain members, particularly in the areas of administration, inventory control, warehouse management, and transportation.[20] Grocery industry managers, for example, believe they can cut $30 billion—10 percent of total operating budgets—via supply chain reengineering.[21]

Firms such as Dow Chemical,[22] SC Johnson Wax,[23] National Semiconductor,[24] Merle Norman,[25] Levi Strauss,[26] and Xerox[27] are but a few of the growing list of organizations to reap the vast benefits of total supply chain reengineering. The main obstacles keeping others from realizing similar benefits are top management's limited understanding of the process, a general resistance to change,[28] the persistence of rigid departmental-based organizational structures,[29] and lack of a customer perspective.[30] The cost of not reengineering can be high. For example, Compaq Computer estimates that it lost between $500 million and $1 billion in sales in the first 10 months of 1994 because its products were not available when and where customers wanted them.[31]

CASE STUDY: DOW CHEMICAL COMPANY[32]

The example of Dow Chemical–North America's efforts to reengineer one of its supply chains through the application of JIT demonstrates clearly how process improvement can result in impressive overall corporate performance. Dow initiated the program in 1993 with the objectives of increasing responsiveness to strategic customers and decreasing the supply chain process costs and capital through waste reduction. The reengineering effort, led by a multifunctional team of Dow managers, employed the Rummler-Brache Process

---

[19] Gary Gagliardi, "Tightening the Flow," *Manufacturing Systems* 14 (October 1996), 104–110; and "From the Editor: Manufacturers Must Strengthen Weak Links in Supply Chain," *Manufacturing Automation* 8 (May 1995), pp. 111–115.

[20] Gagliardi, "Tightening the Flow."

[21] Ronald Henkoff, "Delivering the Goods," *Fortune,* November 28, 1994, p. 64.

[22] Robert L. Cook and Robert A. Rogowski, "Applying JIT Principles to Continuous Manufacturing Supply Chains," *Production & Inventory Management Journal* 37, no. 1, (1996), 12–17.

[23] Tom Andel, "Forge a New Role in Supply Chain: Modern Warehousing," *Transportation & Distribution* 37 (February 1996), 107.

[24] Henkoff, "Delivering the Goods."

[25] "Supply Chain Makeover Doubles Company's Inventory Accuracy," *IIE Solutions* 28 (May 1996), 72–74.

[26] "Reengineering, the Sequel: A New Tool for Growth," *Investor's Business Daily,* March 19, 1996, p. A4.

[27] Tim Minahan, "Xerox Plots a Plan Worth Copying," *Purchasing* 120, no. 11 (1996), 90.

[28] "Reengineering, the Sequel."

[29] Minahan, "Xerox Plots a Plan Worth Copying," p. 39.

[30] Robert W. Kallock, "Logistics Process Reengineering: Getting Started," *Transportation & Distribution* 35 (October 1994), 86.

[31] Henkoff, "Delivering the Goods."

[32] Adapted from Cook and Rogowski, "Applying JIT Principles."

Improvement Approach. This approach involves (1) identification of a critical business issue and a critical process for study, (2) organization and training of the process improvement team, (3) mapping of the current state of the process to be studied, (4) analysis of the process and identification of process wastes and their causes, (5) development of a map detailing what the process should look like, and (6) implementation of recommended process changes and measurement of results. Each step of the reengineering process as undertaken by Dow is discussed in the following section.

1. Process Identification   Dow selected the target supply chain by first performing an ABC analysis, which classified customers by dollar sales and profits. This revealed that approximately 90 percent of sales and profits were attributable to just 10 percent of the customer base. Then a detailed opportunity analysis of these primary customers was conducted with one key application selected. The supply chain selected included a Michigan-based Dow customer using anhydrous hydrochloric acid (AHCL) as a key raw material in the production of a number of products. The selection of this supply chain was further based on the fact that Dow had a long-term, committed relationship with the customer.

2. Organized and Trained Team and 3. Mapping of Current Process   An interorganizational, cross-functional team was assembled to reengineer the important supply chain. A process—as opposed to a functional—perspective was fostered. The interorganizational process improvement team developed a comprehensive process map detailing each step in the flow of AHCL between the two companies.

4. Process Analysis and Identification of Waste Sources and Causes, 5. Mapping of Desired Process, and 6. Actions Taken and Results   Sources of waste identified included over $1.8 million worth of excess inventory. The team's efforts then focused on reducing waste in this part of the process. Consistent with JIT philosophy, waste inventory was targeted for elimination. This required efforts to decrease AHCL demand and lead-time uncertainty significantly. The team then worked together to successfully deal with these issues and realize its waste reduction goals. Within three years of initiation, the results of the reengineering efforts were impressive: (1) Supply chain demand forecast accuracy was improved by 25 percent, (2) distribution lead time was cut by 25 percent, (3) lead-time variability decreased by 50 percent, (4) customer responsiveness increased, (5) working capital decreased by more than $880,000 (due to waste reduction), and (6) a pretax annual total cost savings of $170,000 was realized.

INFORMATION SYSTEMS AND TECHNOLOGY: KEY ENABLERS FOR SUPPLY CHAIN REENGINEERING

Because of the scope and scale of the logistical networks represented by many integrated supply chains, logistical management is increasingly driven by information and information technology. In fact, information technology has significantly changed and improved the organization's ability to manage its logistical activities. A study done by Gustin and colleagues shows that high levels of information availability are closely related to successful implementation of the integrated distribution concept.[33] This level of information availability is every bit as critical in an integrated SCM environment. A 1995 KPMG Peat

---

[33] Craig M. Gustin, Patricia J. Daugherty, and Theodore P. Stank, "The Effects on Information Availability on Logistics Integration," *Journal of Business Logistics* 16, no. 1 (1995), 1–21.

Marwick study on logistics management and technology indicates that the two most important logistics issues for businesses are controlling the costs of logistics-related operations, and concern for information technology selection, deployment, and integration.[34] The deployment of information technology includes tools such as electronic data interchange (EDI), mobile communications system, onboard computers and satellite systems, computer-aided design, electronic funds transfer, point-of-sale systems, bar coding, value-added networks, electronic ordering systems, and decision support systems. Although the use of these tools is important for logistics to function effectively, it is also valuable to note that these tools should not be employed in a vacuum. They must be integrated into a system that brings customers, suppliers, and all activities in the supply chain together.

The central concern to the individual supply chain member from an information systems perspective is to design systems that facilitate open and rapid communication and information sharing across the supply chain.[35] Once a supply chain–wide connection has been established, steps should be taken to (1) eliminate the need to reenter information at each step of order-processing, (2) more closely integrate supply chain partners by providing them real-time status information, and (3) connect the organization more effectively into the larger electronic commerce community.[36]

Automation as a part of supply chain reengineering can also significantly reduce inventory management costs. Gagliardi outlines a two-step process to realize potential cost savings in this regard. First, inventory applications must be mirrored by the correct movement of information in order to properly time orders and minimize stocking levels. Second, order processing should be opened so as to allow stock from other warehouses and in-transit goods to be committed for shipment.[37] Cosmetics giant Merle Norman serves as an example of such process improvements in inventory management. Manual inventory-management processes were automated and the supply chain was fully integrated on a global scale. As a result, inventory accuracy rose from 55 percent to 99 percent. Customer-service measures hit similar levels of excellence.[38] The Planters LifeSaver unit of Nabisco, Inc. experienced similar gains via information technology-driven reengineering of supply chain processes.[39]

Applications of systems technology as a part of supply chain process improvement have recently spread to the Internet. Japanese electronic firms such as Toshiba, Sony, and Brother Industries are at the cutting edge of this movement.[40] Toshiba, for example, lists descriptions and specifications of desired items and invites suppliers to e-mail details of price, availability, and other information to it. Internet usage is a big part of the company's efforts to globalize and streamline procurement operations. Purchasing outside of Japan for fiscal year 1995 amounted to 341.6 billion yen with that figure expected to rise to 500 million yen by the end of fiscal year 1998.[41]

---

[34] Ratliff, "Logistics Management," p. 31

[35] Gagliardi, "Tightening the Flow."

[36] Ibid.

[37] Ibid.

[38] "Supply Chain Makeover."

[39] "Planters LifeSavers Redesigns Procurement and Production Planning," *Food Engineering,* July–August 1995, p. 36.

[40] Dianne Trommer, "Purchasers Use Net to Locate Suppliers—Companies Set Up Web Sites to Enhance Procurement," *Electronic Buyers' News,* September 30, 1996, p. 78.

[41] Ibid.

THE SUPPLY CHAIN OPERATIONS REFERENCE MODEL (SCOR)

Managers responsible for supply chain process improvement planning, implementation, and measurement received a much needed framework to guide their efforts in November 1996 when the 69-member Supply Chain Council introduced its Supply Chain Operations Reference Model (SCOR). Member companies, including diverse industry leaders such as Dow Chemical, Merck, Texas Instruments, Compaq, and Federal Express, worked together for over six months to develop the model. Specifically, they defined common supply chain management processes, matched these processes against "best practice" examples, and benchmarked performance data as well as optimal software applications with the end result being a tool for (1) measuring both supply chain performance and the effectiveness of supply chain reengineering, as well as (2) testing and planning for future process improvements.[42] The model was tested both in a mock supply chain situation and internally at Rockwell Semiconductor Systems with highly positive results.

At the core of the SCOR model is a four-level pyramid that provides a guide for supply chain members to follow on the road to integrative process improvement.[43] Level One consists of a broad definition of the four key supply chain process types (i.e., plan, source, make, and deliver) and is the point at which supply chain competitive objectives are established. Level Two defines the 26 core supply chain process categories established by the Supply Chain Council with which supply chain partners can jointly configure their ideal or actual operational structure. Level Three provides partners with information useful in planning and setting goals for supply chain process improvement. Finally, Level Four focuses on implementation of supply chain process improvement efforts.

The major benefit of SCOR is that it gives interorganizational supply chain partners a basis for integration by providing them, often for the first time, with something tangible to talk about and work with.[44] According to Vinay Asgekar, manager of Business Process Reengineering at Rockwell Semiconductor:

> Various departments are now talking the same language . . . that's a notable achievement. The framework helped to break down functional silos and allowed people to look at real issues and practices holding back supply chain management improvements. It gave people the chance to look at the supply chain with company-wide needs in mind.[45]

The Importance of Time

Superior cost, quality, delivery, and technological performance do not guarantee success for a supply chain. Increasingly, organizations are finding that they must also be able to compete on the basis of time. This does not mean that cost, quality, delivery, and technology considerations are no longer important; they are critically important. However, individual organizations and supply chain organizations must be competitive in these areas and be able to get their products and services to their customers faster than the competition.

---

[42] "69 Manufacturers Launch First Cross-Industry Framework for Improved Supply Chain Management," *PR Newswire,* November 12, 1996; and Dianne Trommer, "Reference Model on Its Way—Allows Firms to Evaluate Supply Chain Processes," *Electronic Buyers' News,* October 14, 1996, p. 59.

[43] Trommer, "Reference Model on Its Way."

[44] "69 Manufacturers Launch First Cross-Industry Framework."

[45] Trommer, "Reference Model on Its Way."

Increasingly, organizations are realizing that they are competing on the basis of time. Reducing the time required to provide the end customer with products or services is one of the major forces that is leading organizations to participate in supply chain management initiatives. Adopting an integrated supply chain management approach provides the means to make significant reductions in the cycle time required to move materials between supply chain members and to the end customer. Time has also been shown by several authors to be a highly effective area to focus overall improvement efforts within an individual organization.[46] The opportunity for improvement appears to be just as abundant in an interorganizational supply chain environment.[47] Organizations have found that in order to compete on the basis of time, a number of other competitive capabilities must simultaneously improve, including quality, flexibility, customer service, cost, and others.

This time-sensitive environment presents new challenges and opportunities for the individual organizations and supply chains. This section introduces the concept of cycle time, presents common causes of "long" cycle times, discusses an approach for making cycle-time improvements, and presents several critical success factors that should be considered as part of the cycle-time reduction initiatives.

CYCLE-TIME OVERVIEW

Cycle time is the total elapsed time required to complete a business process. All too often only a small percentage (e.g., 3 to 5 percent) of the total elapsed time required to complete a process has anything to do with "real work."[48] The rest of the time is typically devoted to a wide range of counterproductive activities and events, all of which take time. Identifying and eliminating these poor uses of time represent one of the major SCM opportunity areas. It should be noted, however, that cycle-time reduction is not just about completing a process quickly (i.e., speed for the sake of speed); it is concerned with completing the given process effectively. By focusing on key processes, supply chain member organizations can make significant improvements in cycle-time performance, improvements that can provide a source of competitive advantage for the supply chain.

CAUSES OF LONG CYCLE TIMES[49]

There are a number of causes of long process cycle times that can be found in a supply chain environment. In examining supply chain processes, typically one or more of the following causes will be present.[50] Several common causes of long process cycle times and key issues that should be addressed when these situations are encountered include, but are not limited to, the following.

---

[46] Joseph D. Blackburn, *Time-Based Competition: The Next Battle Ground in American Manufacturing* (Homewood, IL: Richard D. Irwin, 1991); and George Stalk, Jr. and Thomas M. Hout, *Competing Against Time: How Time-Based Competition Is Reshaping Global Markets* (New York: The Free Press, A Division of Macmillan, 1990); Christopher Meyer, *Fast Cycle Time: How to Align, Purpose, Strategy, and Structure for Speed* (New York: The Free Press, 1993); Robert B. Handfield, *Reengineering for Time-Based Competition* (Westwood, CT: Greenwood Publishing Group, 1995).

[47] Ernest L. Nichols Jr., Mark N. Frolick, and James C. Wetherbe, "Cycle Time Reduction: An Interorganizational Supply Chain Perspective," *Cycle Time Research* 1, no. 1 (1995), 63–84.

[48] Handfield, *Reengineering for Time-Based Competition.*

[49] Adapted from Ernest L. Nichols Jr., "It's About Time!" *Purchasing Today,* November 1996, pp. 29–31.

[50] Ken Kivenko, "Cycle Time Reduction," *APICS—The Performance Advantage,* February 1994, pp. 21–24.

Waiting   In many multistep processes, significantly more time is devoted to waiting between process steps than is spent in all of the processing steps combined! Where are the longest "waits" occurring in the process? What are the causes of these waits? What actions can be taken to reduce or eliminate the time spent waiting? Does the organization or supply chain need additional capacity in terms of facilities, equipment, or personnel?

Non-Value-Added Activities   The key processes found in many supply chains have been in existence for many years. When examining supply chain processes, it is worthwhile to determine the value that is being added by the overall process and individual process activities. It is not uncommon to find processes or activities within a process that were essential at an earlier point in time that add little or no value in the current environment. Is this process necessary? Do all activities in the process add value? Those activities that are not adding value should be eliminated. If the process activity is adding value, is it being conducted in the "best" way possible given current practices? For example, does the organization conduct quality inspections of purchased materials upon receipt, or does it utilize high-performing suppliers that certify that the materials they ship meet all specifications?

Serial versus Parallel Operations   Many supply chains have processes where activities are conducted in a serial manner (i.e., first complete activity 1, then complete activity 2, and so on through activity *N*). Are there opportunities in the process for activities to take place in a parallel (i.e., simultaneous) manner as opposed to the commonly used serial or sequential fashion? For example, within a manufacturing organization in the supply chain, are new products and the processes that will be used to manufacture these products developed concurrently, or is the product designed and then thrown "over the wall" to the manufacturing group? Are the manufacturing organization's key supplier and customer partners in the supply chain involved in the new-product development process?

Repeating Process Activities   A significant cause of poor supply chain cycle-time performance is having to repeat process steps due to product or service quality issues. There are few situations that can increase product cycle times (in terms of both average cycle times and variability) more than problems of this nature. Are there parts of the process that are repeated due to an inability to "get it right the first time"? What are the causes of these problems? What actions are necessary to resolve these problems?

Batching   Batching occurs when some quantity of materials, orders, and so on is accumulated at one step in the process or organization in the supply chain before it is released to the next process step or supply chain member organization. What is the rationale for batching? If the rationale is economic (rather than "that's how we have always done it"), then it should be implemented. An example of an economic rationale might be taking advantage of lower transportation rates for larger shipment quantities. In such circumstances, however, the economics of the situation should be periodically revisited to ensure that the savings associated with the "batch approach" are worth the time required.

Excessive Controls   How much time is spent and potentially wasted following the rules and regulations governing processes within and between supply chain member organizations? A common internal example of this situation is seen in purchase order (PO) processing. How many signatures are needed for a PO? How many of these signatures are merely being "rubber stamped"? We do not mean to imply that all controls should be abandoned. However, organizations would be well served to review the controls that are being utilized to govern both internal and external supply chain processes periodically, and determine if the level of control provided is worth the associated cost. A periodic cost/benefit analysis for intraorganizational and interorganizational controls as they apply to the supply chain is likely to be time well spent. Many organizations discover that their rules and regulations serve only to increase their response time to internal and external customers, and that many of these control mechanisms are more of a burden than a benefit.

Lack of Synchronization in Materials Movement   Are materials being moved across the supply chain in the most effective manner? Are product movements across the supply chain managed in such a way to ensure that the right quantity of the right product is getting to the right location at the right time? Or are materials arriving at the customer's location too early, causing additional storage and materials handling activities, or too late, disrupting the customer's operations and in so doing damaging the supplier's reputation?

Ambiguous Goals and Objectives   Do all supply chain member organizations have a clear understanding of the overall supply chain goals and objectives? Do all supply chain members understand what their organization must contribute for the overall supply chain to be successful?

Poorly Designed Procedures and Forms   Do the procedures and forms associated with a specific process lead to the efficient completion of the process? Or do they significantly increase the time required to complete the process by creating more work while adding little value?

Outdated Technology   Are the supply chain member organizations making the best use of available technology? How is key information communicated across the supply chain? For example, are purchase orders transmitted from the buying organization to the supplying organization by fax, EDI, or Internet, or are they mailed? Are warehousing operations within the supply chain utilizing a high level of automation or are they primarily manual operations?

Lack of Information   The cycle time for supply chain decision making is often lengthy due to the time needed to gather the information required to make decisions. It should be recognized that the required information may originate within the decision maker's organization or in one or more of the other supply chain member organizations. Do decision makers have the information that they need when they need it and in the desired format? How much time is being spent identifying, collecting, and manipulating the information required to make a decision versus making the actual decision?

Poor Communication   Intraorganizational and interorganizational communication are critical to overall supply chain performance. Have the necessary lines of communication been established across the supply chain member organizations? Do managers within supply chain organizations know whom to contact in other functional areas within their own organization, as well as in the other supply chain organizations, if there are problems? A list of key contacts in different organizations across the chain is a very simple but valuable resource in solving problems when they arise.

Limited Coordination   Coordination of supply chain processes is another important factor in determining supply chain performance. Do all parties involved in a given process recognize their respective roles and associated responsibilities? Are the interorganizational processes effectively coordinated? Are there formal "rules of engagement" to ensure that the desired level of coordination is maintained?

Limited Cooperation   Are all supply chain member organizations truly committed to the supply chain management initiative? If not, it is time to reevaluate the membership of those organizations that lack the required level of commitment. Cycle time and overall supply chain performance hinges on the cooperative efforts of the member organizations. Do all organizations have the appropriate cooperative philosophy?

Lack of/Ineffective Training   Proper training reduces the time for people to become proficient in their jobs and can also lead to improvements on an ongoing basis. Have all people involved in supply chain processes and activities received adequate training for their specific jobs? Are there ongoing training opportunities for employees that focus on supply chain performance improvement in general and cycle-time reduction in specific?

OPPORTUNITIES FOR CYCLE-TIME REDUCTION ACROSS THE SUPPLY CHAIN

Very few organizations do not have significant opportunities for cycle-time improvement from a supply chain process perspective. As customers increasingly focus on time-based performance, it is imperative that supply chain member organizations have the capabilities to meet this time-based challenge. SCM represents a challenge that is much like the game of golf: It does not matter how well you perform, there is always room for improvement. (It is also similar to golf in that your customers are not terribly impressed by your organization's past performances. To be competitive the organization must be the top performer every week.) As for future expectations, the level of importance associated with time will only increase.

Given this challenge, where should the supply chain and its member organizations begin in their quest for cycle-time reduction? Opportunities for cycle-time reduction exist on both an intraorganizational and interorganizational basis. Although it requires considerable effort, an examination of the entire supply chain—from raw materials through receipt by the end customer—is usually warranted. If a complete analysis can not be performed, specific supply chain activities that are possible candidates for review include:

Materials planning and scheduling	Manufacturing processes
Purchase order cycle	Customer order processing
Inbound transportation	Warehousing operations
Material receipt/inspection	Outbound transportation
Material review activities	Return materials/reverse logistics

How can the cycle times for key supply chain processes be reduced? It would be great if there were a "secret weapon" that guaranteed significant cycle-time reductions. Unfortunately, the secret weapon has yet to be discovered (at least by the authors). Furthermore, there is no "one right way" to reduce supply chain process cycle times, but rather there are many viable approaches. This does not mean that supply chain organizations must accept current cycle-time performance as a given. However, the specific tools and techniques required will depend upon the current state of affairs within the supply chain.

An approach that has been utilized by the authors in a variety of cycle-time reduction projects is presented in the remainder of this section. This approach is based on the process-improvement approach presented by Harrington[51] and is focused on cycle-time performance. It consists of the following six steps:

1. Establish a cycle-time reduction team.
2. Develop an understanding of the given supply chain process and current cycle-time performance.
3. Identify opportunities for cycle-time reduction.
4. Develop and implement recommendations for cycle-time reduction.
5. Measure process cycle-time performance.
6. Conduct continuous improvement efforts for process cycle-time reduction efforts.

Establish a Cycle-Time Reduction Team (CTRT)   The first step in this process is to identify the people who are going to conduct the cycle-time reduction effort. The composition of this team is extremely important as it will have a significant effect on the probability of success for the initiative. The CTRT should include representatives of each functional area and organization involved in the given process. Therefore, the CTRT will be cross-functional and, if the process includes more than one organization, will be interorganizational in its composition. Further, the CTRT members must possess a thorough understanding of their part of the process. This point can not be overemphasized. The authors have found that in some cases people assigned to CTRTs have a general or high-level understanding of the process but not a detailed understanding. Without a detailed understanding of the process, it is difficult to identify opportunities for cycle-time reduction and to make significant improvements in the process.

Develop an Understanding of the Given Supply Chain Process and Current Cycle-Time Performance   Once the CTRT is established, the next task is to develop an understanding of the current process and its associated cycle-time performance characteristics. A highly effective approach to complete this task is through the development of a process map (flowchart) by the CTRT in a "workshop" format. Each functional area and/or organization represented on CTRT is responsible for researching, documenting (i.e., mapping), and presenting its part of the process to the CTRT. The overall process map is then developed and is a composite of each of these various parts of the process. Current cycle-time performance for the overall process as well as the activities that make up the process are also required. Specific measures should include, but are not limited to, average cycle time, minimum cycle time, maximum cycle time, and standard deviation of the cycle times. Worksheets can be used in this activity to help ensure that all key information is addressed. Sample worksheets are presented in Exhibits 3-1 and 3-2.

Identify Opportunities for Cycle-Time Reduction   Once the CTRT has an understanding of the process and its current performance, the next task is to identify opportunities for cycle-time reduction. If this is the initial examination of the process, a number of opportunities for improvement are often readily apparent. The CTRT should attempt to focus its efforts on the parts of the process with the longest average cycle times and those parts of the process that have the highest levels of cycle-time variability.

Develop and Implement Recommendations for Cycle-Time Reduction   Having identified specific parts of the process that offer opportunities for cycle-time reduction, the

---

[51] H. James Harrington, *Business Process Improvement: The Breakthrough Strategy for Total Quality, Productivity, and Competitiveness* (New York: McGraw-Hill, 1991).

EXHIBIT 3-1   Supply Process Worksheet

Describe the current supply process cycle time between your firm and your supplier for the period from order placement to receipt of product from the supplier.

1. Develop a process flowchart that provides an overview of the current supply process between your firm and your supplier.
2. Describe each of the activities (e.g., order placement, order changes, transit, etc.) in the current supply process. For each activity, please provide the following information:
    A. Activity description
    B. Frequency that activity occurs
    C. Individual or group responsible for activity
    D. Information required to conduct activity (including source, how and when provided)
    E. Average activity cycle time
    F. Minimum activity cycle time
    G. Maximum activity cycle time
    H. Causes of activity cycle-time variability
    I. Activity-specific performance measures and current performance levels
3. What performance measures does your firm currently utilize to assess overall supplier performance?
4. What impact does the current supply process cycle-time performance have on your firm?
5. What potential actions could be taken by your firm to reduce the supply process cycle time?
6. What potential supplier actions could be taken to reduce the supply process cycle time?

CTRT must develop and implement recommendations for cycle-time reduction. This is the creative part of the CTRT's task. Specifically, for the opportunities identified in the previous step, the CTRT must determine what can be done to improve the process cycle-time performance, given its resource constraints. At this point it is good for the CTRT to remember that although it is charged with improving cycle-time performance, this is not time strictly for time's sake. Rather, the CTRT is striving for cycle-time improvements that recognize the cost, quality, and technology requirements of the marketplace. It is also imperative that the effects of any process changes are understood for all parts of the system in question. Computer modeling of the process and proposed changes is highly beneficial.

It is beyond the scope of this book to provide a detailed discussion of specific approaches to process cycle-time reduction. However, the reader is directed to several works available on this topic.[52] A helpful list of tools for cycle-time reduction is presented in Wetherbe's 1995 article, "Principles of Cycle Time Reduction: You Can Have Your Cake and Eat It Too."[53] This article provides an effective summary of 45 techniques that have been demonstrated to reduce process cycle times. These cycle-time reduction approaches address the areas of:

- Organization design and management,
- Human resources,
- Product management,
- Operations, and
- Interorganizational issues.

[52] See Blackburn, "Time-Based Competition"; Stalk and Houk, "Competing Against Time"; Meyer, "Fast Cycle Time"; and Handfield, *Reengineering for Time-Based Competition.*

[53] James C. Wetherbe, "Principles of Cycle Time Reduction: You Can Have Your Cake and Eat It Too," *Cycle Time Research* 1, no. 1 (1995), 1–24.

EXHIBIT 3-2   Customer Order-Fulfillment Process Worksheet

Describe the current customer order-fulfillment process that exists between your customers and your firm for the period from customer order placement to receipt of product by the customer.

1. Develop a process flowchart that provides an overview of the current order-fulfillment process that exists between your customers and your firm.
2. Describe each of the activities (e.g., order placement, order changes, transit, etc.) in the current order-fulfillment process. For each activity, please provide the following information:
   A. Activity description
   B. Frequency that activity occurs
   C. Individual or group responsible for activity
   D. Information required to conduct activity (including source, how and when provided)
   E. Average activity cycle time
   F. Minimum activity cycle time
   G. Maximum activity cycle time
   H. Causes of activity cycle-time variability
   I. Activity-specific performance measures and current performance levels
3. What performance measures does your firm currently utilize to assess overall customer order-fulfillment performance?
4. What impact does the current customer order-fulfillment process performance have on your firm?
5. Describe the type (e.g., raw materials, WIP, finished goods) and amounts (e.g., dollar value, quantities, and days of supply) of inventory held within your organization's portion of the supply chain.
6. For the inventory held within your organization's portion of the supply chain, indicate why this inventory is held.
7. How is the product transported from your organization to the customer? Which organization (e.g., your organization, the customer, third party, etc.) manages this in-transit portion of the supply chain?
8. What potential actions could be taken by your firm to improve the customer order-fulfillment process cycle time?
9. What potential customer actions could be taken to improve customer order-fulfillment process performance?

Once the specific recommendations are developed, the CTRT will then present these recommendations to the management responsible for the functional areas involved. Actual implementation of the changes will typically require people and resources beyond the charter of the CTRT. However, having CTRT members participate in the actual implementation efforts is often worthwhile. These individuals provide context for the implementation effort as well as detailed process knowledge.

Measure Process Cycle-Time Performance   After the initial recommendations have been implemented, it is necessary to determine the effects of the changes on the actual process cycle-time performance. Have the average process cycle times decreased? What effects do the implemented changes have on process cycle-time variability? Key performance measures must be implemented if they do not already exist. These measures need to be monitored on an ongoing basis to determine process performance.

Conduct Continuous Improvement Efforts for Process Cycle-Time Reduction
Process cycle-time reduction is not a one-time event, but rather an ongoing activity. Once

one process or part of a process has been examined and improved, it is time to move on to the next process or attempt to improve further the one at hand.

CRITICAL SUCCESS FACTORS FOR CYCLE-TIME REDUCTION

In conducting research with organizations that have successfully completed cycle-time reduction efforts in a variety of supply chain management areas, several "critical success factors" have been identified that include:

- Top management support;
- A commitment to significant cycle-time reduction goals;
- Use of cross-functional teams with team members that possess thorough process knowledge;
- Application of TQM tools (e.g., process mapping, Pareto analysis, fishbone diagrams, etc.);
- Training in cycle-time reduction approaches;
- Establishing, monitoring, and reporting formal cycle-time performance measures;
- Application of information systems and technology; and
- Collaboration with supply chain members.[54]

In the next section, we discuss a key element in establishing a successful supply chain reengineering effort, via effective performance measurement.

Performance Measurement

One component of SCM that had until recently been relatively neglected was that of supply chain performance measurement. The importance of performance measurement in the context of SCM cannot be overstated. In interorganizational systems such as supply chains, timely and accurate assessment of overall system and individual system component performance is of paramount importance. An effective performance measurement system (1) provides the basis to understand the system, (2) influences behavior throughout the system, and (3) provides information regarding the results of system efforts to supply chain members and outside stakeholders.[55] In effect, performance measurement is the glue that holds the complex value-creating system together, directing strategic formulation as well as playing a major role in monitoring the implementation of that strategy.[56] In addition, research findings suggest that measuring supply chain performance in and of itself leads to improvements in overall performance.[57] In one study of U.S.-Mexican maquiladora operations, improvements to performance were found in the areas of order cycle-time reduction, routing and scheduling, and effective

[54] Nichols, Frolick, and Wetherbe, "Cycle Time Reduction"; Thomas E. Hendrick, *Purchasing's Contribution to Time-Based Strategies* (Tempe, AZ: Center for Advanced Purchasing Studies, 1994); G. Tomas, M. Hult, Mark N. Frolick, and Ernest L. Nichols Jr., "Organizational Learning and Cycle Time Issues in the Purchasing Process," *Cycle Time Research* 1, no. 1 (1995), 25–39.

[55] Stanley E. Fawcett and Steven R. Clinton, "Enhancing Logistics Performance to Improve the Competitiveness of Manufacturing Organizations," *Production & Inventory Management Journal* 37, no. 1 (1996), 40–46.

[56] Ibid.

[57] Daniel C. Bello and David I. Gilliland, "The Effects of Output Controls, Process Controls, and Flexibility on Export Channel Performance," *Journal of Marketing* 61 (Winter 1997), 22; and Theodore P. Stank and Charles W. Lackey Jr., "Enhancing Performance Through Logistical Capabilities in Mexican Maquiladora Firms," *Journal of Business Logistics* 18, no. 1 (1997), 91–123.

handling of border crossings of outbound freight.[58] Another study found that implementation of performance measurement systems lead to improvements in process cycle time, cost, quality, and delivery performance.[59] However, despite its importance, prior to 1990, supply chain performance was measured in oversimplified and sometimes counterproductive (cost reduction–based) terms.[60] Lack of an appropriate performance measurement system has been cited as a major obstacle to effective supply chain management.[61]

RECENT DEVELOPMENTS IN SUPPLY CHAIN PERFORMANCE MEASUREMENT

The concept of SCM requires measuring overall supply chain performance rather than only the performance of the individual chain members. It is the combined performance of the supply chain, the final outcome of the efforts of all integrated members, that is of greatest importance from a measurement perspective. Although measures of supply chain performance differ in terms of individual indicators employed, virtually all have one central, overriding focus: continual improvement of end-customer service.[62] It is this final customer of the supply chain that must be satisfied for the overall supply chain to succeed on a long-term basis. These end customers care little about the time required to move materials between intermediate supply chain members or about the cost associated with this activity. The end customer is concerned with the time required to meet its demands and the cost of doing so. This fundamental concern is reflected most generally in a desire to continually reduce total cycle time.[63] A good performance measurement system also is "actionable": It allows managers not only to identify but also to eliminate causes of supply chain operational problems so that relationships with customers are not permanently harmed.[64] Beyond these general customer-oriented aspects of effective supply chain performance measurement, researchers have stressed the desirability of assessing a wide variety of phenomena indicative of overall supply chain performance. These include measurement of (1) changes in both the average volume of inventory held and frequency of inventory turns across the supply chain over time,[65] (2) the adaptability of the supply chain as a whole to meet emergent customer needs,[66] and (3) the extent to which intrasupply chain relationships are based on mutual trust.[67] Finally, effective measurement of supply chain performance entails looking beyond the in-

---

[58] Stank and Lackey, "Enhancing Performance."

[59] Ernest L. Nichols Jr. and Robert M. Monczka, "Value of Supplier Performance Measurement," working paper from the Global Procurement and Supply Chain Benchmarking Initiative at Michigan State University, 1997.

[60] Thomas A. Foster, "It Pays to Measure Performance: Logistics Performance Compensation Programs," *Chilton's Distribution* 90 (September 1991), 4.

[61] See Hau L. Lee and Corey Billington, "Managing Supply Chain Inventory: Pitfalls and Opportunities," *Sloan Management Review* 33, no. 3 (1992), 65–73.

[62] Stank and Lackey, "Enhancing Performance"; and Garland Chow, Lennart E. Henriksson, and Trevor D. Heaver, "Strategy, Structure, and Performance: A Framework for Logistics Performance." *The Logistics and Transportation Review 31* (December 1995), 285.

[63] Chow, Henriksson, and Heaver, "Strategy, Structure, and Performance."

[64] Stank and Lackey, "Enhancing Performance."

[65] Ibid.; Fawcett and Clinton, "Enhancing Logistics Performance"; and Lee and Billington, "Managing Supply Chain Inventory," p. 65.

[66] Bello and Gilliland, "The Effect of Output Controls, Process Controls, and Flexibility"; Fawcett and Clinton, "Enhancing Logistics Performance."

[67] Fawcett and Clinton, "Enhancing Logistics Performance."

tegrated chain itself in a variety of ways. For example, key members of some integrated supply chains employ outside auditors to conduct random customer-satisfaction surveys at supply chain members' operational facilities in order to ensure objectivity in the measurement process.[68] In addition, managers responsible for performance assessment should continually engage in supply chain benchmarking wherein they compare the results of internal supply chain performance with that of other target supply chains in a wide variety of industries, including their own.[69]

THE "BALANCED SCORECARD" APPROACH
TO SUPPLY CHAIN PERFORMANCE MEASUREMENT

Supply chain management requires that the member organizations have a means to assess the performance of the overall supply chain to meet the requirements of the end customer. In addition, it is necessary to be able to assess the relative contribution of the individual member organizations within the supply chain. This requires a performance measurement system that can not only operate at several different levels but also link or integrate the efforts of these different levels to meeting the objectives of the supply chain. In their 1996 work, *The Balanced Scorecard: Translating Strategy into Action,*[70] Kaplan and Norton present an approach that holds great promise for supply chain performance measurement. The "balanced scorecard" approach incorporates both financial and operating performance measures that are used at all levels of the supply chain. In an interorganizational supply chain environment, the supply chain level represents the starting point for the balanced scorecard.

The balanced scorecard formally links overall supply chain objectives and the strategies undertaken to meet these objectives with supply chain–wide performance measures. Examples of the different levels of balanced scorecards required to manage an interorganizational supply chain are presented in Figure 3-2. Objectives, strategies, and performance measures at the supply chain level can then be linked to the organizational levels (assuming that the supply chain consists of multiple organizations). Here individual organizations develop organizational level objectives, the strategies to achieve these objectives, and associated performance measures. This process is then repeated at the functional level within the individual supply chain member organizations. For example, the procurement function within a manufacturing supply chain member organization will develop its functional objectives, strategies, and performance measures, which are based on the organization's objectives, strategies, and performance measures. This process is then taken to the team or individual level within the various functions where the teams or individuals develop their own objectives, strategies, and performance measures based on those of their respective functional area.

At each level, the balanced scorecard addresses four key performance areas: (1) financial, (2) customer, (3) business process, and (4) learning and growth. Within each of these areas, key objectives are identified that are driven by the objectives and strategies of the next higher level in the scorecard hierarchy; specific performance measures associated

---

[68] Toby B. Gooley, "Partnerships Can Make the Customer-Service Difference," *Traffic Management* 33 (May 1994), 40.

[69] Stank and Lackey, "Enhancing Performance."

[70] Robert S. Kaplan and David P. Norton, *The Balanced Scorecard: Translating Strategy into Action* (Boston: Harvard Business School Press, 1996).

Supply chain Scorecard
Organization Scorecard
Function Scorecard
Team/Individual Scorecard

FIGURE 3-2 Balanced Scorecards for Supply Chain Management

with the objectives, performance targets, and initiatives to achieve the targets are then developed. Figure 3-3 presents an example of the balanced scorecard framework.[71]

WHAT SHOULD WE MEASURE?

There has been considerable debate regarding the specific performance measures required to manage an integrated supply chain. Organizations recognize that future competition is likely to pit different supply chains against each other in pursuit of the

FIGURE 3-3 Balanced Scorecard Framework

Financial Area

Objectives	*Measures*	*Targets*	*Initiatives*

Customer Area

Objectives	*Measures*	*Targets*	*Initiatives*

Business Process Area

Objectives	*Measures*	*Targets*	*Initiatives*

Learning and Growth Area

Objectives	*Measures*	*Targets*	*Initiatives*

[71] Robert S. Kaplan and David P. Norton, "Using the Balanced Scorecard as a Strategic Management System," *Harvard Business Review,* January–February 1996, pp. 75–85.

Performance Area	Primary Measures	Secondary Measures
Customer satisfaction/ Quality	• Perfect order fulfillment • Customer satisfaction • Product quality	• Delivery-to-commit date • Warranty costs, returnrs, allowances • Customer-inquiry response time
Time	• Order fulfillment lead time	• Source/make cycle time • Supply chain response time • Production plan achievement
Costs	• Total supply chain costs	• Value-added productivity
Assets	• Cash-to-cash cycle time • Inventory days of supply • Asset performance	• Forecast accuracy • Inventory obsolescence • Capacity utilization

FIGURE 3-4 Integrated Supply Chain Performance Measures

Source: PTRM Consulting, "Integrated-Supply-Chain Performance Measurement: A Multi-Industry Consortium Recommendation" (Weston, MA: Pittiglio Robin Todd & McGrath, 1994). Used with permission.

end customer's business. Therefore, it is critical to assess and continuously improve the performance of the entire chain. Recognizing the importance of this issue, a consortium of businesses, academics, and consultants developed a comprehensive group of performance measures for supply chain management.[72] These measures address four broad performance areas: (1) customer satisfaction/quality, (2) time, (3) costs, and (4) assets. For each of these areas, primary and secondary performance measures were identified by the consortium. These performance measures are presented in Figure 3-4.

The specific measures necessary to manage supply chain performance will vary according to the customer type, product line, industry, or other factors. However, the importance of maintaining an end-customer perspective (i.e., addressing issues that are truly important to the supply chain's ability to satisfy the end-customer requirements in the most cost-effective manner) when developing these measures cannot be overemphasized. Researchers have identified several supply chain characteristics and activities that significantly increase the likelihood that performance objectives will be attained. Most important is the integration, across the entire channel, of information systems that allows the sharing of information and also facilitates the measurement of performance.[73]

Summary

Although many organizations are involved in a variety of initiatives with key suppliers and customers, relatively few have taken the broader supply chain perspective. Organizations may realize that collaborative supply chain initiatives are the "right" thing to do, but many organizations are not entirely certain how to proceed. This chapter addresses several areas important to the management of supply chain material

---

[72] PTRM Consulting, "Integrated-Supply-Chain Performance Measurement: A Multi-Industry Consortium Recommendation" (Weston, MA: PTRM, 1994).

[73] Fawcett and Clinton, "Enhancing Logistics Performance"; Tom Richman, "Logistics Management; How 20 Best-Practice Companies Do It," *Harvard Business Review,* September–October 1995, p. 11; Ryan Mathews, "CRP Moves Toward Reality: Continuous Replenishment Will Either Be a Blessing or a Curse Depending on How the Process Is Managed on Both Sides of the Table," *Progressive Grocer* 73 (July 1994), 43; and Lee and Billington, "Managing Supply Chain Inventory."

flows. Understanding current supply chains, reengineering logistical processes, reducing cycle times, and performance measurement are all key parts of supply chain management.

Organizations must develop an understanding of current supply chain processes prior to implementing changes. This is an extremely important step in any SCM initiative. Although organizations have experienced over a decade of process reengineering, many organizations do not have a clear understanding of their intraorganizational or interorganizational supply chain processes.

In many cases, interorganizational processes are the product of evolution, rather than the result of a precision design effort. Reengineering interorganizational processes across the supply chain may hold benefits of a similar magnitude to those associated with internal reengineering efforts. However, as with internal reengineering, the appropriate application of information technology enables the reengineering of processes to occur.

Organizations must realize that overall supply chain performance ultimately affects their own individual performance. Furthermore, supply chains are only as strong as the weakest links between organizations in the chain. For example, the linkages between the supply chain manufacturing organization and suppliers may be functioning well. However, if the linkages between the manufacturing organization and the retailing organization are not functioning at a desired level, then the supply chain is not performing well. The critical linkage for the ultimate success of the supply chain is sales to the end customer. It matters little that performance at earlier stages of the supply chain is outstanding if the product is not available as needed to support retail sales.

The ultimate question that needs to be asked when establishing or improving supply chains is, "What are the effects on the end customer and other supply chain members?" If it can't be demonstrated that the proposed change is going to lead to an improvement from the end customer's perspective or that the change will somehow improve the process for the supply chain while not having negative effects on the end customer, don't do it!

Will supply chains be faced with the challenges of time-based competition? The answer for most supply chains is yes. An equally important question that needs to be answered is whether the supply chain is going to be dragged into the fray in a "reactive" manner or will it meet this challenge in a "proactive" manner? This choice faces many supply chains. For supply chains that have not undertaken formal cycle-time reduction efforts, there is no time like the present. The challenges are there, but the opportunities for significant cycle-time improvement are plentiful.

Supply chain performance measurement is also presented in this chapter. Many supply chain initiatives are currently addressing this area. A balanced scorecard approach that includes both financial and operational performance at various levels of the supply chain (i.e., supply chain, organizational, functional, and team levels) appears to hold promise for many SCM initiatives.

Organizations that can successfully incorporate the aforementioned areas into their supply chain management initiatives will be well positioned to manage the flow of materials across the supply chain.

4

Developing and Maintaining Supply Chain Relationships

In discussing the implementation of a truly integrated supply chain, organizations are continually faced with the challenge of managing the "people" part of the equation. As shown in Figure 4-1, relationship management affects all areas of the supply chain and has a dramatic impact on performance. In many cases, the information systems and technology required for the supply chain management effort are readily available and can be implemented within a relatively short time period, barring major technical mishaps. In addition, the inventory and transportation management systems are also quite well understood and can be implemented fairly readily. A number of supply chain initiatives fail, however, due to poor communication of expectations and the resulting behaviors that occur. Managers often assume that managing the personal relationships within and between organizations in a supply chain will automatically "fall into place" once the inventory and information systems are established. However, the management of interpersonal relationships between the different people in the organizations is often the most difficult part of the SCM initiative. Moreover, the single most important ingredient for successful supply chain management may well be a *trusting relationship* between partners in the supply chain, where each party in the chain has mutual confidence in the other members' capabilities and actions. Without a good relationship, all of the other systems (information systems, inventory, contracts, etc.) cannot function effectively. One supply chain manager from a Fortune 500 company expressed this feeling very succinctly:

> Supply chain management is one of the most emotional experiences I've ever witnessed. There have been so many mythologies that have developed over the years, people blaming other people for their problems, based on some incident that may or may not have occurred sometime in the past. Once you get everyone together into the same room, you begin to realize the number of false perceptions that exist. People are still very reluctant to let someone else make decisions within their area. It becomes especially tricky when you show people how "suboptimizing" their functional area can "optimize" the entire supply chain.
>
> Materials Management Vice President, *Fortune* 500 manufacturer

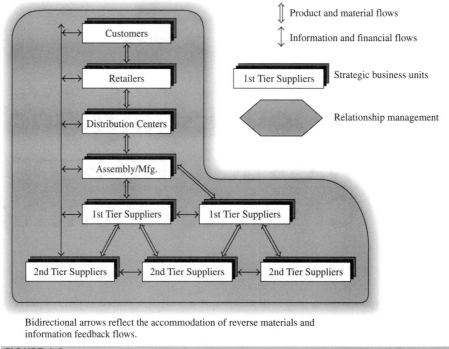

Bidirectional arrows reflect the accommodation of reverse materials and information feedback flows.

FIGURE 4-1 Integrated Supply Chain Model

This experience is not unique to this company. Almost every individual interviewed by the authors who was involved in a supply chain management initiative emphasized the criticality of developing and maintaining good relationships with the customers and suppliers in the chain. In deploying the integrated supply chain, developing trust in your partners and projecting trustworthiness to your partners are critical components for success. In discussing the role of solid relationships in supply chain management, we will emphasize that the trust-building process is an element that must *continually* be managed at all times. One of the most important rules to remember is that trust grows with use and disappears when not used.

In the early stages of supply chain development, organizations will often eliminate those suppliers or customers that are clearly not suitable, because they do not have the capabilities to serve the organization, are too distant, are not well aligned with the company, or are simply not interested in developing a relationship. After these firms are eliminated from consideration, organizations may occasionally encounter a supply chain member that is willing to put forth the time and effort required to create a strong relationship. In such cases, firms may consider developing a special type of supply chain relationship in which confidential information is shared, assets are invested in joint projects, and significant joint improvements are pursued. These types of interorganizational relationships are sometimes called *strategic alliances*. A strategic alliance is a process wherein participants willingly modify basic business practices to reduce duplication and waste while facilitating improved performance.[1] Strategic alliances allow firms to

---

[1] J. M. Schmitz, R. Frankel, and D. J. Frayer, "ECR Alliances: A Best Practice Model," Joint Industry Project on Efficient Consumer Response, 1995.

improve efficiency and effectiveness by eliminating waste and duplication in the supply chain. However, many firms lack the guidelines to develop, implement, and maintain supply chain alliances. This chapter discusses a process developed by case researchers that organizations can use to improve supply chain relationships and that, in the longer run, leads to the development of successful strategic supply chain alliances.

In this chapter, we:

- Develop a conceptual model of how supply chain alliance relationships are initiated and created.
- Identify a "checklist" of traits to look for in selecting an alliance partner.
- Discuss the different types of trust that exist in such relationships.
- Discuss the key practices for developing trust in alliance relationships.
- Suggest solutions for resolving supply chain conflicts when they occur.

A Conceptual Model of Alliance Development

Figure 4-2 is a model showing how organizations typically establish and develop supply chain alliances.[2] The general model has a number of vertical and horizontal components. The vertical components are detailed below:

- The **strategic component** examines how strategic expectations and evaluations of alliance effectiveness evolve as an alliance progresses through development stages.
- The **process component** outlines the stages of alliance development that show the required steps for formation, implementation, and maintenance of an alliance.
- The **operational component** positions the development of search and selection criteria and operating standards for managing an alliance.

Within each of the horizontal stages, we must also consider the vertical stages that occur. At each stage (as we go from top to bottom), managers must consider the strategic and operational issues that coincide with each of the following horizontal stages of development.

- Level One—**alliance conceptualization**—begins when a firm determines a collaborative arrangement has appeal and provides a potential alternative to the current arrangement. This level involves significant joint planning to determine what the "ideal strategic alliance" would be in an "ideal world," and then project what a more "realistic" type of alliance might be.
- Level Two—**alliance pursuance**—The decision to form an alliance is finalized, and the firm establishes the strategic and operational considerations that will be used to select the alliance partner.
- Level Three—**alliance confirmation**—focuses on partner selection and confirmation. Managers determine the strategic and operational expectations for the arrangement through joint meetings with the alliance partner, and the relationship is solidified.
- Level Four—**alliance implementation/continuity**—creates a feedback mechanism to administer and assess performance continually to determine whether the alliance

---

[2] This model was developed by J. M. Schmitz, R. Frankel, and D. J. Frayer, "ECR Alliances: A Best Practice Model," Grocery Manufacturers Association, Washington, DC, 1995. This report was based on case studies of several manufacturer-supplier and manufacturer-distributor alliance relationships.

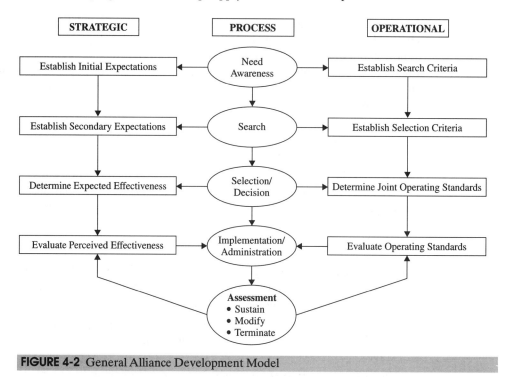

FIGURE 4-2 General Alliance Development Model

Source: J. M. Schmitz, R. Frankel, and D. J. Frayer, "ECR Alliances: A Best Practice Model," Joint Industry Project on Efficient Consumer Response, 1995.

will be sustained, modified, or terminated. Should a conflict occur, the firm may need to explore different types of conflict resolution mechanisms.

In order to understand these processes, we will proceed through the alliance creation process shown in Figure 4-2 from top to bottom and discuss each of the horizontal elements. It is important to note that the first two stages focus primarily on the firm initiating the alliance (the "initiating firm"), whereas the last two stages correspond to both parties, because the alliance partner has now joined the relationship. It is also important to note that such alliances may begin with a single firm, but may then extend to other firms, both customers or suppliers in the supply chain. In each case, the same series of stages has to occur, although the situation is now made more complicated by the fact that there are two or more initiating firms performing the process, not one!

LEVEL ONE: ALLIANCE CONCEPTUALIZATION

Many companies first begin to consider forming an alliance when they realize that a major strategic change is needed to improve performance. This realization is often triggered by the actions of global competitors, industry consolidation, alternative distribution and retail formats, or major technological change in an industry. In some cases, quality problems may cause executive managers to redefine their "core competence" and decide to outsource those processes not considered to be a source of competitive advantage. In other cases, marketing may seek a customer and identify a need that can be met through the development of an alliance relationship.

Any change initiative begins with awareness of a problem. However, problem awareness is not enough to induce change; managers must also be convinced that the possibility for an improved system exists. As we will discuss later, any type of supply chain relationship contains some level of risk or uncertainty, so the potential for improvement due to a change in strategy must appear to be large enough to justify this level of risk. The types of opportunities that initiating firms expect to receive in forming an alliance often vary based on the type of channel relationship involved. The types of channel relationships are one of three types shown in Table 4-1: Manufacturer/Material Supplier alliances, Manufacturer/Distributor alliances, and Manufacturer/Service Supplier alliances.

The criteria for choosing to develop an alliance with a supply chain member organization is typically driven by the expectation of performance improvements in the areas shown in the table. This need is also driven by the expectation that forming an alliance will provide results that are greater than those associated with a traditional adversarial relationship. Managers in such companies share a common belief that a closer supply chain relationship provides the best opportunity for achieving their strategic goals.

The ECR Alliance study previously cited also found that the most typical barriers to alliance conceptualization were the initiating firms' fear of change and an inability to relinquish traditional business practices. Moreover, the creation of an alliance requires a new mindset toward approaching supply chain members that must be nurtured internally. However, successful companies acknowledged that these fears existed and went about resolving them through internal training programs that explained the new types of work practices and their impact on job responsibilities. It is also interesting to note that the alliance was driven by different initiating parties; in some cases, the buying company drove the movement toward an alliance, whereas in other cases the supplying company drove it based on its marketing strategy.

LEVEL TWO: ALLIANCE PURSUANCE

During alliance pursuance, initiating firms will clarify and define their new strategies and finalize the decision to pursue an alliance. This frequently involves a search for detailed information concerning the intended change as well as a detailed evaluation of a potential partner. The initial goals established earlier are reviewed, and secondary goals are created to refine the initial goals and identify the potential degree of achievement. For example, if an initial goal was inventory reduction, the secondary goal was refined to include the specific order of magnitude, such as inventory reduction of at least 20 percent.

These secondary goals then help to identify the strategic and operational characteristics that the selected firm should possess to qualify as a potential alliance partner. For example, if the secondary goal was to improve quality to a specific level, selection criteria could require material suppliers to have a formalized quality control system or be ISO 9000 registered to be considered. This process of defining the selection criteria allows the initiating firm to reduce the number of firms to be considered for alliance partners. The researchers in the study also found that the most successful alliances occurred when the relationship was developed around materials, products, or services that are strategically important to both partners. Once a potential partner was selected, it was also determined whether there was any interest on their part in becoming an

TABLE 4-1	Different Types of Alliance Goals	
	Manufacturer Perspective	**Material Supplier Perspective**
Alliance Goals	• Improve inbound operations • Reduce costs • Reduce inventory • Improve quality • Reduce lead time • Stabilize supply and price • Increase utilization of supplier's technology and expertise • Shorter concept to market product development	• Increase sales volume • Increase customer loyalty • Provide value-added service • Increase switching costs • Reduce costs
	Manufacturer Perspective	**Distributor Perspective**
Alliance Goals	• Increase sales volume • Increase availability • Increase freshness • Reduce damage • New-product innovation • Lower inventory costs • Invoicing accuracy • Improve pricing/promotions • Improve customer service • Improve order commitment	• Increase profitability • Reduce inventory • Increase turns • Fresher product • Reduce delivery cost • Tailor product • Configuration • Improve consumer value
	Manufacturer Perspective	**Service Supplier Perspective**
Alliance Goals	• Improve coordination between transportation operations and product supply • Reduce carrier base • Breakthrough reductions in cost • Breakthrough improvements in service • Improve warehousing and distribution labor productivity and space utilization • Maintain flexibility in product supply • Achieve consolidation benefits • Build support for industry-wide supply chain initiatives	• Increase market share growth in key accounts • Manage operational variability • Provide value-added service • Increase profitability • Develop closer relationships with industry leaders • Satisfy manufacturer customers • Ensure future competitive positioning

Source: J. M. Schmitz, R. Frankel, and D. J. Frayer, "ECR Alliances: A Best Practice Model," Grocery Manufacturers Association, Washington, DC, 1995.

alliance partner. It is important that both partners perceive the potential for significant benefits from forming an alliance. Because the development of such relationships requires a substantial amount of time and resources, the potential benefits of forming an alliance must exceed the costs of doing so.

The initiating firm typically enters into an agreement based on a set of expectations about the potential for benefits, a time frame for achieving them, a history of behavior with the other companies in the supply chain that determines the trustworthiness of the organization, and a set of perceptions about the trustworthiness of the other parties in turn. Initially, these expectations and perceived risks are communicated with the other parties and *alignment* occurs. The term *alignment* is important because it implies that the set of mutual benefits expected on the part of both parties are congruent. Each party enters into the supply chain relationship assuming that every other party has certain responsibilities and duties that they will carry out in the future. This stage of the relationship is critical because it essentially determines the criteria by which the relationship will be deemed successful or not.

In evaluating a partner for possible alliance development, organizations will often perform a detailed assessment of the supplier/customer. In a buyer-supplier alliance, the buyer is purchasing not only the supplier's products and services but its capabilities as well. Within the integrated supply chain, trust must be developed not only between a single alliance or link within the supply chain but also between multiple partners located across the supply chain. Moreover, initiating firms must be able to trust not only their supplier but also their supplier's suppliers! In turn, a supplier cannot simply trust a manufacturer, but must also trust the manufacturer's customers who will dictate demand volumes, pricing, and the like. Managing multiple relationships within a supply chain is a challenging task. Thus, the evaluation of the supply chain partner often looks at multiple criteria in detail to truly identify the long-term potential for an alliance relationship.

Many organizations spend a considerable amount of time evaluating their supply chain partners. This may involve an on-site audit of the supplier, with certain objectives in mind. Some of the different criteria that a company may use to assess the potential for integrating a partner into a supply chain include, but are not limited to, the following:

- Company profile information
- Management capability
- Personnel capabilities
- Cost structure
- Total quality management philosophy and programs
- Process and technological capability
- Environmental regulation compliance
- Financial capability/stability
- Production scheduling and control systems
- Information systems capability
- Supplier sourcing strategies, policies, and techniques
- Long-term relationship potential

It is worthwhile to examine each of these areas.[3] Although it may not be possible to obtain access to information on the potential partner's capabilities in all of these areas, information that can be obtained during the evaluation stage will help to determine the potential for a successful match and can highlight potential problems that need to be addressed in the supply chain relationship. A discussion of these major criteria follows.

---

[3] Adapted from R. Monczka, R. Trent, and R. Handfield, *Purchasing and Supply Chain Management* (Cincinnati, OH: Southwestern Publishing, 1997).

Company Profile Information   The evolution process should include the development of a company profile that provides general background information for the potential partner company. The company profile should include, but is not limited to, the following:

- Company history
- Sales volumes
- Product lines
- Market share by product line
- Number of employees
- Organizational ownership
- Major customers
- Major supplies

Most of this information is available from the company's annual reports and from a variety of publicly available information sources.

Management Capability   It is often important to evaluate the capability of a supplier or customer's management. Different aspects of management capability include management's (1) commitment to continuous process and quality improvement, (2) overall professional ability and experience, (3) ability to maintain positive relationships with its workforce, (4) willingness to make the investments necessary to support future growth, (5) willingness to develop a closer working relationship with the buyer, and (6) vision of the future. Although there is no straightforward "checklist" to follow in evaluating management capabilities, it can be one of the most critical areas to assess. Management capability will affect an organization's ability to satisfy supply chain requirements, both currently and in the future, and will also determine the level of commitment to the overall supply chain initiative.

Some questions that might be asked in assessing management capability include:

- Does executive management practice strategic long-range planning?
- Has management committed itself to total quality management and continuous improvement?
- Has management developed the commitment of all employees to continuous performance improvement?
- Is there a high degree of turnover among managers?
- What is the professional managerial experience?
- Does management have a vision about the future direction of the company that is aligned with your company?
- What is the history of management-labor relations?
- Has management prepared the company to withstand the competitive challenges of the next two decades?

Many of these questions are difficult to answer using strict yes or no criteria. Bear in mind that many organizations are currently undergoing significant reengineering and change and are likely facing a great deal of uncertainty as to their future state. As such, it may be difficult to discern the true state of affairs within a company's management team. Nevertheless, asking these questions can help the supply chain manager to develop a "gut feel" for the strategic posture of the managers in the candidate organization, and determine whether this posture is aligned with that of the initiating organization.

Personnel Capabilities The alliance evaluation process also requires an assessment of nonmanagement personnel. A highly trained and motivated workforce is a critical element of any organization and will be a key factor in determining that organization's performance. An audit team should evaluate: (1) the overall skills and abilities of the workforce, (especially with regard to the level of education and training received); (2) the degree to which employees support the company's quality process and commitment to continuous improvement; (3) the current state of employee-management relations, as well as a history of labor relations within the organization; (4) workforce turnover; and (5) the willingness of employees to contribute to supply chain objectives. All of these data can provide a general idea of how dedicated the organization's employees are to meeting the expectations of the supply chain relationship.

Cost Structure Evaluating a supply chain partner's cost structure requires an in-depth understanding of its total costs. This includes understanding the partner's (1) direct labor costs, (2) indirect labor costs, (3) material costs, (4) manufacturing or process operating costs, (5) overhead costs, and (6) sales and general administrative expenses. Understanding the cost structure helps the initiating firm determine the effectiveness and efficiency of the potential partner's operations. A cost analysis also helps identify potential areas of cost improvement.

Collecting this information can be a challenge during the initial evaluation process. A potential partner may not have a thorough understanding of its costs at the level of detail required. Furthermore, many firms view cost data as highly proprietary. Remember, during the initial evaluation the two firms seeking to develop the alliance usually have not developed any major degree of mutual commitment or trust. (An exception occurs when a firm evaluates a supplier or customer with whom it is already familiar, either through past or current dealings.)

The firm being audited may also fear that the release of cost information will undermine its pricing strategy or flexibility with the evaluation team, and may fear that competitors will gain access to its cost data. This could provide competitors with insight into an organization's source of competitive advantage. For example, a supplier may employ an innovative manufacturing process that allows it to be the low-cost/high-quality producer in its industry. Providing detailed cost data to outsiders might jeopardize the supplier's advantage by allowing competitors to see exactly how much of a cost advantage the supplier's process provides. As a result of these concerns, a buying organization may develop a "total supply chain cost" model that provides estimates of the supplier's cost structure data during the initial supplier evaluation. Although these cost models are never completely accurate, they can be very useful in obtaining more information and querying suppliers further on their cost structure and performance. Even in cases when no data are available, some understanding of a potential partner's cost structure is a critical part of the evaluation process.

Total Quality Management Philosophy A major part of the evaluation process focuses on the potential partner's quality management processes, systems, and philosophy. The evaluation team should not only address the obvious topics associated with quality (i.e., management commitment, statistical process control, number of defects) but also may evaluate safety, training, and facilities and equipment maintenance.

Process and Technological Capability Supply chain evaluation teams often include a member from the manufacturing/industrial engineering or technical staff to evaluate a partner's process and technological capability. Process consists of *the technology, design, methods, and equipment used to manufacture a product or deliver a service.* An organization's selection of a production process helps define its required technology, human resource skills, and capital equipment requirements.

The ability to produce an item economically at the required quality level is critical. A firm that lacks the ability to meet current and expected future technical requirements has a smaller chance of becoming a supply chain member. An exception may occur if other supply chain members are willing to work directly with the candidate organization to increase its technical ability. In such cases, other organizations may provide additional technical (and possibly even financial) support to further develop the supply chain member, if they believe a significant payback can occur in the form of improved supply chain performance.

The evaluation of an organization's technical and process capability should also focus on *future* process and technical ability. This requires assessing an organization's capital equipment plans and strategy and commitment to research and development.

An assessment of the organization's design capability may also take place during the selection process. For example, buyers often expect suppliers to perform component design *and* production. One way to reduce the time required to develop new products involves using qualified suppliers who are able to perform product design activities. Ford, for example, now requires almost all of its suppliers to have not only production but also design capabilities. The company has transferred most of the design of its component and component system requirements to its suppliers. The trend toward the increased use of external design capabilities makes this area an important part of the organizational evaluation and selection process.

Environmental Regulation Compliance   The 1990s brought about a renewed awareness of the impact that industry has on the environment. Government regulations are becoming increasingly harsh on polluters. The Clean Air Act of 1990 imposes large fines on producers of ozone-depleting substances and foul-smelling gases, and the Clinton administration has introduced laws regarding recycling content in industrial materials.[4] As a result, an organization's ability to comply with environmental regulations is becoming an important criteria for supply chain alliances. This includes, but is not limited to, the proper disposal of hazardous waste. It is not in the best interest of an organization to do business with a supply chain partner that fails to comply with environmental regulations.

Financial Capability/Stability   An assessment of a potential partner's financial condition almost always occurs during the initial evaluation process. Some firms view the financial assessment as a screening process or preliminary condition that organizations must pass before a detailed evaluation can begin. A firm can use a financial rating service to help analyze the candidate organization's financial condition. If the organization is publicly held, other financial information found in annual reports and databases is readily available.

Selecting a supply chain partner who is in poor financial condition presents a number of risks. First, there is the risk that the organization will go out of business. This can present serious disruptions in the flow of goods and information occurring in a supply chain. Second, supply chain members in poor financial condition may not have the re-

---

[4] *Business Week,* November 1, 1993, pp. 60–61.

sources to invest in plant, equipment, or research, which leads to longer-term technological or other performance improvement. Finally, organizations must feel confident that they can commit the resources necessary to support continuous improvement.

Circumstances may exist that support selecting a supply chain member who is in a weaker financial condition. For example, a company may be developing but has not yet marketed a leading-edge technology that can provide a market advantage to other supply chain members. A temporarily unstable financial condition may also be a function of uncontrollable or nonrepeating circumstances. In such cases, the candidate organization's financial condition should not be the unique reason for elimination from consideration.

In cases when the organization is a publicly traded company on the stock market, specific financial ratios can be obtained from sources such as 10-K reports, Moody's Industrials, and Dunn and Bradstreet that may help provide insights into the potential partner's financial health. Many of these can also be calculated using income statements and balance sheets. Some of the most common ratios and their implications for partner evaluation are as follows:

LIQUIDITY RATIOS (HOW CAPABLE IS THE COMPANY OF MEETING ITS SHORT-TERM CASH NEEDS?)
- Quick ratio
- Current ratio

ACTIVITY RATIOS (HOW EFFECTIVELY IS THE COMPANY MANAGING ITS ASSETS?)
- Inventory turnover
- Average collection period
- Fixed asset turnover
- Return on net assets
- Installed capacity

PROFITABILITY RATIOS (IS THE COMPANY OVERCHARGING OR UNDERCHARGING?)
- Gross profit margin
- Net profit margin
- Return on equity
- Return on investment
- Earnings before interest and taxes
- Price earnings ratio

DEBT RATIOS (IS THE COMPANY OVERLEVERAGED AND INCAPABLE OF PAYING ITS LONG-TERM DEBTS?)
- Debt ratio
- Times interest earned

In technology-intensive industries, the audit team should also look at the company's research and development (R&D) expenditures as a percent of sales to determine how much it is reinvesting its profits into developing new products. These financial ratios can provide quick and valuable insights into a company's financial health. Moreover, managers should track such ratios for possible "red flags" that may signify a potential financial difficulty. If at any point the manager has reason to believe that the candidate organization is facing a financial crisis of some sort, an appropriate investigation should be carried out.

Production Scheduling and Control Systems   Production scheduling includes those systems that release, schedule, and control a production process. The sophistication of the scheduling system can have a major impact on supply chain performance. Some of the criteria to be investigated include the following:

- Does the organization use a computerized material requirements planning (MRP) system to ensure the availability of required components?
- Does the organization track material and production cycle time and compare this against a performance objective or standard?
- Does the production scheduling system support the supply chain requirements?
- How much order lead time does the production scheduling and control system require?
- What is the on-time delivery performance history?

The purpose behind evaluating the production scheduling and control system is to identify the degree of control the organization has over its scheduling and production process. A well-defined system will use computerized inventory control systems and measure performance against preestablished objectives.

Information Systems Capability   The ability to communicate electronically between supply chain members is rapidly becoming a requirement for entering into an alliance. Many companies now insist that their supply chain partners (1) currently have electronic data interchange (EDI) capability or (2) be willing to develop the capability as a condition for conducting future transactions. Besides the efficiencies that electronic communication provides, these systems support closer relationships and the free exchange of all kinds of information.[5]

Managers should also evaluate other dimensions of the supplier's information technology, including the following:

- Are designers using computer-aided design (CAD) and computer-aided manufacturing (CAM) technologies?
- Is bar coding being used when appropriate?
- Is the company able to communicate via the Internet or the World Wide Web?
- Are its managers networked throughout the company?
- Do they use modern systems such as voice mail, CD-ROM, purchasing credit cards, multimedia computing, and so forth?

Evidence that the organization is using these technologies can provide reasonable assurance that it is keeping up on the information technology curve and will be prepared for the future.[6]

---

[5] Please refer to chapter 2 on systems for a complete discussion of EDI.

[6] R. M. Monczka, E. L. Nichols, and R. B. Handfield, "Information Systems, Technology, Procurement and Supply Chain Management: A View to the Future," *International NAPM Purchasing Conference Proceedings* (Tempe, AZ: NAPM, Inc., 1995), 156–160. See also R. M. Monczka and E. L. Nichols, "Tomorrow's Top Information Technologies," *NAPM Insights,* October 1994, pp. 29–31.

Supplier Sourcing Strategies, Policies, and Techniques   In evaluating a downstream supply chain partner, organizations may also perform a comprehensive assessment of a potential supplier's performance capability, because supplier performance affects total firm performance. The performance of a supplier's suppliers can also affect other downstream supply chain members directly. The same is true of a supplier who receives poor quality from its suppliers.

The concept of managing not just one's suppliers but all of the suppliers in a supply chain is becoming increasingly important. For instance, a recent meeting took place to discuss the manufacture of a part on an airplane. The companies present at the meeting included United Airlines, Boeing (plane manufacturer), Pratt and Whitney (engine manufacturer), and Auto Air (the components manufacturer). In addition, United Airlines was considering bringing along one of its Frequent Flier customers to the meeting! The point of this example is that supply chain management requires an awareness of the sourcing practices of all direct suppliers. In order to truly integrate the supply chain, a firm must gain insights into the sourcing practices of its first-, second-, and sometimes even third-tier suppliers as they relate to critical purchased items. Evaluating a potential supplier's sourcing strategies, policies, and techniques is one way to gain greater insight and understanding of the supply chain. Because so few firms actually have an understanding of their second- and third-tier suppliers, those that do can gain an important advantage over competitors. For instance, firms that integrate their information systems across multiple tiers of suppliers and customers can improve planning and forecasting, reduce lead time throughout the supply chain, reduce in-transit inventory, and significantly reduce costs. On the technology side, engineers can obtain advance information on new innovations being developed by second- and third-tier suppliers, thereby improving the design of their own new products.

Longer-Term Relationship Potential   Firms today increasingly evaluate a supply chain partner's willingness to develop longer-term relationships. A major flaw in managers' conceptualization of supply chains is that all potential supply chain members will want to develop closer relationships; however, this may not always be the case. In particular, many smaller organizations were started and in some cases are still owned by entrepreneurs. As a result, there is a desire on the part of management at some companies to remain independent of larger supply chain members. A company seeking a relationship with a smaller organization that requires the sharing of sensitive information should address management's willingness to enter into such an arrangement.

A company that wants to establish a longer-term relationship or partnership with a supplier or customer must go beyond evaluating the performance areas just discussed. When evaluating the possibility of a closer relationship with a potential supply chain candidate, an initiating organization should ask a number of questions about commitment to joint planning and problem solving[7]:

- Has the organization signaled a willingness or commitment to a partnership-type arrangement?
- Is the organization willing to commit resources that it cannot use in other relationships?

---

[7] Robert E. Spekman, "Strategic Supplier Selection: Understanding Long-Term Buyer Relationships," *Business Horizons,* July–August 1988, pp. 80–81.

- How early in the product design stage is the organization willing or able to participate?
- What does the organization bring to the relationship that is unique?
- Will the organization immediately revert to a negotiated stance if a problem arises?
- Does the organization have a genuine interest in joint problem solving and a win-win agreement?
- Is the organization's senior management committed to the processes inherent in strategic partnerships?
- Will there be free and open exchange of information across functional areas between companies?
- Does the organization have the infrastructure to support such cross-functional interdependence?
- How much future planning is the organization willing to share with us?
- Is the need for confidential treatment of information taken seriously?
- What is the general level of comfort between the companies?
- How well does the organization know our business?
- Will the organization share cost data?
- What will be the organization's commitment to understanding our problems and concerns?
- Will we be special to the organization or just another customer/supplier?

This is not a complete list of questions that can be asked when evaluating the possibility of a closer longer-term relationship. This list does provide, however, a framework concerning the types of issues that are important in this area.

LEVEL THREE: ALLIANCE CONFIRMATION

Having thoroughly evaluated a supply chain partner using the selection criteria described above, the initiating firm can narrow down the small group of finalists to a single finalist who is most closely aligned with the initiating firm, and who has the most promise in terms of potential alliance success. Having approached this final partner, both firms are committed to forming an alliance. This commitment can be communicated through verbal agreement or with a formal written contract. When used, written contracts may vary substantially in terms of length of time over which the relationship will take place, content, and level of detail.

In addition to a written contract, both partners must determine the expected effectiveness standards for the alliance. Partners must specify a number of criteria for managing the relationship and the processes that will be used to resolve any foreseeable problems that may arise. Some of the factors that must be managed include the following:

- How to manage the length of the relationship and under what conditions the alliance should be terminated.
- How to manage power imbalances when one party has more power than the other in the relationship.
- How to manage managerial imbalances when alliance partners fail to provide equal managerial support in terms of the number of key contacts within each of their organizations.
- How to manage conflict when one supply chain member is engaged in behavior designed to injure, thwart, or gain scarce resources at the expense of the other partner.

- How to jointly allocate actual net benefit, in terms of the costs required to develop and manage the alliance, as well as the resulting benefits that accrue to each party.
- How to develop a suitable match between the parties, in terms of developing a cohesive arrangement based on management styles and corporate cultures. Building trust is an important part of this stage of the process and is discussed in the next section in further detail.

Although the potential alliance partners may not establish specific detailed expectations in all of these areas, it is important for them to develop a mutual understanding of how the alliance will be strategically managed to achieve its goals. This understanding enables partners to consider any potential problems that may limit the alliance's effectiveness. For example, partners must assess how potential power imbalances and managerial imbalances will be overcome, knowing full well that one partner may be devoting a greater share of time and effort to the alliance. Although such situations cannot always be changed, it should be recognized that the situation exists and be managed within the context of the relationship.

In addition to these agreements on strategic effectiveness, the parties must also develop a mutual agreement on a number of specific joint operating standards. These operating standards refer to the minutae or details of the actual "mechanics" that will occur as the partners do business on a day-to-day basis. Some of the specific details that must be worked out at this stage of the relationship development process include the following:

- What are the defined procedures that enable each alliance partner to know exactly what its roles and responsibilities are in order to reduce duplication of effort and establish accountability? This includes procedures for unexpected events, emergency procedures, and well-defined procedures that eliminate any questions or misunderstandings regarding each partner's roles and responsibilities.
- How will the partners measure, specify, and quantify operational performance? These measures must be tracked on an ongoing basis to improve operational activities, and include frequent joint appraisal to solve any problems as they arise.
- What type of information will be shared, and how frequently will information transfer occur? This refers to the day-to-day requirements necessary for each party to adhere to the operating standards. The amount of information shared will often depend on the level of trust that exists between the two parties (discussed in the following section).
- How responsive will each partner be to special requests from the other party, and how can communication be improved through technology adoption? Responsiveness refers to the speed of interaction between parties and the ability to handle problems quickly as well as accurately. This means that the partner is taking corrective action to ensure the problem is solved and will not happen again. Technology adoption refers to the willingness of the supply chain partner to adopt specific technologies that enable quicker response. This includes EDI, Intranet connections, or even facsimile. Although it is often taken for granted that such technologies are widely used, it is always possible that a supply chain partner may be unwilling to introduce electronic connectivity with an unknown firm.

Although the actual investment in physical resources (e.g., equipment) and human resources (e.g., training and dedicated personnel) is not always necessary in an alliance, it is important that partners discuss the need for such investments at this stage in the process. If a significant level of investment is required to proceed, the partners should agree on the arrangement prior to financial commitment.

LEVEL FOUR: ALLIANCE IMPLEMENTATION/CONTINUITY

Once the initial agreement occurs with all parties concurring on the terms, resources are committed, and the alliance between the parties is "kicked off." Each party begins to commit the promised resources and hopefully begins to open up communications.

After a certain period of time, the parties either meet or fail to meet performance expectations. In cases where results meet or exceed expectations, everyone is satisfied. The level of trust between the parties increases because everyone in the agreement is "true to his or her word." Needless to say, this occurrence is the exception rather than the rule, simply because of the fact that unexpected occurrences always happen. Projected volumes do not accrue, or parties are unable to meet performance expectations due to mitigating circumstances. The test of a truly successful supply chain relationship is, therefore, not whether it always succeeds *but how the partners manage the relationship when problems inevitably occur.* In cases in which the relationship is not managed well, the relationship dissolves, and parties write off the whole experience as a loss. In such cases, the parties are unlikely to enter into such a relationship again!

The secret to successfully deploying the integrated supply chain is through joint problem solving, which occurs when each party trusts that the other party is committed to making the relationship work. Through a process of examination of the problem, re-alignment of priorities, and continuous measurement of performance and activities over time, the relationship will continue, and the integrated supply chain will not only grow but also provide unexpected benefits beyond initial expectations. For this to occur, however, key alliance contacts must visit each partner's facilities to meet face-to-face and develop a better understanding of both operations. These visits allow the partners to manage changes within the relationship and facilitate the development of personal relationships between key contacts. If this process is unsuccessful, partners may try a variety of other methods to resolve the conflict (discussed in the latter portion of this chapter).

As mentioned earlier, the ECR Alliance study found that a major barrier to implementation of successful alliances is the inability to abandon traditional strategic and operational practices. This includes the fear of organizational and personal change, incompatible systems of doing business, and in some cases, the inability to secure the required resources committed to in the early stages of alliance confirmation.

To avoid the possibility of an alliance breakup, the authors of the study found that successful partners used a feedback mechanism continually over time to ensure that the ongoing relationship was successful. Following initial implementation, alliance partners evaluated the strategic aspects of the alliance by comparing perceived and expected effectiveness, and also evaluated the operational aspects by determining each partner's adherence to predetermined operating standards. These comparisons were formally assessed by both parties in the relationship.

If the comparisons reflect a *positive evaluation of strategic and operational dimensions,* it is likely the alliance was sustained in its current form. If sustained, the partners:

- Perform ongoing assessments of perceived alliance effectiveness and adherence to operating standards.
- Revise strategic goals and operating standards based on competitive conditions and changing needs.
- View the alliance as a permanent system that continually moves between assessment (to evaluate strategic effectiveness and operating standards) and administration.
- Agree to sustain the alliance as is until (1) the alliance needs to be modified or (2) the alliance needs to be terminated because it has outlived its strategic effectiveness and/or failed to meet operating standards.

If, however, the comparisons reveal a *negative or neutral evaluation of strategic and operational dimensions,* it is likely the alliance will be modified. If modified, the partners determine what changes are required and implement them. Next, the partners assess the new changes. If the modifications are successful, the new assessment will determine if the alliance is sustainable, and continuous administration and assessment will occur. If the modifications are unsuccessful, further modifications or termination of the alliance will result.

If evaluation of *strategic and operational dimensions are extremely negative,* it is likely that the partners will terminate the alliance by jointly agreeing to end the collaborative relationship. It should be noted that termination does not always indicate performance failure but may be due to a change in one or both partners' strategic goals. In other cases, the goal may simply have been achieved, and there is no longer a need to continue the alliance. This is particularly true in dynamic industries with very short technological and product life cycles.

In the next section, we discuss an important attribute of supply chain relationships that occurs over time, as an alliance relationship matures and is sustained: trust. We discuss how trust develops and how it can be maintained and increased over time between supply chain partners.

Developing a Trusting Relationship with Partners in the Supply Chain

As discussed in the prior section, trust is not something that simply "happens." Especially in the early stages of a supply chain relationship, partners must trust not only one another but also other members higher or lower up in the supply chain. Trust can be initiated when a company's performance history and reliability of its supply chain linkages can be demonstrated. If another party does not perceive your supply base or customers as being reliable, then a strong convincing factor is an "open book" policy of past performance data.

Trust is not something that can be easily measured or identified. For instance, what are the specific criteria that you as an individual use in "trusting" another individual? The elements of trust will typically vary considerably depending on the situation. You may trust someone out of a sense of loyalty, or because he or she has "always come through" for you, or simply because you get a "good" feeling about his or her integrity, even though you haven't known the individual very long. In fact, any one of these types of feelings is important in assessing trust. A number of studies have been carried out on the types of actions and behaviors that lead to trusting relationships between individuals, and this has enabled researchers to develop a "taxonomy" of different types of trust.[8] If we are to understand how organizations learn to trust one another in a supply chain, we must first understand how *individuals* come to trust each other, in both the short-term and the long-term. Once we understand how trust develops, we can then begin to understand the types of actions that can lead to a trusting relationship, resulting in the important benefits achieved through supply chain integration.

In this section, we describe the major types of trust, how they are developed, and illustrate each type with a supply chain example. In addition, we provide a number of "Rules of Thumb" that supply chain managers can employ in their efforts to develop greater levels of trust with their supply chain partners. In other words, we will consider how people can become more "trustworthy" in the eyes of their customers and suppliers, and thereby increase confidence that their joint goals and objectives can be achieved.

RELIABILITY

This element of trust depends on the prior contact that an individual has experienced with another individual over time. If someone has acted in a consistent and predictable manner over an extended period, that person is likely to be considered reliable by the other party.[9] However, reliability is also often based on the integrity or honesty of the other party. Integrity refers to the extent to which a person repeatedly acts according to a moral code or standard. If a person consistently follows this code, even in unusual situations, he or she is perceived as being reliable, and, therefore, trust in that individual is likely to increase.

In discussing reliability, it is important to note that a supplier or customer who applies coercion or stress to get a partner to act reliably will not improve the relationship. For instance, if a supply chain partner *forces* a supplier into a supply chain relationship, then it is less likely that the supplier will act in a reliable manner. On the other hand, if the supplier *promises* on-time delivery but repeatedly fails to follow through with this promise, it is unlikely that the partner will gain confidence in and trust that supplier. A basic rule of thumb for managers to follow in helping to improve the level of trust in the relationship is, therefore, the following:

Rule of Thumb 1: **Follow through on your commitments, and act in a predictable manner.**

Parties in a supply chain who repeatedly "say what they do" and "do what they say" are more likely to instill confidence, because they can be relied on to act in a predictable

---

[8] For more reading, see the following: Christian Bechtel, "The Development of Trust in Strategic Supplier Alliances," Ph.D. dissertation, The Eli Broad Graduate School of Management, Michigan State University, East Lansing, MI, 1998; J. M. Schmitz, R. Frankel, and D. J. Frayer, "ECR Alliances: A Best Practice Model," Grocery Manufacturers Association, Washington, DC, 1995; R. M. Kramer and T. R. Tyler, *Trust in Organizations: Frontiers of Theory and Research* (Berkeley, CA: Sage Publications, 1995).

[9] M. Deutsch, "Trust and Suspicion," *Journal of Conflict Resolution* 2 (1958), 265–279.

manner. A lack of congruence between words and action can lead to a deterioration of the relationship. For this reason, many managers seeking to create an integrated supply chain will first approach those suppliers who have a demonstrated track record in terms of on-time delivery, quality, ramp-up, mix flexibility, and so on. These suppliers have demonstrated that they are able to meet performance expectations reliably as set out in the contract. In addition, these suppliers have established a long-term relationship, and very often the primary contacts in the buying company and the supply company have established a personal relationship in which they know the other person will keep his or her word and act with integrity according to a mutually defined set of standards. This is an important point to remember: If you cannot follow through on a commitment, it is better to state up-front, "I cannot commit to that promise." It is far better to do this than to make a commitment and fail to follow through.

COMPETENCE

Competence is one person's perception of the ability of another person to meet commitments. This form of trust is somewhat different than reliability. Competence-based trust can be broken down into three key areas.[10] The first area, *specific competence,* is trust in the other person's specific functional area. For example, a buyer purchasing a transmission system from a supplier trusts that the supplier can answer any relevant question he or she might have with regard to the specific mechanics of the transmission system. If the supplier cannot answer such questions, there is reason to wonder if the supplier really knows what he or she is doing! The second area is *interpersonal competence,* which is the ability of a person to work with people. This often refers to an individual's "people skills," such as the abilities to listen effectively to another person, to negotiate effectively, to communicate and make a presentation, to reach a consensus with a group, and other types of related skills necessary when dealing with others on a day-to-day basis. In managing a supplier or customer, these types of skills are especially important, as the majority of communication in the early stages of supply chain integration occur at face-to-face meetings. The third area of competence involves *business sense*, which refers to an individual's experience, wisdom, and common sense.[11] This may also occur in specific technological or functional areas. For instance, if you are working with an engineer in the supplier's organization who has worked for many years with a given technology and who understands the intricate details of his or her organization's product, you are more likely to trust that engineer's opinion when you ask him or her about a problem you are having with the product. Competence-based trust is therefore a powerful integrating mechanism between two parties in a supply chain.

**Rule of Thumb 2:   Choose a supply chain partner with a documented record of
experience in the technology. Also ensure that the partner
is assigning competent, knowledgeable, and experienced
people to managing the relationship.**

---

[10] Kramer and Tyler, *Trust in Organizations,* 1995.

[11] D. Gambetta, "Can We Trust Trust?" in *Trust: Making and Breaking Cooperative Relations,* ed. D. Gambetta (Cambridge, MA: Basil Blackwell, 1988).

This rule of thumb is especially important when you are working with a new supplier or customer. In some cases, companies will conduct a thorough audit of their partner prior to entering into a relationship (described earlier in the chapter). This can help support the decision to integrate the partner into the supply chain and will avoid many problems that may occur after significant resources have been invested in developing the relationship. If a supplier or customer is unwilling to commit its experienced and knowledgeable people to the relationship, one should approach it with caution, as this may indicate that it is not fully committed to an integrated supply chain, and you may be better off looking for a different partner, if possible. Alternatively, discussions with top managers at the partner company may help them understand the need for such a person in developing the relationship.

AFFECT-BASED TRUST ("GOODWILL")

This dimension of trust is somewhat difficult to define fully because it refers to the emotional investment that develops between individuals that trust one another. The importance of interpersonal relationships is recognized as a vital element in developing trust between organizations.[12] Authors describe the shift to affect-based trust as the movement from an economically based reliance on contracts, to a psychological reliance on developing and building the relationship between two parties.[13] Affect-based trust can be broken down into two elements. The first, *openness with the other party,* describes a situation when each party feels that it can share problems or information with the other party. For instance, a supplier who provides information on internal costs, or a buyer who provides information on future forecasts, may instill greater trust on the behalf of the other party. Second, affect-based trust requires *benevolence*, which refers to the assumption by one party of an acknowledged or accepted duty to protect the rights and interests of the other party. Moreover, this type of trust can best be described as a faith in the moral integrity or goodwill of others, which is produced through repeated personal interactions. Over time, this leads to a certain "bond" between the individuals, defined by common mutual norms, sentiments, and friendship.[14]

Rule of Thumb 3: **In selecting the primary interface with your supply chain partner, choose an individual who has a high level of knowledge in the technology or function, good "people" skills, and good "commonsense" knowledge.**

Although this rule of thumb perhaps seems a bit obvious, it emphasizes the need for skilled people in the supply chain area, who are often difficult to find. Supply chain managers who do not possess all of these skills may need to go through different types of technical or managerial training before being appointed full time to a supply chain position.

---

[12] D. McAllister, "Affect- and Cognition-based Trust as Foundations for Interpersonal Cooperation in Organizations," *Academy of Management Journal* 38 (1995), pp. 10–36.

[13] P. Ring and A. Van de Ven, "Developmental Processes of Cooperative Interorganizational Relationships," *Academy of Management Review* 19 (1994) pp. 18–40.

[14] Ibid.

Because supply chain relationships will undoubtedly be tested by conflict at some point in the future, it is important to get the best people involved who can manage these conflicts when they occur through their controlled interactions with supply chain partners, supplemented by their technical knowledge required to brainstorm and solve technical problems. It is important to remember that inappropriate behaviors such as shouting, ignoring the problem, or glossing over it can harm the relationship and result in a deterioration in supply chain performance. The perception of "fairness" on the part of the supply chain partner in the manner that your organization deals with problems when they occur can influence its behavior and help resolve the problem. In addition, the supplier must feel that the representative from your company is "involved" in core activities and can elicit a response if necessary from other members of your organization. For instance, if the supply chain partner requires additional forecasting information but the liaison claims that "my boss won't let me release it," the supplier or customer may feel that it cannot trust this individual to look out for its needs. By appointing the "best" people to supply chain liaison positions, organizations can help ensure that they are putting their "best foot forward" in maintaining a positive relationship with suppliers or customers.

VULNERABILITY

It has been said that trust without some kind of vulnerability simply cannot exist, and that trust involves adhering to commitments to others or a stated course of action even if the probability of failure is greater than the probability of success.[15] Moreover, vulnerability suggests that some form of risk is present in committing to a supply chain partner, which goes beyond the common types of uncertainties that accompany any supply situation. Vulnerability projects a feeling of being unprotected or exposed in addition to uncertainty or risk. There is also a difference between risk-taking action and vulnerability. For instance, if one goes to work without an umbrella, then one is assuming the risk that it will rain. However, if one goes to work and asks an associate to bring an umbrella for he or she to use, then one is depending on that individual and is therefore vulnerable to the fact that that person may forget the umbrella.

Within a supply chain situation, three types of vulnerability arise. The first, *adverse selection*, involves the inability to evaluate accurately the quality of the assets the other partner brings to the relationship. For instance, it may be difficult to assess whether a supplier's production system is truly capable of meeting your cycle-time requirements. The second form of vulnerability is *moral hazard,* which refers to the inability to evaluate the assets committed when a relationship exists. If a supplier promises to increase the capacity of its system to meet your future requirements, and you have no way of auditing it to ensure that it is actually investing in this capacity, then a moral hazard exists. Finally, an *asymmetric investment* occurs when one partner commits more to the relationship than the other. For example, if a supplier has invested in an information system that links directly into your production plan, yet your company has failed to upgrade its computer systems to the level required to support the supplier's system, then your organization is guilty of an asymmetric investment. Any one or a combination of the three types of vulnerability may be present when a supplier and customer enter into a supply chain relationship.

Unfortunately, there is no such thing as an integrated supply chain free of any form of vulnerability. By definition, when parties begin to rely on one another for information,

---

[15] Deutsch, "Trust and Suspicion."

joint problem solving, integrated materials management, and interdependent managers, vulnerability is present.

Rule of Thumb 4: **The perception of vulnerability needs to be carefully managed by supply partners through information sharing, which assures the other partner that its interests will be protected.**

It is not surprising that supply chain partners are less likely to commit to trusting behavior unless there is some type of risk involved. In such situations, trust can exist without action, but trusting behavior involves actions based on trust. When there is no risk involved at all, the commitment to the supply chain may dwindle. In turn, this suggests that managers should not totally "roll over" and give suppliers or customers everything they ask for, but should also have an active role in maintaining the interests of their own organization. For instance, if a supplier asks for a price increase without providing sufficient evidence of why higher prices are necessary, the buying company should not simply "trust" that the supplier is providing it with accurate information, but should ask for supporting documentation for the price increase, and otherwise refuse to accept it. This would send a message to the supplier that it is still vulnerable to a market-based attitude on the part of the buyer.

LOYALTY

This type of trust occurs after a period of reliable performance, when one party develops a certain degree of faith in the other party. This leads one party to believe that the other party is not only reliable but will perform well in extraordinary situations, and can be relied on when "it really counts." This goes back to the old adage, "You find out who your true friends are when you're really in trouble." One can only be certain that someone really cares when a situation makes it possible for that person not to care.[16] This often occurs through strong interpersonal bonds. For instance, if your organization suddenly gets a rush order from a major customer that requires material currently not in stock, you may need your supplier to expedite the material on overnight delivery. To do so, the supplier may need to schedule workers an extra shift in order to meet the delivery window. In such a situation, the supplier has demonstrated a loyalty to your organization in responding in an extraordinary situation.

Rule of Thumb 5: **Show genuine responsiveness to your partner's needs and demand the same of your partner if necessary. Be willing to "go out on a limb" if the situation requires it.**

By actively working to meet a partner's needs, the relationship will continue to grow, as the other party will also feel indebted to you as you "helped him when he re-

---

[16] Kramer and Tyler, 1995.

ally needed it." On the other hand, organizations should not fall into the habit of consistently requiring extraordinary support, because the supplier or customer may fail to see the benefits of doing business with such an organization that does not respond in kind. This form of trust typically develops after a relationship has been developed for several years. A partner's predictable actions, complemented by an occasional willingness to help the other party in a bind, will most often lead to a deeper sense of trust by the other party and a greater commitment to maintaining the relationship in the future.

By now, it is fairly obvious that trust is really a multidimensional concept. It is also obvious that trust occurs through the actions of *both parties* within the supply chain. Companies who are initiating a supply chain relationship from a neutral standpoint can get the relationship off to a good start by:

- Employing a decision-making process that results in a high level of perceived fairness and equity.
- Becoming involved in a broad level of activities with the supplier/customer.
- Increasing the level of competence within the organization, especially for individuals who will be acting as the key liaison with partners in the supply chain.

However, in developing supply chain relationships, a number of other specific practices can be employed to nurture the relationship and develop a greater sense of trust with supply chain partners.

Resolving Conflicts in a Supply Chain Relationship

All contracts, no matter how carefully worded and prepared, can be subject to some form of dispute or disagreement between the parties. It is virtually impossible to negotiate a contract that anticipates every potential source of disagreement between two parties in a supply chain. Generally speaking, the more complex the nature of the contract and the greater the dollar amounts involved, the more likely it is that a future dispute over interpretation of the terms and conditions will occur. Supply chain managers must, therefore, attempt to envision the potential for such conflicts and prepare appropriate conflict resolution mechanisms to deal with such problems should they arise.

The traditional mechanism for resolving contract disputes is grounded in commercial law, which provides a legal jurisdiction in which an impartial judge can hear the facts of the case at hand and render a decision in favor of one party or the other. Due to the uncertainty, cost, and length of time required to adjudicate a dispute in the U.S. legal system, most organizations prefer to avoid the problems associated with litigation and deal with the situation in other ways. Taking a dispute into the jurisprudence system should be viewed as a last resort, not an automatic step in resolving contractual disputes.

LEGAL ALTERNATIVES

New methods of settling supply chain disputes have evolved in the last several years. These techniques, although diverse in form and nature, have a number of similar characteristics.[17]

---

[17] Linda R. Singer, *Settling Disputes: Conflict Resolution in Business, Families, and the Legal System* (Boulder, CO: Westview Press, 1990), p. 5.

- They all exist somewhere between the polar alternatives of doing nothing or of escalating conflict.
- They are less formal and generally more private than ritualized court battles.
- They permit people with disputes to have more active participation and more control over the processes for solving their own problems than traditional methods of dealing with conflict.
- Almost all of the new methods have been developed in the private sector, although courts and administrative agencies have begun to borrow and adapt some of the more successful techniques.

Perhaps the simplest method of resolving a contractual disagreement involves straightforward, face-to-face negotiation between the two parties involved. In the alliance model discussed earlier in the chapter, we saw how continuous monitoring of performance and feedback systems are an important part of alliance management, so that problems can be prevented whenever possible. When conflict occurs, however, parties should attempt to be as open as possible in addressing it, and explicitly deal with the issue rather than hoping it will go away. Frequently, other factors surrounding the dispute can be brought into consideration by the parties, even though these factors are not directly involved in the dispute at hand. For example, if the buying and selling parties to a contract disagree on the interpretation of the contract's terms and conditions of delivery, then perhaps they might be able to collaborate on other terms and conditions such as price or scheduling. In many cases, the buying and selling executives involved in the dispute are seeking to avoid a legal altercation. Both parties explore alternatives that are less time-consuming and less costly. A process of changing all of the possible variables in the relationship, including the terms, prices, conditions, and so forth, can often produce an agreement that is not only satisfactory to both parties but also more robust and more likely to withstand the test of time.

In some situations, no amount of negotiation produces a solution. When this alternative is exhausted, both parties become aware of the fact that it may be practically infeasible to agree on suitable alternatives. In such cases, it may be virtually impossible for the parties to negotiate an acceptable resolution of the dispute on a good-faith basis without additional assistance from outside parties.

ARBITRATION

The use of an outside arbitrator, or third party, to help settle contractual disputes is the fastest-growing method of conflict resolution among contracting parties, both in the United States and overseas. Because of the parties' inability to reach a negotiated settlement, emotional reactions to the problem (i.e., frustration, disappointment, and anger) may prevent rational examination of the true underlying causes of the source of disagreement. In such cases, arbitration may be a solution. Arbitration is defined as "the submission of a disagreement to one or more impartial persons with the understanding that the parties will abide by the arbitrator's decision."[18] Arbitration, if set up and handled properly, can serve to protect the interests of both parties to the dispute better because it is relatively inexpensive, less time-consuming, private, and typically a reasonable solution for all involved.

---

[18] Robert Coulson, *Business Arbitration: What You Need to Know*, 2nd ed. (New York: American Arbitration Association, 1982), p. 5.

When writing and negotiating supply chain contracts, many supply chain managers include an arbitration clause in the boilerplate terms and conditions contained on their purchase orders and other contract documents. Such a clause typically spells out how the disputing parties will choose an appropriate arbitrator and the types of disputes for which arbitration will be considered. A good source for commercial arbitrators is the American Arbitration Association, which can also handle the administrative burden of the entire process from an impartial point of view. It is important to ensure that the arbitrator's opinion will be binding on both parties to the dispute. A key point to remember here is that adequate advance planning for potential disputes can prevent significant problems later should an unforeseen conflict arise. Also, it is a good idea to spell out the location and method of conducting the arbitration hearings, particularly if the dispute involves companies or individuals from different states or overseas countries. In addition to the basic procedures, other considerations include arbitrator authority, how notices are to be sent to the other party, whether a single arbitrator or a panel of arbitrators is to be used, and the time frame within which the process is to be completed.

OTHER FORMS OF CONFLICT RESOLUTION

Along with the rising popularity of arbitration between supply chain members, a number of different forms of conflict resolution have been introduced. When people think of the arbitration process, the process of mediation generally comes to mind. Mediation involves the intervention between conflicting parties to promote reconciliation, settlement, or compromise. The mediator's responsibilities include listening to the facts presented by both parties, ruling on the appropriateness of documents and other "evidence," and rendering judgment on a solution that reconciles the legitimate interests of both the disputing parties. Mediation varies from arbitration in that the arbitration is binding on the parties. In the mediation process, however, the disputing parties preserve their right of final decision on the solution proffered by the mediator. The mediator utilizes a variety of interpersonal skills and techniques to help the disputing parties come to a settlement but is not authorized to impose a solution.

A second type of dispute resolution mechanism is called the *minitrial,* which is not actually a trial at all.[19] The minitrial is a form of presentation involving an exchange of information between managers from each organization involved in the dispute. Once the executives hear both sides of the presentation, they then attempt to resolve the dispute through negotiation with their executive counterparts. Because minitrials are generally more complicated than other forms of negotiation, they are typically used when the dispute between the parties is significant and highly complex. One of the benefits of such a process is that it turns a potential legal conflict into a business decision and promotes a continuing relationship between the parties. A major advantage of the minitrial process is that it can be customized to fit the situation at hand. In essence, the process is a form of self-mediation with rules and conditions agreed to beforehand by the disputing parties. The process may or may not include the use of a mediator, depending on the requirements of the disputing parties.

Another related conflict resolution mechanism is the *rent-a-judge,* which is a popular name given to the process by which a court, on the agreement of the parties involved, refers a lawsuit pending between the parties to a private, neutral party. The neutral

---

[19] Singer, *Settling Disputes,* pp. 61–66.

party (often a retired judge) conducts a "trial" as though it were conducted in a real court. If one or both of the parties are dissatisfied with the outcome of the rent-a-judge decision, then the verdict can be appealed through normal channels. In this process, the parties agree to hire a private referee to hear the dispute. Unlike the binding arbitration process, rent-a-judge hearings are subject to legal precedents and rules of evidence.

A final alternative to dispute litigation and the dispute resolution mechanisms discussed earlier is one that is gaining popularity in the business press. Dispute prevention is a key factor in the concept of collaborative business relationships such as long-term contracting, partnering, and strategic alliances. When contracting parties initially agree to dispute resolution processes, a progressive schedule of negotiation, mediation, and arbitration followed by litigation as a last resort can be defined and delineated in the agreement. The "baring of souls" involved in this type of close, collaborative relationship dictates that the two parties fully recognize and agree upon the mechanisms for dispute resolution that are to be utilized under certain conditions.

A supply chain manager needs to consider several factors when deciding whether to use a dispute resolution mechanism and which mechanism to choose.[20] The first and, perhaps, foremost consideration is the status of the relationship between the parties in the dispute. When the relationship between the parties is ongoing and expected to continue for the foreseeable future, the disagreeing parties will prefer to resolve the contract dispute through means that will hopefully preserve the relationship.

Second, the choice of mechanism should be based on the type of outcome desired. There may be a need to establish an appropriate precedent to govern actions in future disputes as well as the one at hand. Many contractual disputes that end up in litigation are often settled out of court anyway. In this case, it is likely that an out-of-court or adjudicated settlement will be achieved under some level of duress and may not be as favorable as one that might have been derived in a mutually agreed-upon mediation or arbitration process.

A third consideration is whether it is desirable to have the disputing parties themselves involved in generating the outcome or resolution. The presence of the disputing parties is important to successfully resolving disputes using techniques such as negotiation, arbitration, mediation, minitrials, and rent-a-judge proceedings. Active participation by all parties involved in a dispute generally results in a more equitable and harmonious resolution (as opposed to having third parties such as attorneys involved).

The level of emotion displayed by the principals is another important consideration in selecting the type of dispute resolution mechanism. If emotions such as anger and frustration are high, the total cost of litigation, in terms of time, money, and management effort, may be more significant than originally anticipated. The harsh realities of a past prolonged court battle has convinced more than one set of potential litigants to consider less costly and more timely dispute resolution alternatives.

The importance of speed in obtaining a resolution can be a determining factor in the choice of whether to litigate, arbitrate, or mediate. In many instances the alternatives to court adjudication are quicker than litigation. Time pressures may force the disputing parties to be more creative and understanding in reaching an appropriate resolution short of meeting in court. There is a direct relationship between the time involved in settling a dispute and the cost involved: Quicker resolution is generally cheaper.

---

[20] Ibid, pp. 82–83.

The information required to reach a settlement may dictate the mechanism preferred. The closer the parties come to having the courts settle their dispute, the more formal and more voluminous the information requirements. Strict rules of evidence in the courtroom setting may not be desirable to parties because of publicity. Companies involved in the dispute may not be willing to spread their dirty linen or trade secrets out in public for all to see. In addition, the credibility of experts and other witnesses may be more difficult to achieve or maintain in a trial. All of the conflict resolution mechanisms or settlement options presented here allow a greater degree of privacy to the parties involved than that which can be attained in a court.

Summary

In this chapter, we have presented a general framework for managing supply chain relationships. It is clear that the concepts proposed are by definition very broad and general in nature. There is a very good reason for this: Every supply chain relationship is unique and carries with it a unique set of benefits, challenges, and potential conflicts. Companies who go into a close relationship with supply chain members must be aware of the fact that such relationships require a great deal of time, effort, and resources to manage. Just as in a marriage, parties to a supply chain relationship must be prepared to spend a great deal of time communicating, improving the relationship, and resolving conflicts within the relationship as they occur. It is for this reason that we stated early in the chapter that supply chain relationships are probably one of the most difficult elements of the supply chain to manage, as they are dynamic in nature and very fragile in countenance. The processes described in this chapter can help managers select the right partners in the first place and conduct business in a manner that will foster trust within the relationship. Finally, we presented a set of tools that can be used to resolve conflicts if and when they occur. Although these concepts appear to be rather straightforward in nature, they are certainly not always easy to apply. However, we believe they constitute a good set of ground rules for implementation of the other strategies described in this text.

C H A P T E R

Cases in Supply Chain Management

Case One   Consumable Computer Supplies[1]

INTRODUCTION

Incredible growth in the use of computers and related peripheral equipment has created a new industry—consumable computer supplies and accessories. The market for toner cartridges, magnetic media, impact printer supplies, and other essential consumable items found in today's automated office is sizable and growing. In 1995, estimates of the market for nonpaper consumable computer supplies were approximately $15.5 billion per year in the United States and Canada. This industry is expected to grow to approximately $22 billion per year by the turn of the century. Daisytek International, Inc. is the largest wholesale distributor of nonpaper consumable computer supplies and accessories in North America.

COMPANY HISTORY AND OVERVIEW

Originally established in 1977 as a manufacturer of printer "daisywheels," the early years of Daisytek's existence were focused on being a supplier for daisywheels and a variety of other computer and software products. In 1982, British executive David Heap pur-

[1] This case is adapted from Ernest L. Nichols Jr., "Computer Supplies Overnight: Distribution Operations at Daisytek International, Inc.," *Cycle Time Research* 2, no. 1 (1996), 53–58.

chased the firm and developed alliances with major computer hardware manufacturers. Throughout the 1980s, the company's business was split between hardware products and consumable computer supplies. By 1989, recognizing both the fierce competitiveness within the hardware industry and the seemingly untapped potential within the supplies market, Heap shifted Daisytek's focus exclusively to nonpaper consumable computer supplies and accessories.

Headquartered just north of Dallas in Plano, Texas, Daisytek is a wholesale distributor of over 6,000 nationally branded nonpaper consumable computer supplies and accessories. Companies such as Canon, Digital, Epson, Hewlett-Packard, IBM, Kodak, 3M, Sony, and Xerox are among the approximately 150 original equipment manufacturers whose products are sold by Daisytek. In addition, Daisytek works with over 14,000 customers, including value-added resellers, computer and office superstores (e.g., Office Depot, OfficeMax, and CompUSA), buying groups, and merchandisers across North America.

In developing client relationships, the Daisytek sales force makes use of a highly customer-oriented promotional program, leading-edge technologies, and a consistent, aggressive stream of promotions to down-channel organizations. Monte White, Daisytek's director of product management, sums up the company's promotional philosophy by saying Daisytek's exciting future is based on "the services we offer to our customer base." White goes on to emphasize the company's optimism about the future and its exciting industry: "As there are more and more computers, copiers, and fax machines that go out into the market, the need for offerings like Daisytek's consumables increases proportionally."

Daisytek has earned a reputation in its industry as a highly innovative and low-cost distributor. Testimonials to the firm's success include the positive reception of its first public stock offering in January 1995 and the fact that Daisytek was named one of *Inc.* magazine's 500 fastest growing companies on two different occasions. Daisytek's revenue for the 1994 fiscal year was $276 million. Revenue for the 1995 fiscal year grew to $353 million, an increase of 27.6 percent.

Daisytek's success did not happen overnight. Nearly two decades and two entirely different distribution systems have come and gone since the company began operations. The transformation of Daisytek's distribution operations, an important catalyst to Daisytek's current favorable market position, is discussed below.

DECENTRALIZED DISTRIBUTION

In the late 1980s and into the early 1990s, Daisytek promoted itself primarily as the industry's low-price supplier. The firm established a network of regional distribution centers (DCs) across the United States. By 1990, Daisytek had five distribution centers in the United States, which were located in Dallas, Los Angeles, Atlanta, Chicago, and Parsippany, New Jersey. Figure 5-1-1 illustrates Daisytek's U.S. distribution network. At this point, orders were transported via a traditional, ground-based shipping system.

As Daisytek's order volume and customer base grew, so did the complexity of its operations. Increasingly, complaints were lodged by customers who inquired about orders that seemed to vanish. The regional DCs with their small staffs and low levels of automation in the order-handling and shipping process, along with a series of difficulties with their ground carrier, were causing Daisytek considerable problems and were

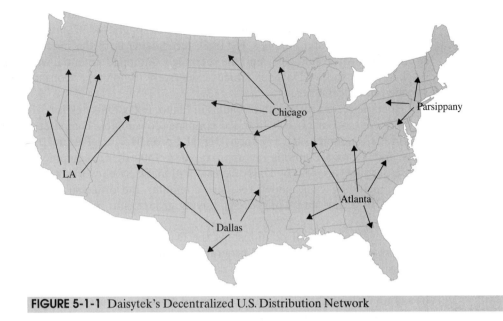

FIGURE 5-1-1 Daisytek's Decentralized U.S. Distribution Network

significant obstacles to further growth. Daisytek's senior management was faced with a critical decision regarding its distribution operations. The choice came down to two options: (1) Build more regional DCs and maintain the status quo of existing distribution and order systems that were barely sufficient, or (2) break from traditional industry practices and consolidate distribution activities at a single "superhub" facility to realize economies of scale in both technology and operations. The latter option was selected.

DAISYTEK'S CONSOLIDATED DISTRIBUTION STRATEGY

The consolidation decision radically changed Daisytek distribution in terms of both geographic location (see Figure 5-1-2) and operations. This decision shifted Daisytek's distribution activities to a superhub DC located in Memphis, Tennessee. The choice of the Memphis location was based on several factors, including:

- Memphis has an excellent transportation infrastructure. Positioned on the Mississippi River, Memphis offers local distributors access to virtually every form of freight transportation: air freight, trucking, and rail facilities, along with access to ocean transport via the river.
- Most important to Daisytek, Memphis is home to FedEx, the world's largest air distribution company and Daisytek's strategic partner.

These factors made Memphis a natural choice for Daisytek's superhub. In fact, the Daisytek superhub and FedEx's Memphis hub are almost neighbors. Daisytek's 176,000-square foot DC, which houses more than $35 million of inventory, is located 4 miles from FedEx's Memphis hub. This facility handles approximately 3,000 orders that include over 5,000 packages every day.

As a result of their strategic partnership, Daisytek has been able to integrate its own advanced information system capabilities with FedEx's sophisticated freight track-

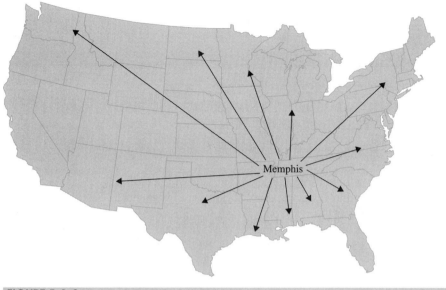

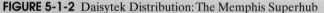

FIGURE 5-1-2 Daisytek Distribution: The Memphis Superhub

ing system and "time-definite" transportation services. Integration of these distinctive information systems competencies allows Daisytek to track any customer's order at any time, at any point in the delivery cycle, within minutes. Utilization of FedEx as its exclusive carrier allows Daisytek to guarantee next-day delivery of in-stock items.

These advantages place Daisytek far ahead of its competition in terms of handling customer orders, which significantly improves customer satisfaction. Once a real problem for the firm, instant order information has become a unique advantage in doing business with Daisytek.

DAISYGRAMS: A PROACTIVE APPROACH TO CUSTOMER ORDER INFORMATION

Recognizing the importance of customer order information in today's business environment, Daisytek actually goes one step further than most of its competition. Rather than waiting for customers to call regarding the status of their orders, Daisytek takes a "proactive" approach and sends its customers "DaisyGrams." DaisyGrams provide current order, backorder, shipment, and delivery information for all orders and are faxed or sent via electronic data interchange (EDI) nightly. DaisyGrams are available to all Daisytek customers.

NEXT-DAY DELIVERY

Because of the efficiency of Daisytek's superhub operations and proximity to FedEx, it is able to guarantee its customers next-day delivery on orders received by 9:00 P.M. (Eastern). Not only can the company boast a 95 percent fill rate on customers' orders, it is often able to exceed customers' expectations in terms of delivery time. The distribution system also allows Daisytek to ship orders to its customers or to "drop ship" orders directly to the Daisytek customer's customer. Beginning with the first customer shipment sent out of the superhub on July 6, 1992, the results have been tremendous. The next section illustrates several of the benefits associated with Daisytek's distribution strategy and also identifies key principles of cycle-time reduction incorporated in this strategy.

DAISYTEK'S DISTRIBUTION STRATEGY: RESULTING BENEFITS AND ASSOCIATED PRINCIPLES OF CYCLE-TIME REDUCTION

Daisytek's innovative distribution strategy incorporates a number of key principles of cycle-time reduction.[2] These approaches have been shown to be effective means for reducing the time required to complete organizational processes. Specific principles observed in the Daisytek distribution strategy include consolidating, automating, "informating" (i.e., innovative application of information technology to allow the free flow of information between organizations), co-locating, and partnering. In the following paragraphs, cycle-time reduction principles are presented and resulting benefits realized by Daisytek are discussed.

Consolidating

Creation of a consolidated superhub DC has allowed Daisytek to take advantage of economies of scale in terms of personnel, automation, and technology. Specific benefits that have resulted include the following: (1) a reduced amount of safety stock by consolidating inventory from the multiple DCs in the previous system, (2) an increase in inventory turnover rate from approximately 9 turns to approximately 12 turns (fiscal year 1994), (3) an improved order fill rate of approximately 95 percent, (4) an improvement in labor productivity, (5) a reduction in shipping errors and their associated cost, (6) an improvement in delivery times to most geographic areas, and (7) a reduction in facility-related expenses.

Automating

The move from small regional DCs to a superhub facility provided the order volume necessary to justify investment in "state-of-the-art" warehouse automation. Specific automation employed includes automated conveyors, in-line scales for automatic accuracy checking, computerized sorting equipment, scanning and bar-coding systems, an automated package routing system, and a paperless order-picking system. Order volumes in the regional DCs could not justify investments of the magnitude required for this level of automation. The high level of automation employed in the superhub is a key enabler allowing Daisytek to provide next-day delivery for 95 percent of its orders.

"Informating"

Linking Daisytek's information systems with the FedEx order tracking system has significantly reduced the time required to provide tracking information for customer orders. At one point, nearly 30 percent of the time spent on a given Daisytek order was devoted to customer "WISMO" (Where Is My Order?) requests. The time devoted to

---

[2] For an insightful discussion of the principles of cycle-time reduction, see James C. Wetherbe, "Principles of Cycle Time Reduction: You Can Have Your Cake and Eat It Too," *Cycle Time Research* 1, no. 1 (1995), 1–24.

tracking orders has been all but eliminated. Now when a customer calls, or when an order must be tracked for any reason, it can be done within minutes of the request. This development has not only reduced the time required to provide its customers with requested information; it has also reduced the cost associated with providing this information. Furthermore, the use of the DaisyGrams provides critical order information in a cost-effective manner before it is even requested.

Co-Locating

Locating the superhub in Memphis to take full advantage of the capabilities of FedEx has allowed Daisytek to extend its order cutoff time. Under Daisytek's earlier decentralized DC configuration, customer orders had to be placed before 4:00 P.M. (Eastern) to make the cutoff time for a given day's shipping. Now, located practically in FedEx's backyard, Daisytek's customer order deadline has been extended to 9:00 P.M. (Eastern). Even with the 9:00 P.M. cutoff, Daisytek still has 4.5 hours (12:30 A.M. Central) to process these orders before the end of its daily shipment window with FedEx. The Memphis location also allows FedEx to provide Daisytek with favorable rates, given the relatively low cost associated with getting Daisytek's freight into the FedEx system. Daisytek, in turn, charges its customers ground transportation rates but provides them with air transportation performance.

Partnering

Daisytek and FedEx are true partners committed to a mutually beneficial, long-term relationship. Evidence of this partnership can be seen in the long-term agreement between Daisytek and FedEx, which runs through the end of 1999, as well as the co-location of FedEx personnel at Daisytek to facilitate the processing of Daisytek orders into the FedEx system.

CONCLUSION

Daisytek's president and COO, Mark C. Layton, states that the company's mission is ". . . to be a low-cost, high-growth distributor." The benefits of Daisytek's distribution strategy and the Memphis superhub are being realized. Armed with a leading-edge distribution strategy, a strategic alliance with FedEx, and its innovative use of information technology, Daisytek appears well positioned to accomplish its mission. These factors will enable Daisytek to remain the industry's low-cost distributor while meeting steadily increasing demand for its products "overnight." ■

REFERENCES

Daisytek International, common stock prospectus. New York: Dillon, Read & Co. Inc., January 26, 1995.

Daisytek International, promotional videotape. Daisytek International, Inc., 1994.

Memphis Superhub Distribution Center, promotional videotape. Daisytek International, Inc., 1994.

Personal interviews with Jim Forrest, distribution director, Daisytek International, Inc., 1995, Memphis, TN.

Wetherbe, J. C. "Principles of Cycle Time Reduction: You Can Have Your Cake and Eat It Too." *Cycle Time Research* 1, no. 1 (1995), 1–24.

Case Two   Computer Hardware and Software[1]

INTRODUCTION

Although most companies have automated many of their functions (e.g., accounting, manufacturing, etc.), organizations are now exploring the final frontier of automation —the sales process (Kay 1995). In an attempt to become more profitable, companies are seeking new ways to reduce sales/order-processing cycle times, cut the costs associated with sales/order processing, and make salespeople more productive, all while trying to provide better service to customers.

Although the automation of sales/order processing holds a great deal of promise, it is a huge task to consolidate the information needed to integrate all parts involved in the process. For the organizations that have the technical expertise, however, the pay-offs can be substantial. For example, Campbell's Soup reengineered and automated its sales process. For its effort, Campbell's is now saving more than $18 million annually through reduced order cycle times, more accurate invoicing, and better control of funds (Kay 1995). This improvement in sales/order processing through the use of automation is now being explored by organizations in many industries.

Few industries are more competitive than computer hardware and software distribution. Although most distributors of hardware offer multiple configurations of their products, the number of computer software programs available seems almost limitless. With new software packages and new versions of existing programs being released with ever-increasing frequency, it is extremely difficult for distributors to keep these products in stock.

Insight Direct, a Tempe, Arizona–based hardware and software distribution organization, felt that it had to improve the performance of its sales/order-processing system. It needed a system that could support a broader product offering, while reducing the sales/order-processing cycle time and making the process more profitable. The result was an on-line inventory status and electronic data interchange–based sales/order-processing system that has met each of these requirements and has dramatically increased customer satisfaction.

THE COMPANY

Insight Direct was founded in October 1987 in Tempe, Arizona, as a distributor of computer hardware and software. Its business has grown substantially over the years to the point where it now has approximately 1 million customers. Insight Direct has grown from $1 million in sales in 1987 to sales of $250 million in 1995. Its customers, who are the ultimate end consumers of software products, place an average of 2,000 orders per day with peaks of up to 3,000 orders per day. Insight Direct has 400 order-entry termi-

---

[1] This case is adapted from Mark N. Frolick, "Cycle Time Reduction in the Order Processing of Packaged Computer Software," *Cycle Time Research* 2, no. 2 (1996), 81–87.

nals, which allow its salespeople to serve their customers' orders efficiently for over 5,700 product stock keeping units (SKUs) offered by the firm. Insight Direct, like most companies experiencing rapid growth, has had its share of the growing pains associated with an increasing customer base and product offering.

THE CHALLENGE

Insight Direct wanted to broaden its software product base to address customer demand for the latest software products. If a customer wanted to order a software product that Insight Direct did not have in stock, there was always a possibility that the customer would take his or her business elsewhere. To ensure that the software needs of its customers were met, Insight Direct wanted to broaden its software product offering tenfold. Although an admirable objective, this strategy would have dramatically increased the complexity associated with managing its business from both an order-entry and inventory-management perspective due to limitations of its existing order-processing system. To add to the problem, although there are hundreds if not thousands of software titles available, only 25 of these titles had a turnover rate high enough to justify holding them in inventory at Insight Direct's distribution center.

Basically, Insight Direct wanted to sell every conceivable computer software package available under the sun, but it did not want to have to hold the required inventory. This situation was problematic given its existing systems and practices.

THE ORIGINAL ORDER-PROCESSING SYSTEM

Lead times for software products orders at Insight Direct for out-of-stock products were extremely long and could often take up to seven days to fill. In a best-case scenario, it would take Insight Direct three days from the time a customer placed an order to get that software product into its DC. Then shipping the software to the customer took an additional two days. The total cycle time for this best-case scenario was five days. In the worst-case scenario, it would take five days to get the software product into the DC, with an additional two days for shipping the product to the customer for a total cycle time of seven days.

A significant problem with this order-processing system was that salespeople would take orders for computer software packages without knowing if the products were actually in stock. It was not until the evening after the order was taken that the order-processing system would check customer orders against current inventory. If the product was not available, it would be back ordered. The salespeople would then be alerted to the back-order condition the next morning when a purchasing report was generated.

In the back-ordered situation, the purchasing department had to generate a purchase order that would be faxed to the appropriate software vendor. The software vendor would then have to enter the purchase order information into its own order-processing system, which would trigger the software product being express shipped to Insight Direct (see Figure 5-2-1).

Upon receiving the software product from the vendor, Insight Direct would have to perform the product-receiving process, which includes bar coding the software product, placing the product in the appropriate location in the DC, and entering the software's availability into the computer. The computer would then release the order to the DC for

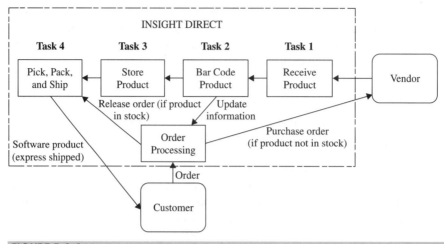

FIGURE 5-2-1 Order Processing prior to the Interorganizational Information System

shipping. The software product then had to be picked, packed, and express shipped to the customer. This process is very expensive and time-consuming when one considers that one piece of software retailing for $55 typically has a gross profit of approximately $8.

Insight Direct realized that for reducing order-processing cycle time and cost, as well as increasing customer satisfaction, this system was not adequate. Therefore, Insight Direct set out to solve the order-processing dilemma by reengineering the sales/order process and developing a new information system to support it.

THE INTERORGANIZATIONAL ORDER-PROCESSING SYSTEM

To solve the problems associated with the sales/order process, Insight Direct decided that it needed an easy-to-use system that would allow it to access its vendors' software product inventory information in an on-line manner. Therefore, Insight Direct developed an interorganizational information system (IOIS) that allowed it to interact better with its software vendors. This IOIS approach to order processing has allowed Insight Direct to create a competitive advantage in the field of packaged computer software distribution. The use of IOIS to exploit technology for competitive advantage is becoming increasingly popular (Gomes-Casseres 1994; Kanter 1994; Levinson 1994; Levinson & Meier 1988; Nichols et al. 1995).

An IOIS is an integrated data-processing/data-communication system utilized by two or more separate firms (Barrett 1986–1987). Use of IOIS has allowed business partners to reengineer their relationships in a beneficial way to all parties involved (Riggins & Mukhopaphyay 1994). IOIS benefits include higher levels of operating efficiency both internally and interorganizationally, better bargaining power for products, lower product costs, and improved customer service (Johnston & Vitale 1988). The IOIS at Insight Direct, which took three months to develop, has had a significant positive impact on both customer service and profitability.

The IOIS initiative at Insight Direct required significant collaboration between Insight Direct and its software vendors. One of the things that is often true of interorganizational relationships is that they are "out of alignment" (Wetherbe 1995). Often the different organizations in a supply chain hold very different perspectives on the world in which they compete. A key to reducing cycle time is for the organizations in an interorganizational relationship to understand each other's needs better. Therefore, it was important for Insight Direct and its vendors to understand the problems and concerns that each were experiencing in the software product order-fulfillment process.

The IOIS at Insight Direct was developed to allow salespeople to determine product availability interactively for every product SKU that they have in the system on a real-time basis, regardless of inventory location. For example, some products may be stored in Insight Direct's DC while others reside at a software vendor's location. The IOIS displays cumulative inventory availability for software products from vendors. This system allows salespeople to serve customers better by providing timely and accurate product availability and delivery information.

Order processing at Insight Direct is now a much smoother process. Salespeople now know the availability and location of products. If the product resides in a vendor's warehouse, the salesperson simply answers the system prompt, "Do you want to drop ship this line item? Y/N." It is at that point that the IOIS takes over the order process. The system reads through all line items with a "Y" answer and compares the products to vendor availability. If all of the interorganizational partner software vendors have the product in stock, the system then chooses the vendor with the lowest price. Once the vendor has been selected, the order is transmitted to the vendor via electronic data interchange. All vendors have agreed to same-day express ship orders directly to customers for all orders placed by 4 P.M. (see Figure 5-2-2). The application of EDI as part of an IOIS interface is becoming more commonplace (Bakos & Brynjolfsson 1993; Riggins 1990; Riggins & Mukhopaphyay 1994; Williamson 1995).

This interorganizational order-processing system has allowed Insight Direct to grow its packaged software distribution business in a manner that is both profitable and customer service–oriented. This new system has yielded several benefits for Insight Direct (see Table 5-2-1). The order-processing cycle time at Insight Direct is now two to five days shorter, which has lead to increased customer satisfaction. Software inventory levels at Insight Direct's DC have dropped by 80 percent. The IOIS allows Insight Direct to sell virtually any product it wants without having to hold it in inventory. This system has allowed Insight Direct to widen its total product offering to 35,000 products versus the 6,000 products that were sold with the original order-processing system.

Perhaps the largest contribution the IOIS has made at Insight Direct is its contribution to the bottom line. By using the IOIS to drop ship software products from vendors

FIGURE 5-2-2 Order Processing after the Interorganizational Information System

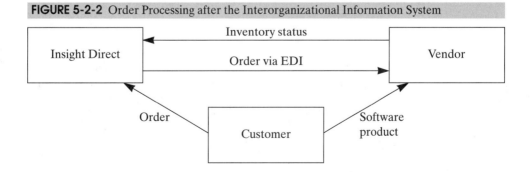

TABLE 5-2-1   Summary of IOIS Benefits at Insight Direct

	Before IOIS	*After IOIS*
Cycle time from customer order to product delivery	Best case—3 days Worst case—7 days	Best case—1 day Worst case—2 days
Percentage of product SKUs sold that are held in Insight Direct's inventory	100%	20%
Number of software products offered	6,000 titles	35,000 titles
Cost to process an order	Several dollars	A few cents

directly to customers, Insight Direct has lowered its order-processing costs by nearly 95 percent. A process that once cost several dollars per order now can be done for pennies.

KEYS TO SUCCESS

In order to be successful, it was determined that the system needed to simplify the order process, reduce order-processing cycle time, increase customer service, and reduce the costs associated with order processing. There were several keys to the success of the IOIS initiative at Insight Direct:

- Transforming the original order-processing system into an IOIS.
- Automating the order-entry process.
- Simplifying the process.

Transforming the Original Order-Processing System into an IOIS

Insight Direct realized that its ability to compete was being constrained by its original order-processing system. Therefore, it felt the need to change the way the order process was structured through a reengineering effort. This reengineering effort included better alignment with its vendors through better understanding of the roles each played in the process. This effort also required a closer working relationship, or partnering approach, where the software vendors had to be willing to share inventory and price information in order to increase their share of Insight Direct's business.

In return for their willingness to share inventory and pricing information, the software vendors are provided a report at the end of each month detailing the total number of orders sent to vendors and the percentage of those orders the particular vendor received. This allows vendors to change their pricing on a regular basis to compete for business. It also ensures that Insight Direct will continue to obtain the best possible price for products.

Automating the Order-Entry Process

A key to the success of the IOIS at Insight Direct was "informating" (Wetherbe 1995), or the free flow of information. Without vendors agreeing to share their inventory and pricing information, there would have been little need to develop an IOIS as it would have accomplished little that was not done with the original order-processing system. However, with vendors agreeing to provide their inventory and pricing information, technology was the "enabler" for improving the order process by providing access to this critical information as well as the EDI conduit to place orders.

One of the keys to success for the software vendors in this automation process was the realization that they could increase the sales of a particular software product by lowering their price under that of the other vendors. By doing so, the Insight Direct system would automatically send them all of the orders for that particular product.

Simplifying the Process

The original order processing system was limiting salespeople's effectiveness. They were often unable to answer customer questions concerning product availability and would not realize out-of-stock situations until the day after orders were placed.

The IOIS allows Insight Direct to offer every software product it wants, not have to inventory the product, give salespeople real-time inventory information regardless of location, and simplify the order process so that the salespeople only have to make one yes/no decision concerning drop shipping the products. After that one decision, the system determines which vendor is best for the order and transmits the order to that vendor. Not only does this simplify the process, but it ensures the highest order fill rate and the best possible price at all times.

CONCLUSION

In an effort to increase customer satisfaction, become more efficient, lower costs, increase profits, and reduce order-process cycle time, many organizations are beginning to examine their order-fulfillment processes. Insight Direct is one such company.

The original order-processing system at Insight Direct was slow, stressful on salespeople, and costly when dealing with out-of-stock items. Through an intensive reengineering effort, Insight Direct developed an IOIS to better handle the 2,000 to 3,000 orders that it receives each day from its customer base of 1 million. Information sharing proved to be a key to success in implementing the IOIS. Information often proves to be a key factor required to improve cycle time between organizations (Nichols et al. 1995).

More important than the development of the IOIS was the establishment of partnering arrangements with software vendors. When all organizations involved in a supply chain realize the role that they play in the supply chain's ultimate success, they are more willing to share information, helping to improve performance to the ultimate customer.

By developing its IOIS, Insight Direct has turned order processing into a process that better meets the needs of customers by reducing the order-processing cycle time. This new system has also lowered transaction costs, increased operating efficiency, and made Insight Direct much more profitable. ■

REFERENCES

Bakos, J. Y. and E. Brynjolfsson. "Information Technology, Incentives, and the Optimal Number of Suppliers." *Journal of Management Information Systems* 10, no. 2 (Fall 1993), 37–53.

Barrett, S. S. "Strategic Alternatives and Interorganizational System Implementations: An Overview." *Journal of Management Information Systems* 3, no. 3 (Winter 1986–1987), 5–16.

Gomes-Casseres, B. "Group Versus Group: How Alliance Networks Compete." *Harvard Business Review* 72, no. 4 (July–August 1994), 62–74.

Johnston, H. R. and M. R. Vitale. "Creating Competitive Advantage with Interorganizational Information Systems." *MIS Quarterly* 12, no. 2 (June 1988), 153–165.

Kanter, R. M. "Collaborative Advantage: The Art of Alliances." *Harvard Business Review* 72, no. 4 (July–August 1994), 96–108.

Kay, E. "Selling Enters the Information Age." *Datamation* 41, no. 8 (May 1, 1995), 38–42.

Levinson, N. S. "IOIS's: New Approaches to Global Economic Development." *Information & Management* 26, no. 5 (May 1994), 257–263.

Levinson, N. S. and R. Meier. "Toward the 1990's: Information Management Trends." *Xerox Corporation,* 1988.

Nichols, E. L., M. N. Frolick, and J. C. Wetherbe. "Cycle Time Reduction: An Interorganizational Supply Chain Perspective." *Cycle Time Research* 1, no. 1 (1995), 63–84.

Riggins, F. J. *The Boeing Company: The Material Division, Case Report.* Carnegie Mellon University, April 1990.

Riggins, F. J. and T. Mukhopaphyay. "Interdependent Benefits from Interorganizational Systems: Opportunities for Business Partner Reengineering." *Journal of Management Information Systems* 11, no. 2 (Fall 1994), 37–57.

Wetherbe, J. C. "Principles of Cycle Time Reduction: You Can Have Your Cake and Eat It Too." *Cycle Time Research* 1, no. 1 (1995), 1–24.

Williamson, M. "Entering the Fast Lane." *CIO* 8, no. 13 (April 15, 1995), 53–58.

Case Three   Upscale Men's Shoes[1]

INTRODUCTION

Successfully selling upscale products with traditionally low inventory turnover requires having the right inventory mix, while simultaneously keeping total inventory low. These objectives often conflict. Ensuring that items are in stock for immediate customer fulfillment helps sales but inflates inventory, which can be disastrous for inventory turnover and lead to large volumes of discontinued inventory. Alternatively, keeping inventory low frequently can cause out-of-stock situations, hurting sales. Selecting the right inventory strategy can be a pivotal business decision in this environment.

This complex business problem was encountered by a retailer of upscale men's shoes with retail stores nationwide. Sales volumes are relatively low, as compared to the average shoe store, whereas the number of stock keeping units carried is high as a result of the many combinations of pattern, color, size, and width. The distribution center carries approximately 10,000 active SKUs. Thus, it is not unusual for a particular retail store not to sell any of an individual SKU during the course of a year. Not surprisingly, this tends to lead to large volumes of discontinued product inventory and low inventory turnover.

Three different retail inventory strategies, which together represent a broad spectrum of inventory stocking levels, are compared. At one extreme is the traditional ap-

---

[1] This case is adapted from Donna Retzlaff-Roberts, Ernest L. Nichols Jr., and James C. Wetherbe, "Complete, Pareto, and No Inventory: Alternative Strategies for Retail Inventory," *Cycle Time Research* 1, no. 1 (1995), pp. 41–61.

proach of stocking all items in the retail store for immediate customer fulfillment, termed the *complete inventory.* In this scenario, if items (where an "item" is defined as a particular SKU) are stocked in sufficiently large quantities, stockouts and special orders are a rarity. At the other extreme, the *no-inventory* scenario refers to having a display-only inventory where customer demands are met through express special orders from the DC. An express special order is defined to mean next-day (or perhaps second-day) delivery directly to the customer via air freight. The intent here is to come as close as possible to providing the desired item when and where the customer wants. The "when" is generally limited to no sooner than the following morning. However, the "where" is virtually unlimited and is left to the customer's discretion. For example, the shoes could be shipped to the customer's home or office, or picked up at the store location. The particular shoes displayed could be selected to represent the entire size distribution, such that customers could try shoes on to check fit. (Size and fit are quite consistent between different patterns.) Thus it could be said, "If the shoe fits—ship it."

Between these two extremes are varying degrees of stocking items in the retail store. The third strategy, the *Pareto inventory approach,* lies here. This involves displaying all stock numbers, but stocking only the best-selling SKUs.[2] About 20 percent of the items often accounts for 80 percent of the sales, according to the Pareto principle. Empirical data shows that this pattern holds true for this case. Thus by stocking only the top-selling 20 percent of the items, the retail store should be able to fulfill approximately 80 percent of customer demand on the spot. The remaining 80 percent of items would be held at the DC, with the associated 20 percent of customer demands fulfilled by express special order, as in the no-inventory scenario. By increasing the percent of SKUs stocked, the percent of demands immediately fulfilled also increases.

The company used a Monte Carlo computer simulation to evaluate the impact and desirability of the alternative inventory strategies discussed above. Simulation offers a very effective method of answering "what if" questions. As is demonstrated in the following analysis, the Pareto strategy is recommended because of the significant improvement in inventory turnover. The display-only strategy may offer possibilities for some locations, such as airports, where the certainty of delayed fulfillment is not a hindrance, but this option is unlikely to be a plausible replacement for the complete inventory shoe store located in a shopping mall.

CURRENT SITUATION

The supply chain for the shoes is shown in Figure 5-3-1. Shoes are manufactured and obtained from both domestic and overseas manufacturing sites and shipped to a central DC. The shoes are then shipped from the DC to each of the retail stores. As previously mentioned, there are approximately 10,000 active SKUs at the DC. These represent approximately 300 stock numbers. The average stock number is available in approximately 33 size and width combinations; however, the actual size and width availability varies considerably by stock number with the most popular stock numbers being available in over 100 size and width combinations. There are up to 7 widths ranging from 2A

---

[2] A stock is a combination of pattern and color. If display space is limited, displaying at least one of each pattern would suffice, with the most popular color(s) chosen for each pattern.

to 3E, and up to 20 sizes ranging from size 5 to 16. Less popular stock numbers are available in considerably fewer sizes and widths.

To reduce inventory and improve inventory turnover, retailers neither stock nor display all 300 stock numbers. Rather, they stock and display about 100 stock numbers. In addition, they carry a limited size selection. Although no two stores are identical, the average retail store currently carries approximately 1,180 active SKUs, about 12 percent of the SKUs available at the DC. Thus, the average stock number is available in only about 11.8 different sizes in the retail store. In other words, about one third of the stock numbers are available in about one third of the sizes, which makes about one ninth of the SKUs available in the retail store.

The numbers describing the current situation have been based upon empirical data where possible. However, where exact data were unavailable, reasonable assumptions as determined by management were made. For example, retail data has been tracked by revenue, rather than by pairs of shoes as follows. The average number of pairs of shoes in inventory is about 1,800, with approximately 1,200 pairs (67 percent) being from active SKUs, and approximately 600 pairs (33 percent) being from discontinued SKUs. For active inventory, having 1,200 pairs from 1,180 SKUs means the vast majority have a stock-up-to level of 1. Only a handful are stocked 2 deep, meaning 2 pairs per SKU, which is the maximum. Based on average sales of 9 pairs per day (net of returns), and a 360-day year, the average annual inventory turn is based on sales of 3,240 pairs and inventory of 1,800 pairs, for an inventory turns value of 1.8.

Sales of discontinued shoes (about 3 pairs per day) account for approximately one third of retail sales. The remaining 6 pairs per day represent sales from active inventory, which means that turns on active inventory is also about 1.8 (based on inventory of about 1,200 pairs). However, as a result of the low stock-up-to levels for active items, the desired item is sometimes out of stock. In such a situation a special order is offered to the customer, where the desired pair of shoes will be shipped directly to the customer from the DC. Special orders are generally not available for discontinued items. In addition, special orders are offered for some nonstocked items, such as when a customer wants a size or color of a stocked pattern, which is not stocked. This means that more than the stocked 1,180 SKUs are actually being sold from the retail store. A special order currently takes 5 to 7 days, so it is not an express special order. Special orders are

FIGURE 5-3-1 Distribution Network

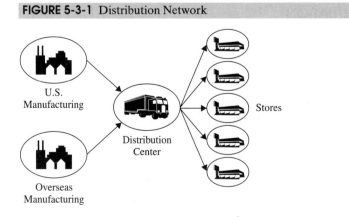

estimated to account for approximately 1.5 pairs per day, leaving 4.5 pairs per day being sold from active in-store inventory.

When a special order is offered, approximately 45 percent of customers accept with the remaining 55 percent representing lost sales. So, the 1.5 special orders per day currently being realized in sales is only 45 percent of the demand for out-of-stock and non-stocked active SKUs. This means approximately 3.3 pairs per day are actually being demanded from active inventory that are not available for immediate fulfillment. Combined with the average 4.5 pairs per day being sold from active in-store inventory, this indicates the overall demand from active inventory is approximately 7.8 pairs per day. If the discontinued sales are also included, total demand for the average retail store is about 10.8 pairs per day.

COMPARISON OF TRADITIONAL VERSUS PARETO STOCKING POLICIES

In the traditional approach, as a result of the large number of SKUs and relatively low sales volume, some stores may never sell a particular SKU all year. The shoes have been placed in the retail stores in anticipation of a demand that never occurs. The very low probabilities of selling for many of the SKUs means that a large gamble is being taken for a large number of shoes. This is the "just-in-case" approach to retail inventory. As a result, the retail stores have large inventories and low inventory turns, which have traditionally led to significant markdowns of discontinued shoes.

By using the Pareto inventory approach, some portion of the SKUs, say 20 percent, would be held at the retail store with the remaining 80 percent held only at the DC. This means that for less popular items, the risk of placing shoes where they will not sell is greatly reduced. In addition, it may be that fewer of the less popular items need to be manufactured because one pair is not needed for every retail store. Thus retail inventories are reduced and inventory turnover increased considerably. This should also lead to considerably less discontinued inventory in the long run.

MAKING SPECIAL ORDERS ATTRACTIVE

Success of the Pareto as well as the no-inventory strategy hinges on improving the acceptance rate on special orders. Providing the shoes when and where the customer wants leads to satisfied customers. In the case of special orders, the lower bound on "when" will, in most cases, be the following morning. Shipping the shoes overnight or second day, rather than the current five- to seven-day fulfillment, would increase costs, but it should also improve acceptance rates. Where to ship is easily solved by simply asking the customer. If the customer is concerned about fit and comfort and does not mind returning to the store, he may prefer the shoes be shipped to the store. In this case, the store could give the shoes a high-quality shine as an added customer service. However, many customers would likely prefer having the shoes shipped to their home or office and thus avoid the return trip to the store.

There also might be incentives offered that encourage future purchases. For example, "With your special order, here's a coupon for $10 off your next purchase." This sort of incentive might be used in conjunction with shipping time to tailor the scenario to what the customer wants. For example, "We could have the shoes to you tomorrow, or if you don't mind waiting, we could have those shoes to you in about five days and offer you a coupon for $10 off your next purchase."

THE INVENTORY DECISION MODEL

To further clarify the current situation, empirical data were used to develop a representative demand distribution for 1,140 SKUs. A size distribution was first developed, including both size and width, based on what portion of sales each size represents in the empirical data. Similarly, a stock number distribution was developed based on what portion of sales each stock number represents. These produce probabilities of customer size and shoe (stock number) preference. The probability of a particular SKU being chosen is the product of the size probability and stock number probability. This yields 1,140 probabilities ranging from 0.030116 to 0.000001. When these probabilities are sorted into descending order, the cumulative values reveal that these data very closely fit the Pareto principle, as may be seen in Table 5-3-1. The top 20 percent of the items account for 81.39 percent of the demands on active inventory. The cumulative curve is shown in Figure 5-3-2, where it may be seen that the curve levels off considerably beyond 20 percent of the SKUs. This means that the incremental demand filled by an additional SKU becomes increasingly small as more SKUs are added.

TABLE 5-3-1 Distribution of SKU Probabilities

% of SKUs	Cumulative % of Demand	Incremental % of Demand
0	0.00	65.78
10	65.78	15.61
20	81.39	7.27
30	88.65	4.58
40	93.23	2.87
50	96.10	1.74
60	97.84	1.03
70	98.87	0.65
80	99.82	0.46
90	99.86	0.14
100	100.00	—

FIGURE 5-3-2 Plot of Cumulative Demand Distribution

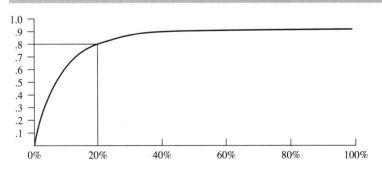

Although discontinued products represent a significant portion of the sales and inventory, we do not attempt to model them for several reasons. First, there are insufficient data available to model what might currently be in inventory. Second, this varies considerably by store. Third, the purpose of the study is to evaluate future inventory strategy, which means we are primarily concerned with active inventory. Changing from the traditional to the Pareto inventory approach would almost certainly affect the discontinued inventory in the long term.

The active inventory situation is modeled using a decision tree, shown in Figure 5-3-3. The first question (question A in Figure 5-3-3) is whether the customer wants a stocked item or a nonstocked item. If a nonstocked item is desired, a special order is immediately offered. If a stocked item is desired, the next question (B) is whether it is currently in stock. If so, the demand is immediately fulfilled. If not, a special order is offered. Given the demand distribution, the probability of answering question A affirmatively (P_A) is controlled by the choice of which SKUs to stock in the retail store. The probability of answering question B affirmatively (P_B) is controlled by the stock-up-to policy. Thus, both of these probabilities are controllable by management. For question C, however, the probability of a customer accepting a special order (P_C) is determined by the customer, but is controllable by management to the extent to which a special order is made appealing.

Values shown in Figure 5-3-3 are those for which approximations were initially available for the current situation. Missing values, such as P_A, were not known because

FIGURE 5-3-3 Decision Model

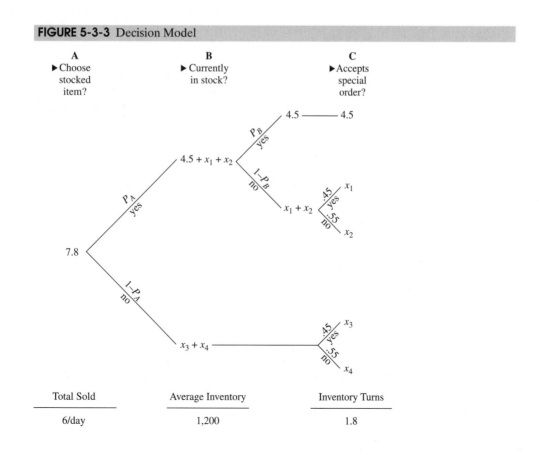

Total Sold	Average Inventory	Inventory Turns
6/day	1,200	1.8

relevant data had not been collected. However, enough is known about the relationships between the values that it is possible to estimate the missing values. The decision tree defines many of the relationships. When moving from left to right in the tree, one multiplies by the probability on a particular branch to find the expected outcome. For example, beginning with the average demand of 7.8 pairs per day, the expected average number of pairs per day demanded from stocked items is: $7.8 \, P_A = 4.5 + x_1 + x_2$. In addition, other key relationships are known, such as:

- The total number of special orders accepted per day is approximately 1.5 (i.e., $x_1 + x_3 \sim 1.5$).
- Approximately 58 percent of those desiring to buy from active inventory receive immediate fulfillment (i.e., $P_A P_B \sim 4.5/7.8 = 0.58$).

THE SIMULATION MODEL

This simulation models a representative retail store's active inventory. As indicated in Figure 5-3-4, only the portion of the network within the box is studied. Each simulation was run for one year to observe the long-term effects of an inventory strategy. Queuing behavior, store management practices, and discontinued inventory are not addressed. Customers arrive randomly with their interarrival times following the exponential distribution with an average arrival rate that varies according to the day of the week and month of the year, based upon empirical data. For example, sales are highest on the weekend (almost 25 percent of sales occur on Saturday), and late fall and early winter are the busiest times of year (October through January). Based on earlier discussion, the average demand per day is 7.8 pairs. As in Figure 5-3-3, a random probability is used to determine whether the desired item is a stocked item. If so, the customer's shoe size and stock number preference are randomly generated using the discrete probability distributions discussed earlier. Again there are 1,140 different SKUs involved, which agrees very closely with the 1,180 SKUs that the average store carries.

If the desired SKU is in stock, a purchase is recorded and inventory reduced. If the item is not in stock, then a special order is offered to the customer. Given a specified probability for willingness to accept a special order (currently .45 but likely to improve as a result of quicker, more flexible shipments), customer acceptance is randomly de-

FIGURE 5-3-4 Portion of Network Simulated

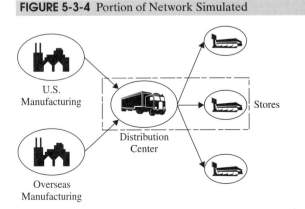

U.S. Manufacturing

Overseas Manufacturing

Distribution Center

Stores

termined whether the customer accepts the special order or if the sale is lost. Similarly, if the desired item is a nonstocked SKU, a special order is offered with the same random behavior regarding its acceptance.

Once a week inventories are reviewed and a replenishment order is placed, based on a specified stock-up-to level for each item. Orders are placed at the close of business each Sunday (because sales are highest during the weekend) and arrive one week later, being available for purchase Monday morning. The current practice is to stock the vast majority of items only 1 deep (i.e., 1 pair per SKU) and stock only the most popular items 2 deep. In the simulation, only the top 1 percent of the SKUs used a stock-up-to of 2. During the peak October through January period, stock-up-to's were increased by one for the top 2 percent of the SKUs.

Results for each simulation include the annual totals for the five outcomes shown on the right side of Figure 5-3-3. In addition, the average annual inventory is provided, which allows the inventory turns to be calculated. Another result of interest is the number of stocked SKUs that were "not hit," meaning not demanded during the entire year. For the simulations run with all 1,140 items stocked, the average number not hit was about 670 (about 59 percent).

By applying the simulation model to the current inventory strategy, the missing values in Figure 5-3-3 were estimated to be those shown in Figure 5-3-5. Figure 5-3-5 presents both the average number of pairs per day and the average number of pairs per

FIGURE 5-3-5 Current System

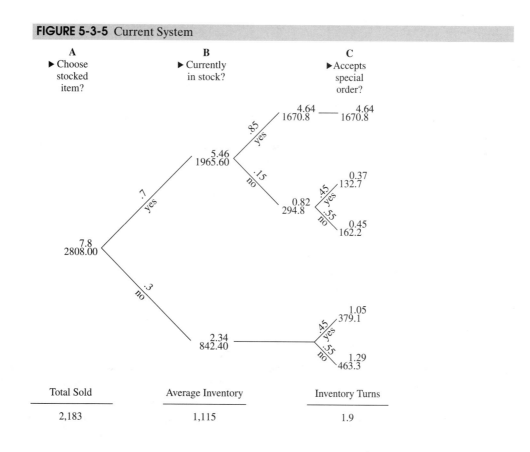

Total Sold	Average Inventory	Inventory Turns
2,183	1,115	1.9

year. In the simulation, the stock-up-to policy led to out-of-stock situations approximately 15 percent of the time (i.e., $P_B = .85$) for demands from stocked active inventory. This means that the previously unknown split between out-of-stock special orders and nonstocked special orders is approximately 1 to 3. Overall results agree quite strongly with reality, especially because many of the estimated averages were not known with certainty. For example, the results of Figure 5-3-5, which are based on the simulation, indicate an overall special order average of 1.42 per day, which is lower than the estimated 1.5 per day. Also, the average sales from in-store inventory are 4.62 per day, which is higher than the estimated 4.5 per day. Notice, however, that their total demand from store inventory does come very close to the estimated 6 pairs per day. The average inventory in the simulation was 1,115 pairs versus the estimated average 1,200. Such differences are actually quite small in light of the uncertainty of the estimate values. Overall, the amount of agreement between the simulation results and estimates of the current situation is surprisingly high.

We now have the probabilities associated with the answers to questions A and B in Figure 5-3-3. Thus, by stocking about 12 percent of the active SKUs available at the DC, about 70 percent of the demand is being captured by the retail inventory. This also agrees strongly with the Pareto principle and the probability distribution presented in Table 5-3-1. This indicates that the current inventory strategy is to some extent a Pareto strategy already, with respect to all 10,000 SKUs held at the DC.

THE COMPLETE INVENTORY STRATEGY

One easily made improvement in examining Figure 5-3-5 is to reduce the probability of a stocked item being out-of-stock (P_B) because 15 percent of the time is rather high. This is accomplished by increasing the stock-up-to levels. However, this is not equally true of all items. During the simulation runs, the more popular items were frequently out of stock. These best-selling items move quickly, so there is relatively little risk associated with increasing their stock-up-to levels. After repeated simulation runs and fine-tuning the stock-up-to levels, we found that P_B could be increased to .96 by using stock-up-to levels as high as 6. Only the top 3 items (0.26 percent) used a stock-up-to of 6, the next 11 items (0.96 percent) were stocked 4 deep, the next 15 (1.32 percent) were stocked 3 deep, the next 50 (4.39 percent) were stocked 2 deep, and the remainder (93 percent) were still only 1 deep. During the peak period, the practice of increasing stock-up-to's by 1 for the top 2 percent of SKUs was continued. This resulted in increased inventory and increased sales, while maintaining inventory turns, as shown in Figure 5-3-5. Increasing stock-up-to levels further allows P_B and sales to be increased, but inventory turns begin to diminish as inventory growth begins to outpace sales growth.

In deciding which of the active SKUs to stock at the retail store, there does not seem to be any reason to increase beyond the current number. Of the 1,140 SKUs in the simulation, on average 670 (58.8 percent) were not hit in a one-year period. This agrees with behavior observed in the retail store. Therefore, the scenario shown in Figure 5-3-6 will be considered the complete strategy, with its only difference from the current reality being the increased stock-up-to's for top sellers. This scenario is summarized in the right-hand column of Table 5-3-2. If special orders were made more attractive so that the proportion of customers accepting increased to 60 or 75 percent, the results would match those summarized in the right-hand column of this table.

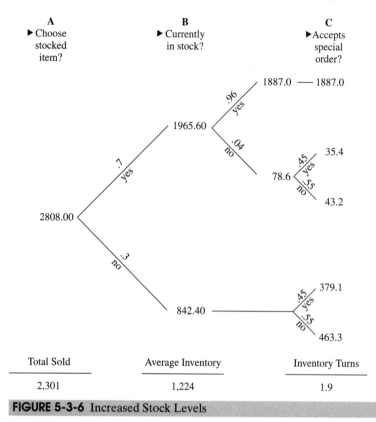

	A	B	C
	► Choose stocked item?	► Currently in stock?	►Accepts special order?

```
                                                    .96
                                                    yes
                                            1965.60        1887.0 —— 1887.0
                                                    .04
                                    .7              no
                                    yes                        .45
                                                               yes    35.4
                                                        78.6
                                                               .55
                    2808.00                                    no     43.2


                            .3
                            no
                                            842.40            .45
                                                             yes     379.1
                                                        842.40
                                                             .55
                                                             no      463.3
```

Total Sold	Average Inventory	Inventory Turns
2,301	1,224	1.9

FIGURE 5-3-6 Increased Stock Levels

TABLE 5-3-2 Summary of Pareto and Complete Inventory Options

Special Order Accept Rate (P_C)		Percent of 1,140 of SKUs Stocked				
		20% ($P_A = .570$)	30% ($P_A = .621$)	40% ($P_A = .653$)	50% ($P_A = .673$)	100% ($P_A = .700$)
	In-store sales	1,536	1,673	1,759	1,813	1,887
	Ave. inventory	330	431	540	656	1,224
	Items not hit	3.5%	12.5%	21.9%	28.9%	58.8%
	Sp. orders	572	511	472	448	414
45%	Tot. sales	2,108	2,184	2,231	2,261	2,301
	Inv. turn	6.4	5.1	4.1	3.4	1.9
	Sp. orders	763	681	629	597	542
60%	Tot. sales	2,299	2,354	2,388	2,410	2,429
	Inv. turn	7.0	5.5	4.4	3.7	2.0
	Sp. orders	954	851	787	746	677
75%	Tot. sales	2,490	2,524	2,546	2,559	2,564
	Inv. turn	7.5	5.9	4.7	3.9	2.1

THE PARETO STRATEGY

Moving on to the Pareto scenario, the same decision tree model may be used. The probability of a stocked item being desired (P_A) will diminish based on the portion of the 1,140 items stocked. The probability of a stocked item being in stock (P_B) will again be dependent on the stock-up-to policy. Finally, the probability of a customer accepting a special order (P_C) will depend on the customer and how attractive a special order is made. Simulations were run for an array of values for P_A and P_C as shown in Table 5-3-2. Notice that P_A equals the product of 0.7 (the demand captured by the 1,140 SKUs) and the percent of this that is captured by the portion of stocked items. For example, with only 20 percent (228) of the 1,140 SKUs stocked, as in Table 5-3-1, we can expect 81.39 percent of these demands to be fulfilled by retail inventory (except for out-of-stock situations), so we have $P_A = 0.7 * 0.8139 = 0.570$. Using the same stock-up-to policy and doing nothing to make special orders more attractive (i.e., P_C still equals 0.45), the simulation results indicate that total sales would be 2,108 and inventory turns would increase to 6.4. In general, the simulation results for in-store sales (those with immediate fulfillment), average inventory, and percent of items not hit, are unaffected by the special-order acceptance rate. Thus, these three numbers, shown in the upper portion of Table 5-3-2, apply to all of the special order acceptance rates. In moving from left to right in Table 5-3-2, increasing the portion of items stocked, one can see that while in-store sales improve, the amount of improvement diminishes, which is not surprising given the nature of the probability distribution. The opposite is true of inventory turns.

THE NO-INVENTORY STRATEGY

The same decision model also applies to the no-inventory or display-only inventory strategy, but with P_A being 0.0. Hence, the model simply reduces to offering special orders. However, unlike the other scenarios, the customer would know beforehand that a special order is the only option. Even the Pareto scenario with only 20 percent fulfills the majority of demands immediately. To avoid angering customers, it would probably be unwise to attempt to present the store as a traditional shoe store. Customers would need to be aware that this is a display-only store. Thus, anyone who found that unacceptable would be unlikely to express a desire to purchase. Hence, P_C would be likely to equal essentially 100 percent. This leaves the question of what happens to demand. We can certainly not assume that it remains unchanged. The profitability could be analyzed for an array of demand rates.

Such a store would be similar to catalog shopping except that the customer could see, touch, and experience the product. The display shoes could be from the full array of sizes so that he might also try one on. It would be unlikely to be the pattern desired, but the shoes are very consistent in size between patterns. So, how the shoe feels and what size is appropriate could be determined. In a traditional shopping setting, such as a mall, it seems unlikely that such a strategy would be successful. However, in settings where having the shoes shipped is less problematic or even desirable, it may have possibilities. One such example is an airport where business travelers often have "time to kill." This possibility is helped by the fact that the average buyer of upscale men's shoes is much more likely than the average person to be a business traveler.

DISCUSSION

Several aspects of the models used and other issues warrant additional discussion.

No "Switching" Behavior

The models did not incorporate customer switching. In reality a customer may initially demand a particular shoe that is not in stock. The customer may then switch to another similar shoe to avoid a special order. For example, there may be a similar pattern available in the appropriate size and color. Alternatively, if the shoe is available in a number of widths, it is possible that another width may suit the customer. A problem with attempting to model switching behavior is identifying the likely customer preferences for which SKUs are substitutable for one another, both for size and for pattern. Information was not available for customer switching and would be extremely difficult to obtain accurately due to variations in personal preferences. If the Pareto inventory strategy were to be implemented, increasing the company's understanding of customer-switching behaviors and adjusting to them would be useful.

Probabilities Are Treated as Known

As previously discussed, empirical sales data were used to determine the probability distributions regarding the likelihood of a particular item being chosen. Such an estimate is needed for stocked items to determine the stock-up-to level. In reality, forecasts must be made using a best guess of probabilities. As in the model used here, two distributions are needed: the size distribution (including both size and width) and the stock number distribution. The probability of a particular SKU being chosen is the product of these two. Fortunately, some of the historical data should provide accurate information. The size distribution should be very accurate from historical data. Men's dress shoes are not generally trendy items, so the stock number distribution may use many of last year's sales proportions for existing patterns and those with slight changes for old patterns. For example, the popularity of wing tips and penny loafers is unlikely to change dramatically in one year. Although the popularity of a new pattern is always uncertain, the greatest uncertainty will typically be associated with casual and contemporary styles.

In any inventory scenario, it is important to collect data "on the fly" so that probabilities can be updated. A pattern that is selling much better than expected should have its stock-up-to level increased. Conversely, a pattern that is selling less well than expected should have its stock-up-to level decreased.[3] Thus, in the Pareto inventory approach, which items are stocked and to what level should be viewed as flexible, and customer preferences should be continually monitored (from in-store sales, special orders, and lost sales, too, if possible). It should also be noted that the core stock could certainly vary by store.

Choice of Stocked SKUs

Given the above discussion regarding estimating the probability of each SKU being selected, these probabilities should be used even in the complete inventory scenario to select which SKUs are stocked. As previously discussed, the retail stores currently stock about 1,180 SKUs, which represent about 12 percent of the active SKUs at the DC. It was

---

[3] It is suggested that this be accomplished by reduced reorders and not by shipping inventory back to the DC.

found that these SKUs are capturing about 70 percent of the demand for active SKUs. The current practice is to determine which stock numbers to carry (about the top 100), and then to select a number of sizes for each stock number (on average 11.8 sizes). This process makes use of the probability distribution for stock numbers and the distribution for sizes, but in a 2-step process that does not make use of the SKU probabilities. If one instead were simply to use the SKU probabilities and pick the largest 1,180, a slightly different set of SKUs would result. For example, using the current method a particular stock number, say the 95th most popular, might be stocked in 8 sizes. Using the SKU probabilities, this stock number might instead be chosen in only 3 sizes, whereas a very popular stock number, in the top 10, might currently be stocked in 15 sizes. Using the SKU probabilities, this stock number might be stocked in an even larger variety of sizes.

Selecting each SKU based on its own probability would deviate from using a more standard size selection per stock number. However, the sum of the individual SKU probabilities yields the total demand being captured by those SKUs. Thus, for whatever number of SKUs management desires to stock, the total percent of demand captured will be maximized by selecting the SKUs with the largest probabilities. Using such a process, it may be possible to increase the 70 percent of demand currently being captured without increasing the number of stocked SKUs.

No Interaction between Special-Order Aversion and SKU

How likely a particular customer, on a particular day is to accept a special order will be random. It is possible that there could be an interaction between this likelihood and the probability of selecting the desired item. For example, a customer who wears an unusual size (for example, an SKU with a small probability of being selected) may be much more willing to accept a special order than the customer who wears a common size. The same may be true of the pattern. A more unusual pattern may be harder to find, thus, the customer may be more willing to accept a special order. It seems logical that the more unusual the item the more willing the customer may be to accept a special order. A relationship of this sort could easily be incorporated into the simulation model.

If such an interaction does exist, then the probability of accepting a special order P_C would be based on the probability of selecting the particular SKU. Thus, results for the Pareto inventory approach would be even better than those reported because the nonstocked items would be those with smaller probabilities of being chosen. Hence, these special orders would be more likely to be accepted.

No Lack of Availability at Distribution Center

It should be noted that if a Pareto or no-inventory strategy is implemented for a number of retail stores, availability at the DC is critical. Another study would be useful for evaluating the levels at which items should be stocked in the DC. However, for any particular item, the DC level certainly should be lower than the current total over all retail stores.

TOTAL COST ANALYSIS

To evaluate which inventory strategy is most beneficial, financial considerations are of primary importance. The various possible scenarios summarized in Table 5-3-2 might be transformed to a total cost model in the following way:

$(R - C) * \text{(In-store sales} + \text{Special orders)} - H * (\text{Avg. inventory}) - C * (\text{Avg. inventory})$
$S_1 * (\text{In-store sales}) - S_2 * (\text{Special orders}) = \text{Preliminary Operating Income}$

where

R = Revenue per pair (average)

H = Holding cost per pair per year

C = Cost per pair to manufacture or purchase (average)

S_1 = Regular shipping cost per pair from DC to store

S_2 = Express shipping cost per pair from DC to customer

Only costs that would differ between inventory scenarios need be included to observe the net financial impact of changing from one scenario to another, so this income calculation is not net operating income. For example, overhead costs of running the retail store are not included because these costs would be unaffected by the inventory strategy. Manufacturing (or purchase) cost is included because the total number of pairs manufactured would be reduced by the Pareto and no-inventory scenarios. For example, as shown in Table 5-3-2, moving from 100 percent to 40 percent of the SKUs in the retail store reduces the average inventory from 1,224 to 540. This reduces total inventory over all retail stores considerably, but is not expected to significantly increase DC inventory. The reason the DC inventory is not expected to increase considerably is that the SKUs that have been "backed up" to the DC are the less commonly chosen SKUs. If there were 100 retail stores, each of which previously had one pair of a particular SKU, the DC does not need to increase its stock-up-to level for this SKU by 100 pairs in order to supply demand. Therefore, the total number of pairs manufactured is reduced, and this reduction is primarily showing up in reduced retail inventory. Because manufacturing cost is not equal over all scenarios, the above income calculation must include it and account for the fact that manufacturing cost is incurred not only for what was sold but also for what is in inventory that did not sell.

Depending on how the above costs are quantified, any of the Table 5-3-2 scenarios might be considered "best." However, Table 5-3-2 shows that operating in the Pareto mode at 30 percent or 40 percent provides the majority of the sales of operating at 100 percent. The fact that almost 60 percent of the items are "not hit" in the complete mode (stocking all 1,140 SKUs) implies that stocking only the top 40 percent should suffice. In fact, moving from 100 percent to 40 percent at the 45 percent acceptance rate for special orders, sales decrease only 3 percent (from 2,301 to 2,231) while inventory decreases 56 percent (from 1,224 to 540) and inventory turnover increases 216 percent (from 1.9 to 4.1). The special-order acceptance rate is currently 45 percent, which should be easily increased if special orders are made more attractive by express shipment and/or some of the other previously discussed possibilities. In which case, reducing the number of stocked SKUs would be even less detrimental to sales, as shown by the 60 percent and 75 percent rows.

Using the cost values below, the net revenue for the Table 5-3-2 scenarios may be calculated. It is estimated that the average per pair costs are:

R = \$200

H = \$15 to \$23 (based on 20 to 30 percent of C)

C = \$75

S_1 = \$1

S_2 = \$5 to \$25 (depending upon method of shipment)

The annual holding cost of 20 percent to 30 percent of an item's value is based upon commonly used standards in the logistics field.[4] In addition to the cost of capital, this cost takes into account the risk of obsolescence of the item, which is a very relevant factor in this type of inventory situation. As mentioned earlier, about one third of the average retail store's inventory is comprised of discontinued shoes. The special-order shipping cost will depend on how quickly the item needs to arrive. The low end of the range involved using ground transport at a cost of about $5 and taking about four days, which is the current method and cost. The upper end involves overnight air freight for next-morning delivery at a cost of about $S = 25. In between are other alternatives such as second-day delivery.

The preliminary operating income results are summarized in Figures 5-3-7, 5-3-8, and 5-3-9. Each figure corresponds to a different special-order acceptance rate. Within each

FIGURE 5-3-7 Preliminary Operating Income: 45% Special-Order Acceptance Rate

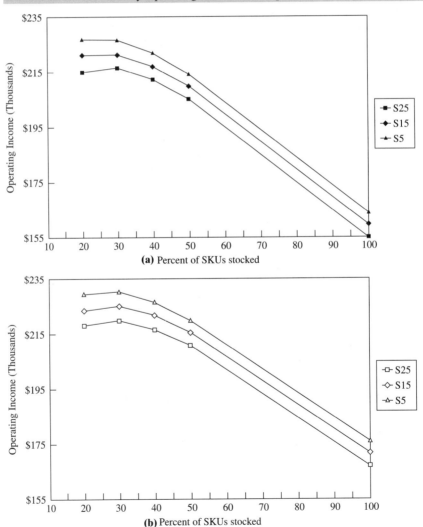

(a) Percent of SKUs stocked

(b) Percent of SKUs stocked

---

[4] See for example Stock and Lambert (1987) or Bowersox, Closs, and Helferich (1986).

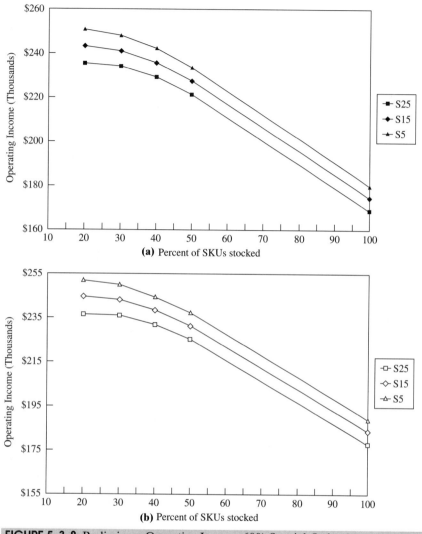

FIGURE 5-3-8 Preliminary Operating Income: 60% Special-Order Acceptance Rate

figure, two different holding costs and three different shipping costs are used. Thus, the current situation may be found at the right of Figure 5-3-7, for $S = 5$, using either holding cost. In all scenarios, income appears to be maximized by a stocking level between 20 percent and 30 percent.[5] Looking between the three graphs, it may be observed that the best stocking level decreases as the special-order acceptance rate increases. At the 45 percent acceptance rate, the best stocking level appears to be about 30 percent, whereas at the 75 percent acceptance rate, the ideal stocking level seems to be closer to 20 percent.

Results from marketing research will determine what special-order costs are necessary in order to improve the special-order acceptance rate. For example, if special-order acceptance could be improved to 60 percent at an average cost of $15, the two

---

[5] At these low stocking levels, it is possible that the savings in manufacturing cost is overestimated because of the earlier discussed probable need to increase DC.

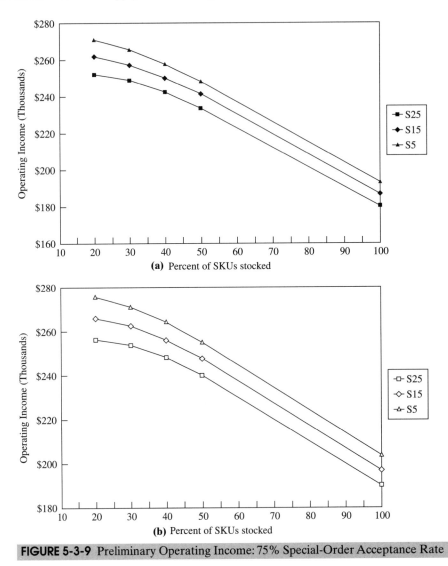

FIGURE 5-3-9 Preliminary Operating Income: 75% Special-Order Acceptance Rate

curves for $S = 15$ in Figure 5-3-8 are relevant. This indicates that stocking in the 40 percent to 45 percent range would be best, which would be approximately 500 SKUs. This also indicates a net revenue increase of approximately 11 percent and inventory turnover would increase approximately 225%.

CONCLUSION

This investigation of the trade-offs between inventory availability for immediate customer fulfillment and inventory costs has shown that notable improvements could be achieved by adopting the Pareto inventory approach. These improvements include significantly reduced inventory, associated savings in manufacturing costs, improved inventory turnover, and improved profitability. The success of such a strategy hinges upon choosing the right items to stock such that the majority of customers receive immediate fulfillment and making special orders sufficiently attractive for nonstocked items, in order to keep lost sales to a minimum.

Some of the values used in these models are approximations because exact data were unavailable. In addition, there are a number of unresolved implementation issues such as the previously discussed issue of determining stocking levels at the DC. Despite these caveats, there is clear indication that the above improvements are possible. Such a strategy could be applied to a number of other retail inventories where the risk of an individual item not moving is large. ■

REFERENCES

ARENA *Users' Guide.* Sewickley, PA: Systems Model Corporation, 1994.

Bowersox, D. J., D. J. Closs, and O. K. Helferich. *Logistical Management,* 3rd ed. New York: Macmillan, 1986.

Law, A. M. and W. D. Kelton. *Simulation Modeling and Analysis.* New York: McGraw-Hill, 1982.

Stock, J. R. and D. M. Lambert. *Strategic Logistics Management,* 2nd ed. Homewood, IL: Irwin, 1987.

Case Four   Biochemicals[1]

INTRODUCTION

This case reports the results of an important project conducted by the biochemical division of a major international medical products firm. This case consists of three main sections. The first section presents an overview of the major project activities and provides a useful model for firms interested in conducting a cycle-time reduction project. The second section presents the results of project "action team" efforts, which addresses specific cycle-time reduction opportunities. A discussion of key principles of cycle-time reduction associated with the action team initiatives is also provided. The final section presents the project conclusions.

PROJECT OVERVIEW

Major project activities included an initial meeting, a cycle-time reduction workshop, action team initiatives, and a meeting in which the action teams presented their findings. In this section, a brief overview of each of these activities is presented.

Initial Meeting

The key feature of the initial project meeting was the identification of potential cycle-time research problems. A "brainstorming" session yielded a number of project

---

[1]This case is adapted from Ernest L. Nichols Jr., Donna Retzlaff-Roberts, and Mark N. Frolick, "Reducing Order Fulfillment Cycle Time in an International Supply Chain," *Cycle Time Research* 2, no. 1 (1996), 13–31.

candidates. This list of potential projects was narrowed to two candidates through evaluation of required resources, potential for successful completion, potential benefits, and customer impact. Following the meeting, the firm's executive management determined the project would address the customer order-fulfillment process for a key product line within its international supply chain. A project plan was developed and project team selected.

Cycle-Time Reduction Workshop

A two-day cycle-time reduction workshop was held at an off-site location. Workshop activities included: (1) education and training regarding the principles of cycle-time reduction; (2) development of a supply chain process map; (3) identification of potential opportunity areas or "points of leverage" to reduce the time required to complete the customer order-fulfillment process; and (4) prioritization of these potential points of leverage.

Education and training.   Education and training were key elements of the cycle-time reduction workshop. Participants were introduced to over 40 strategies that have been shown to be effective in reducing process cycle times.[2] This session also drew comparisons between cycle-time reduction initiatives with business process reengineering and total quality management (TQM) programs and introduced the concept of points of leverage.

Process mapping.   An important part of the workshop was the development of the supply chain process map. The process map presents the key steps in a given process and the time required to complete each step.

Prior to the workshop, the functional groups involved in the customer order-fulfillment process were asked to complete two supply chain cycle-time worksheets. These worksheets provide a framework for project team members to examine current processes and cycle-time performance across the supply chain. The worksheets are presented in Appendix A.

During the workshop, the project team used the information captured by the supply chain process worksheets to develop a supply chain process map. A high-level process map for the firm's current order process is presented in Figure 5-4-1.

Identification of "points of leverage."   Upon completion of the supply chain process map, the group focused its efforts on identifying points of leverage. The points of leverage concept for a cycle-time reduction project is analogous to the flaps and rudder on an aircraft. A pilot steers an aircraft through the use of the flaps and rudder. Although these are relatively small parts of the aircraft, use of these points of leverage allows the pilot to turn the aircraft. Similarly, in examining business processes, there are often a few specific parts of the overall process (or points of leverage) that can provide opportunities for significant cycle-time improvement.

In examining the customer order-fulfillment process map, the project team developed a list of potential points of leverage to improve order cycle-time performance. Specific areas identified included:

- Direct shipment of U.S. customer orders from the European division,
- Increased inventory held in the U.S. division's distribution center (DC),

---

[2] For a discussion of the principles of cycle-time reduction, see James C. Wetherbe, "Principles of Cycle Time Reduction: You Can Have Your Cake and Eat It Too," *Cycle Time Research* 1, no. 1 (1995), 1–24.

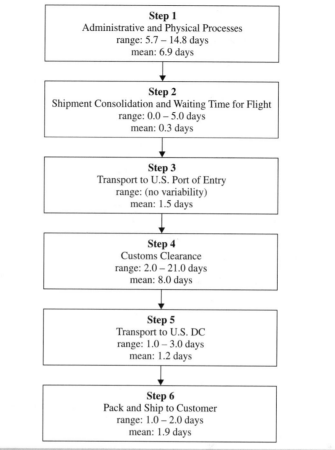

FIGURE 5-4-1 Current Order Process

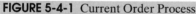

- Review of customs broker activities,
- Utilization of electronic data interchange to link U.S. and European division information systems,
- Integrated information systems,
- Use of more frequent product shipments from the European division to the U.S. division,
- Reduction in product line through standardization of package sizes and product concentration strengths,
- Alteration of working hours, and
- Use of different U.S. ports of entry.

Prioritization of points of leverage. Having identified the points of leverage and recognizing that the project team did not have the resources to address all points of leverage that were identified, the next activity was to prioritize these opportunities. To accomplish this task, each member of the project team was allowed to vote for the specific area he or she thought would provide the greatest potential for cycle-time reduction. When casting their votes, project team members were asked to keep two criteria in mind: (1) the "overall impact of the opportunity area on the firm's business" and (2) "probability of implementation." As a result of the voting process, four points of leverage were selected for further review:

- Direct shipment of U.S. customer orders from the European division,
- Increased inventory held in the U.S. division's DC,
- Review of customs broker activities, and
- Utilization of electronic data interchange to link U.S. and European division information systems.

Several other areas offered significant opportunities for cycle-time reduction but were not considered to have high likelihood of implementation. Other opportunity areas, such as integrated information systems, were already being addressed by the firm.

An action team was assigned to each of the selected opportunity areas. These teams worked independently to identify specific opportunities for cycle-time reduction and to develop actionable recommendations for each of the four areas.

Reports from the Action Teams

Each action team worked on its specific cycle-time initiative for approximately six months. At the end of this period, the entire project team met to present and discuss the action teams' findings. An overview of each of the action team initiatives is presented in the next section.

ACTION TEAM INITIATIVES

The action team initiatives included modeling the customer order-fulfillment process, reviewing the customs clearance process, and utilizing EDI technology to link the firm's U.S. and European information systems. This section presents an overview of each of the action team initiatives.

Customer Order-Fulfillment Process

An action team analyzed both the direct shipment of U.S. customer orders from the European division and the impact of an increase in inventory held in the U.S. division's DC through the use of a computer-based simulation model. The direct shipment option represented an effort to reduce the cycle time required to fill an order for products that are not currently held in inventory at the U.S. division's DC. The inventory analysis attempted to reduce average customer order cycle time by increasing the probability that the ordered product would be in-stock. This section discusses the modeling effort and its results.

Current Process and Alternative Approaches   The firm's products are manufactured and inventoried at its European division. A limited product inventory is also held at the U.S. division's DC. U.S. customer orders are received by the U.S. division sales office. If the customer order is for a product that can be filled from inventory held at the U.S. DC, then the customer receives the order in approximately two days. If the required product is not available at the U.S. DC, the customer order is relayed to the European division.

As shown in Figure 5-4-1, the current process consists of several activities. Various administrative and physical processes are performed at the European division. The product is then air-freighted to the United States, typically in a consolidated shipment that includes multiple orders and multiple products. Upon arrival in the United States, the shipment goes through customs, which sometimes causes considerable delays, as indicated in step 4 of Figure 5-4-1. After clearing customs, the product is shipped to the U.S. DC, and upon arrival is repacked and shipped to the customer.

This process can be lengthy, ranging from 2.2 to 9.5 (five-day) workweeks. The majority of orders are filled in 3.2 to 5.6 weeks, and the average is 4.0 weeks. Customers frequently express frustration at this lengthy lead time, but often they must wait because they have no alternative. However, when possible, many customers will switch to suppliers that provide shorter order-fulfillment times. Another sentiment expressed by customers is that they would increase their orders if they could receive their orders faster. Thus, it is critically important that customer order-fulfillment cycle time be reduced.

As mentioned earlier, when a U.S. customer places an order, if inventory is available at the U.S. DC, then only the "pack and ship" part of the process (step 6 in Figure 5-4-1) is required. In fact, order-fulfillment time can be as short as one day if the product happens to be packaged in the appropriate quantity. In general, if inventory is available in the United States, order-fulfillment time is two days.

One way to reduce customer order-fulfillment cycle time is to maintain a bulk stock of inventory in the United States. From the customer's perspective, the steps related to the manufacture of the product and shipment to the U.S. division's DC (steps 1 to 5 in Figure 5-4-1) are eliminated. These five steps would become the reorder process for restocking the U.S. DC's inventory.

Another alternative involves express shipment of the product from the European division directly to the U.S. customer. Each of these alternatives was considered in the simulation modeling analysis and is discussed in the following sections.

Bulk stock, standard shipment of reorders.   In evaluating a U.S. bulk stock inventory, customer order-fulfillment time would be one to two days if sufficient inventory were available. An important question is, how much inventory would be needed in the United States to maintain a high service level? The goal is to achieve a service level of 99 percent; that is, 99 percent of customer orders can be filled immediately. A specific inventory policy must be determined so the firm can achieve this service level with a minimum amount of inventory. The inventory policy consists of the reorder point, the stock-up-to level, and the frequency of inventory review. The initial proposal suggested that inventory levels be reviewed weekly, the reorder point be a four-week supply, and the stock-up-to level be an eight-week supply. Six different products within the product line were included in the analysis. The results presented here are the average results for all six products.

Due to the random nature of customer orders (both arrival time and order size) and random lead time for reorders, computer simulation was utilized for evaluating a number of scenarios. Simulation is useful because it allows for an accurate assessment of the impact of the specific inventory policy. Assumptions utilized in the simulation model are summarized in Appendix B. Simulation of the reorder process (steps 1 to 5 in Figure 5-4-1) shows the average lead time for a reorder is 3.6 weeks, ranging from 2.0 to 9.0 weeks, with the majority taking between 3 and 5 weeks. The inventory policy used in the simulation is as follows:

- Inventory levels are reviewed weekly;
- A reorder is placed if a product's inventory has fallen below the reorder point; and
- The size of a reorder is calculated by subtracting the current inventory level from the stock-up-to level.

When a customer places an order, the order is filled immediately if there is sufficient inventory. If there is insufficient inventory to fill the *entire* order, the order must wait until a replenishment order arrives at the U.S. DC. The firm's products are lot-specific, so partial orders are never shipped. Thus, when inventory is low, it is possible that a larger customer order may experience a stockout, whereas a smaller order could be filled immediately.

For each inventory scenario, the following information was collected for each product:

- The service level,
- The number of replenishment orders required, and
- The average inventory level.

The values are collected for each product separately because these values will vary based upon the frequency of customer orders. The reorder point was varied from 4 weeks of supply up to 10, and the stock-up-to level was varied from 8 weeks of supply up to 16. Service levels for the specific inventory policies examined are presented in Table 5-4-1. Scenarios that were clearly not feasible or unattractive were omitted.

The first inventory policy examined was the (4, 8) policy (which means the reorder point is 4 weeks of supply and the stock-up-to level is 8 weeks of supply). The resulting service level is 73.2 percent, indicating that this policy causes stockouts 26.8 percent of the time, which is far too often. As shown in Table 5-4-1, both inventory parameters were gradually increased, causing the service level gradually to approach 100 percent. Table 5-4-2 presents the average annual number of reorders per product that resulted for each of the scenarios. This value decreases (and thus reorder cost is minimized) as one moves toward the lower-right corner of the table. Table 5-4-3 correspondingly shows the average inventory level for the scenarios. This value decreases (and thus holding cost is minimized) as one moves toward the upper-left corner of the table. If minimizing cost were the objective, one could use the values in Tables 5-4-2 and 5-4-3 to find the minimum cost inventory policy. However, the objective was to minimize customer order-fulfillment time, so service level was the major factor in selecting the "best" inventory policy. It ap-

TABLE 5-4-1   Service Level (percentage of orders that are filled immediately)

		Stock-up-to Level (in weeks of supply)				
		8	10	12	14	16
	4	73.2				
Reorder Point	6	78.3	91.3	95.7	96.5	
(in weeks of supply)	8			97.8	99.3	99.4
	10				99.3	

TABLE 5-4-2   Average Number of Reorders per Product

		Stock-up-to Level (in weeks of supply)				
		8	10	12	14	16
	4	9.3				
Reorder Point	6	11.2	9.3	7.2	5.6	
(in weeks of supply)	8			9.3	7.1	5.6
	10				9.3	

TABLE 5-4-3   Average Inventory Level (in weeks of supply)

		Stock-up-to Level (in weeks of supply)				
		8	*10*	*12*	*14*	*16*
	4	2.3				
Reorder Point	*6*	2.4	3.7	5	5.9	
(in weeks of supply)	*8*			5.6	7.1	6.1
	10				7.7	

pears that the (8,14) policy is best, given the goal of achieving a 99 percent service level. These values could be further refined for each of the various products, with the more frequently ordered products achieving the desired service level with less inventory.

Bulk stock, express shipment of reorders.   The major contributor to the high inventory level is the lengthy lead time of reorders. If this lead time could be reduced by using express air freight, the reorder point and stock-up-to levels could be reduced significantly. In the current order process, considerable time is devoted to customs clearance activities (step 4 of Figure 5-4-1). Also, there is a self-imposed delay due to shipment consolidation and waiting (step 2 of Figure 5-4-1). If reorders could be shipped the day they were ready, the time range for this part of the process would be reduced. The express reorder process is presented in Figure 5-4-2. If product shipments were handled by an express air-freight company with express customs clearance capabilities, the product shipments would be delivered to the U.S. DC in one to three days, with an average of two days. The simulation shows this process reduces the average lead time to under two weeks.

Computer simulation of this alternative shows that a (4, 8) inventory policy using daily inventory review achieves a service level of 98.7 percent and leads to an average inventory level of 4.3 weeks of supply. This scenario would have a higher reorder cost due to the increased expense of express air freight; however, this process allows the U.S. inventory to be kept considerably lower.

Direct shipment to U.S. customers.   An alternative to maintaining bulk stock inventory at the U.S. DC is to ship orders using an express air freight carrier directly from the

FIGURE 5-4-2 Express Reorder Process

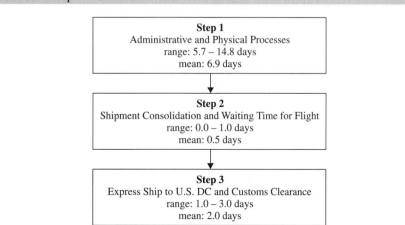

European division to the U.S. customer. This process is presented in Figure 5-4-3 and is essentially the same as the express reorder process (Figure 5-4-2), with the difference being that delivery is being made directly to the U.S. customer (step 3). The administrative and physical processes (step 1 of Figure 5-4-3) would also be lengthened by one day due the need for customized packaging for the final customer. Simulation of this alternative shows that customer order-fulfillment time averages 2 weeks, and ranges from 1.5 to 4.0 weeks. A potential drawback of this alternative is that the addressee typically is responsible for resolving any customs problems. In the other alternatives, customers are not involved with customs issues associated with their product shipments.

Comparison of alternatives. The four alternatives discussed here are summarized in Table 5-4-4. The two bulk stock alternatives clearly are best for customer order fulfillment, but they would increase worldwide inventory levels. Using express reorders would involve a smaller increase in inventory but would have higher shipping costs. Direct shipment would not increase inventory; however, it would not reduce customer order-fulfillment time to the extent of the bulk inventory approaches. It also holds the potential problem of the customer needing to deal with customs issues that may occur.

The key principles of cycle-time reduction utilized in this portion of the project include *eliminating, anticipatory-scheduling,* and *prototyping* (Wetherbe 1995). *Eliminating* is utilized with the direct shipment of U.S. customer orders from the European division of the firm. The U.S. division's involvement in the customer order-fulfillment process has been eliminated.

Anticipatory-scheduling is utilized in the bulk inventory scenarios. In this situation, the objective is to identify the key factors that influence inventory availability, including reorder points, stock-up-to levels, and frequency of inventory reviews.

Prototyping is the overall simulation effort utilized to analyze and compare new alternatives with the firm's current practices. The new practices are being prototyped through the use of the simulation model to determine if they offer significant potential for cycle-time reduction prior to actual implementation.

FIGURE 5-4-3 Direct Shipment Process

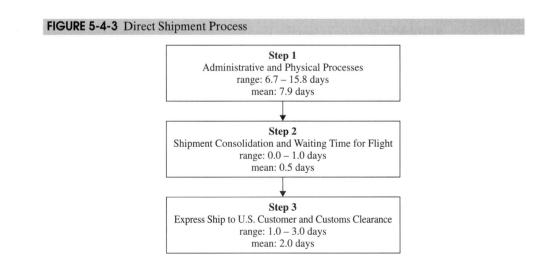

TABLE 5-4-4   Summary Comparison of Alternatives

Alternative	Order-Fulfillment Time	Other Issues
1. Current Process	2.2–9.5 weeks Mean = 4.0 weeks	
2. Bulk stock, standard shipment	1–2 days	✓ Higher worldwide inventory than #1
3. Bulk stock, express reorders	1–2 days	✓ Lower inventory than #2 ✓ Higher shipping costs than #2 for reorders
4. Direct shipment to U.S. customers	1.5–4.0 weeks Mean = 2 weeks	✓ Customers may have to deal with customs clearance issues ✓ Higher shipping costs than #1

Customs Clearance

The customs clearance part of the order-fulfillment process was one of the longest (an average of 8 days) and the most variable (a range of 2 to 21 days). The action team assigned to the customs clearance process conducted a detailed review of these activities in an effort to improve the cycle-time performance in this area.

The team made a field visit to the firm's customs broker at O'Hare Airport in Chicago, Illinois, to observe the processing of its shipments. The objective for this visit was to observe the customs broker's internal processes and resources in action. Key observations made included:

- The customs broker could not begin the clearance process until all packing lists and invoices had been received from the firm's U.S. division office. The U.S. division received these documents from the European division and reviewed them prior to sending them to the customs broker. The U.S. division was unable to fax these documents to the customs broker due to problems with illegible copies. These documents were sent to the customs broker via an overnight delivery service.
- It takes customs broker personnel up to four hours to enter the firm's documentation into their system. Therefore, if the customs broker receives the documentation at 1:00 P.M. or later, the chances of a shipment clearing that day are zero.
- Because another division of the firm is regulated by the Food and Drug Administration (FDA), the firm's biochemical division shipments are subject to a greater level of scrutiny. During the period from January 1995 through September 1995, the firm's biochemical division experienced 18 customs "intensive" reviews and 23 FDA "holds," which can take from 3 to 30 days to complete.
- Chicago is a training site for FDA inspectors, and due to the rapid turnover of personnel at this location, the inspectors have limited knowledge regarding the firm's products and their uses.

The firm's goal is to reduce customs processing time to an average of three days as well as reduce the variability associated with this activity. To accomplish this objective, the action team developed the following recommendations:

- Shipment documentation should be sent directly from the European division to the customs broker via EDI. This approach would reduce the cycle time by at least three days.

- The firm should begin working more closely with U.S. customs and the FDA to determine which products they repeatedly question in an effort to provide these agencies with the information they need to avoid FDA holds and customs-intensive reviews.
- The firm should identify products that cause a "red flag" and ship these products under a separate airbill to avoid one product delaying an entire shipment that typically contains multiple orders and multiple products.
- The firm should consider alternative clearing points that have an established record for timely customs clearance.

Each of these recommendations incorporates key cycle-time reduction principles (Wetherbe 1995). The use of EDI to transmit documentation directly from the European division to the customs broker involves *eliminating* and *automating*. The direct EDI transmission of shipment documentation from the European division *eliminates* the involvement of the U.S. division. The EDI approach also *automates* the manual entry of the firm's documentation into the customs broker's system.

The firm's efforts to work closely with the governmental agencies is an example of *partnering*. The firm is willing to work on a cooperative basis with the FDA and customs to ensure that it provides them with all the information they require to perform their duties, whenever, wherever, and however they need it. (In a perfect world, *eliminating* these regulatory agencies would be the preferred option. However, this option, although appealing, is not likely to occur in the near future.)

Identifying products that are likely to result in additional review and sending these products under a separate airbill apart from the main shipment is an effective means to improve the average cycle time.

The final recommendation incorporates two cycle-time reduction principles, *measuring* and *benchmarking*. The firm will measure the customs processing time performance at its current point of entry and benchmark this level of performance against that of other points of entry where similar products are being cleared. If the firm identifies an opportunity to reduce significantly the customs clearance process through the use of another point of entry, it will do so.

Electronic Data Interchange (EDI)

This firm, like many others, must deal with the limitations of legacy information systems. Specifically, the firm's various information systems around the world are old and incompatible. This fact has proven particularly problematic for the customer order-fulfillment process within the firm. The firm's European division receives customer orders from more than 100 sales offices around the world. The European division handles an average of 45,000 customer orders per year with a total of 380,000 line items. To complicate this issue, the firm has experienced an 11 percent decrease in its order-processing staff while at the same time experiencing a 15 percent increase in the number of line items that must be processed.

Customer order processing. Due to the incompatibility of information systems within the firm, order processing was slow and plagued with problems. When one of the firm's sales offices received a customer order, it would enter the customer order into its own information system. If the specific location was unable to fill the customer order from inventory held in its DC, then a printout of the customer order was faxed manually to the European division. This process often required the European order-processing staff to make several phone calls to resolve questions about the order. Once the European division received the customer order, it would enter it manually into its own order-processing information system, pick and pack the order, print out a delivery note/invoice, and manually fax it back to the originating sales office. This process took an average of 48 hours. In fact, the European division had 2 people devoted to order processing on a full-time basis. These individuals could enter a maximum of 180 to 200 line items per hour. As a result, no more than 20 customer orders could be handled per day. This manual order processing was also plagued with low accuracy. Another significant cycle-time problem with this order-processing approach was that several other people merely acted as order "mailmen."

To help streamline the order-handling process, increase order-entry accuracy, and reduce the cycle time of the order process, the European division decided to implement an intraorganizational EDI-based order-processing system that would work in conjunction with an organization-wide implementation of an integrated information system. In addition, the firm's management felt that only people who add value to an order should handle it.

EDI and order processing. EDI has been touted as a useful component of an interorganizational information system (e.g., Gomes-Casseres 1994, Kanter 1994, Levinson 1994, Levinson and Meier 1988, Nichols et al. 1995). The benefits of implementing EDI interorganizationally facilitate opportunities for business partners to refine their relationship in a way that is beneficial to all parties involved (Riggins and Mukhopaphyay 1994). These benefits include higher levels of operational efficiency, lower costs, and improved customer service (Johnson and Vitale 1988).

The European division decided to implement EDI as a means of reducing cycle time for its global order processing. With this new intraorganizational EDI order-processing system, the sales force will enter orders into its local information system. For example, the U.S. division would enter orders at its location. If the order cannot be filled from U.S. inventory, the system will transmit automatically the customer order to the European division. After a short validation process, the European system automatically generates the required production order. The firm estimates that less that 1 percent of the customer orders will require additional manual intervention. In addition, each line item will now have an associated comments section. This feature will help to overcome the need for telephone conversations for explanations. Once the order has been accepted by the system, a production order is generated automatically and sent to the manufacturing facility. Invoices are created automatically and sent to the system of origin. A system-generated declaration is also forwarded automatically to the firm's customs broker (see Figure 5-4-4).

This new order-processing system reduces the total order-processing cycle time to 24 hours, has a much higher accuracy rate than the old system, requires less human involvement due to line items being automatically entered without manual processing, and costs less than faxing the orders.

The key cycle-time reduction principles illustrated here are once again *automating* and *eliminating* (Wetherbe 1995). By *automating* the customer order transmission process through the use of EDI, the firm has *eliminated* the non-value-added steps of manually faxing customer orders and multiple entry of the customer order information. The use of

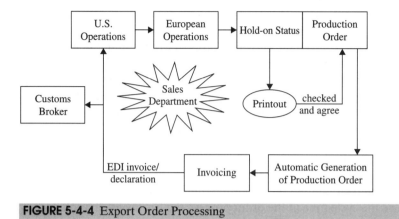

FIGURE 5-4-4 Export Order Processing

EDI has also improved the quality of the information utilized within the customer order-processing system. This feat has been accomplished by decreasing the opportunity for input errors associated with multiple entries of a single customer order.

CONCLUSION

This case provides an overview of a successful supply chain cycle-time reduction project. The project was successful in that the firm was able to identify a number of opportunity areas or points of leverage to reduce the time required to complete the order-fulfillment process.

The firm's multifaceted attack on order-fulfillment process cycle time proved highly effective. By utilizing several action teams in a parallel manner, the firm was able to address several points of leverage concurrently. Each of the action teams was able to develop actionable recommendations to reduce the customer order-fulfillment cycle time. In the EDI case, the implementation of an intraorganizational EDI-based order-processing system has already reduced order-processing cycle time. Although they differ in magnitude of effect, each of the action team initiatives provides significant opportunities for cycle-time reduction. ■

REFERENCES

Gomes-Casseres, B. "Group versus Group: How Alliance Networks Compete." *Harvard Business Review* 72, no. 4 (July–August 1994), 62–74.

Hammer, M. and J. Champy. *Reengineering The Corporation: A Manifesto for Business Revolution.* New York: HarperCollins, 1993.

Johnson, H. R. and M. R. Vitale. "Creating Competitive Advantage with Interorganizational Information Systems." *MIS Quarterly* 12, no. 2 (June 1988), 153–165.

Kanter, R. M. "Collaborative Advantage: The Art of Alliances." *Harvard Business Review* 72, no. 4 (July–August 1994), 96–108.

Levinson, N. S. "IOIS's: New Approaches to Global Economic Development." *Information & Management* 26, no. 5 (May 1994), 257–263.

Levinson, N. S. and R. Meier. "Toward the 1990's: Information Management Trends." *Xerox Corporation,* 1988.

Nichols, E. L., M. N. Frolick, and J. C. Wetherbe. "Cycle Time Reduction: An Interorganizational Supply Chain Perspective." *Cycle Time Research* 1, no. 1 (1995), 63–84.

Riggins, F. J. and T. Mukhopaphyay. "Interdependent Benefits from Interorganizational Systems: Opportunities for Business Partner Reengineering." *Journal of Management Information Systems* 11, no. 2 (Fall 1994), 37–57.

Wetherbe, J. C. "Principles of Cycle Time Reduction: You Can Have Your Cake and Eat It Too." *Cycle Time Research* 1, no. 1 (1995), 1–24.

APPENDIX A   Supply Chain Cycle-Time Worksheets:

Supply Process

Use this worksheet to describe the current supply process between your organization and your supplier for the period from order placement to receipt of product from the supplier.

Supplier: _____

Product Supplied: _____

Average Supply Process Cycle Time: _____

Minimum Supply Process Cycle Time: _____

Maximum Supply Process Cycle Time: _____

Supply Process Cycle Time Variance: _____

1. What are the specific supply process components (e.g., supplier processing time, transit time, etc.) and associated cycle times?

2. What are the causes of supply process cycle-time variability?

3. What information is provided to the supplier? When is it provided? How is it provided?

4. What information is received from the supplier? When is it provided? How is it provided?

5. How is the product transported from the supplier to your organization? Which organization (e.g., supplier, your organization, third party, etc.) manages this in-transit portion of the supply chain?

6. What are the performance measures that your organization currently utilizes to assess supply process performance?

7. What impact does the current supply process cycle-time performance have on your organization?

8. What are potential actions that could be taken to reduce the supply process cycle time?

Customer Order-Fulfillment Process

Use this worksheet to describe the customer order-fulfillment process for the period from customer-order receipt to customer receipt of finished goods.

Supplier: _____

Product Supplied: _____

Average Customer Order-Fulfillment Cycle Time: _____

Minimum Customer Order-Fulfillment Cycle Time: _____

Maximum Customer Order-Fulfillment Cycle Time: _____

Customer Order-Fulfillment Cycle Time Variance: _____

1. What are the specific customer order-fulfillment process components (e.g., order processing, planning, fabrication, etc.) and associated cycle times?

2. What are the causes of customer order-fulfillment cycle-time variability?

3. What information is received from the customer? When is it provided? How is it provided?

4. What information is provided to the customer? When is it provided? How is it provided?

5. Describe the type (e.g., raw materials, WIP, finished goods) and amounts (e.g., dollar value, quantities, and days of supply) of inventory held within your organization's portion of the supply chain.

6. For the inventory held within your organization's portion of the supply chain, indicate why this inventory is held.

7. How is the product transported from your organization to the customer? Which organization (e.g., your organization, the customer, third party, etc.) manages this in-transit portion of the supply chain?

8. What are the performance measures that your organization currently utilizes to assess customer order-fulfillment performance?

9. What impact does the current customer order-fulfillment cycle-time performance have on your organization?

10. What are potential actions that could be taken to reduce the customer order-fulfillment cycle time?

APPENDIX B   Simulation Model Assumptions

Customer Order Assumptions

- The prorated quantity shipped through July 1995 is the average annual demand.
- Customer orders arrive randomly (exponential distribution) without significant seasonal pattern.
- The prorated number of orders for 1995 is the average annual number of orders.
- The average order size is (annual demand)/(prorated number of orders for 1995).
- The order size range is ±30 percent of the average order size.
- Order size is normally distributed, and the randomly generated values will be rounded off to the nearest 0.1 units of measure (UOM).

Inventory Assumptions

- Inventory levels are reviewed once a week.
- If an item's inventory is below the four-week supply (e.g., 1/13th of average annual demand), a reorder is placed. If inventory is greater than or equal to the four-week supply, nothing happens.
- Reorder size = eight-week supply minus the current inventory; this is then rounded up to the nearest whole number of normal package sizes.
- No reorder is placed if a replenishment order is pending.
- If there is insufficient stock to fill an order, the order waits until a replenishment order arrives from the European division (as opposed to placing the customer order with the European division).
- Replenishment orders placed with European division follow the current process (Figure 5-4-1) except for step 6 (packing and shipping to customer).

Packaging Assumptions

- U.S. division inventory will be held in the normal package sizes (rather than in bulk).
- Repackaging is necessary when order size does not equal the normal package size (e.g., the exact amount the customer ordered is sent).
- The entire quantity ordered is sent together (for example, if an order is for 4.1 kilograms and the normal package size is 0.5 kilograms, then repackaging is needed for the 0.1 kilograms and the 4 standard packages wait until the entire order is ready).
- Odd amounts left over from repackaging remain in inventory to be used for other orders requiring repackaging.
- For products available in two package sizes, only the smaller package size was used in the model (for simplicity). This will not affect model results as the total inventory quantity at any given point in time is unchanged.

Case Five   Solectron[1]

Integrated Supply Chain Management

BACKGROUND

In 1977, Ray Kusamoto founded Solectron, a manufacturer of solar energy products, in the midst of the solar energy boom. The name Solectron is a combination of "solar" and "electron." Today it is a worldwide provider of electronics manufacturing services to original equipment manufacturers (OEMs). The company provides customized, integrated manufacturing services that span all three stages of the product life cycle, including premanufacturing, manufacturing, and postmanufacturing (see Table 5-5-1). These services are integrated to the point where Solectron is now responsible for all supply chain processes associated with sourcing parts, building, and distribution of electronics and systems for almost every major OEM customer in the industry. A list of primary OEM customers is shown in Table 5-5-2, which spans the telecommunications, networking, computer systems, peripherals, semiconductors, consumer electronics, industrial equipment, medical electronics, avionics, and automotive electronics industries. These industries are in different stages of maturity, with network manufacturers fairly new, and computer systems fairly mature. The diversity of major customers in this list is testimony to Solectron's success.

In 1991 and again in 1997, Solectron won the Malcolm Baldrige National Quality Award for manufacturing, reflecting the high level of performance achieved within this company. The company has also been honored with more than 140 customer quality and business awards, 25 of which were received in 1997 (see Table 5-5-3).

The financial growth of Solectron in recent years has been remarkable by any standard (see Table 5-5-4). Most recently, profit before taxes exceeded 6 percent, with gross margins increasing to 12 percent. Compounded annual sales growth rates have exceeded 60 percent over the last 5 years, and 66 percent over 18 years. Sales in 1997 exceeded $3.7 billion. The company employs more than 20,000 people worldwide.

The reason for this growth? A commitment to establishing long-term partnerships with customers and suppliers, supported by consistent quality, responsiveness, continuous improvement, and technology leadership. In deploying this strategy, Solectron has essentially created a new market, and thereby developed a new way of managing its

TABLE 5-5-1 Customized Services Provided		
Premanufacturing	*Manufacturing*	*Postmanufacturing*
Product design and engineering	Supply base and logistics management	Product fulfillment and distribution
Interconnection and packaging consulting	Printed circuit and flex assembly	Repair and refurbishment
Concurrent engineering	Systems assembly and services	Product upgrades
Test development	Testing	End of product life support
Product prototyping	Packaging	

[1]Used with permission from Solectron.

TABLE 5-5-2   Primary Customers Served by Solectron and Number of Years

Original Equipment Manufacturer	Number of Years Served
IBM	16
Hewlett-Packard	14
Sun	10
Apple	10
Applied Materials	8
3Com	8
Anspex	6
Honeywell	6
SGI	6
Megatest	5
Buy Networks	5
Picture Tel	4
Cisco	4
Ericsson	1

TABLE 5-5-3   Awards Received by Solectron

Supplier Quality Awards	Other Awards
Sun Microsystems	1991 Malcolm Baldrige National Quality Award
Hewlett-Packard	1994 California Governor's Award
Allied Signal	1996 Industry Week—100 Best Managed Co.'s
Honeywell	1996 Texas Quality Award
Megatest	1996 Malaysian Quality Management Excellence Award
Picturetel	1996 North Carolina Quality Leadership Award
IBM (Gold Award)	1997 Malcolm Baldrige National Quality Award
Arthur Andersen	
Intel	
LTX	
Synoptics	
Pinnacle	
3Com	
Vixel	
Norcomp	
Watkins Johnson	
National Semiconductor	
Unisys	
Silicon Graphics	
Acuson	
Apple	
Exabyte	
Maxtor	
NCR	
Phillips	
Toshiba	

TABLE 5-5-4	Financial Growth since 1992 (millions of dollars)		
Year	*Net Sales*	*Net Income*	*Total Assets*
1992	$ 407	$ 14	$ 309
1993	836	31	603
1994	1,457	56	766
1995	2,066	80	941
1996	2,817	114	1,452

customer and supply base, through an evolving *total business strategy* known as supply chain management.

CONTRACT MANUFACTURING IN THE SUPPLY CHAIN

The evolution of Solectron as a contract manufacturer represents a cutting-edge strategy, which has driven the company to continuously reengineer its supply chain processes. The entrepreneurial nature of the company has led to an ever-increasing expansion into turnkey solutions, as OEMs continued to simplify their supply chains and outsource "gray areas" not considered to be core competencies. These changes have occurred largely in response to the changing nature of the computer industry. The evolution of this strategy is shown in Figure 5-5-1, where the thickness of the lines between entities represents the strength of the relationship. In the 1970s, suppliers shipped parts to OEMs via truck to consigned operations, which assembled parts into products shipped to customers. This process was largely labor-intensive. Some parts were also shipped to distributors for sales to customers. Suppliers' primary strategy for success involved trying to get "designed in" to a particular OEM's product through direct sales.

In the 1980s, assemblies were shipped from suppliers to OEM turnkey operations, which were largely capital- and process-intensive. Solectron emerged as a printed circuit board assembler during this period and began introducing leading-edge surface mount technology. The company made a major transition in the early 1980s to become a 100 percent turnkey contract manufacturer after producing Atari's Christmas overflow of video games. The company's entrepreneurial spirit played a major role in driving this transition. If a customer who was already doing business with Solectron decided to outsource a process previously not performed, Solectron almost always jumped at the chance. The chairman, president, and CEO of the company, Dr. Koichi Nishimura, foresaw two major trends. First, he believed quality would be a key differentiator and made it part of the "company religion." Second, he strenuously believed that customers would increasingly outsource more of their processes and that a company's responsiveness to its customers would be a strategic differentiator. As a result, a key element of Solectron's growth strategy involved performing an increasing number of new manufacturing services for its customers. However, as a contract manufacturer, Solectron was responsible only for the quality of products produced internally, with minimal responsibility for supply-base management. Because the OEM dictated which suppliers were to be used, the components were simply kitted and shipped to Solectron for assembly.

In the early 1990s, OEMs began offering systems and technological resources to end users via distributors, often entailing full-service support and partnerships with distributors. As this occurred, they outsourced increasing levels of manufacturing and supply

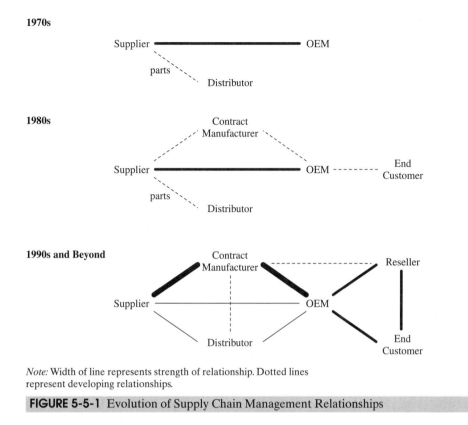

1970s

1980s

1990s and Beyond

Note: Width of line represents strength of relationship. Dotted lines represent developing relationships.

FIGURE 5-5-1 Evolution of Supply Chain Management Relationships

chain management activities to Solectron, who was now establishing closer relationships with suppliers. Many OEMs were also starting to focus on their core competencies of product design and marketing, through the development of closer relationships with the emerging group of large-scale resellers such as Comp USA, Circuit City, and Best Buy. These important new channels offered electronics equipment directly to customers at low prices. Top management at Solectron realized that by establishing closer relationships with leading-edge suppliers, they could offer OEMs access to these preferred suppliers of computer components, instead of having to use an OEM's designated suppliers, which were not always the best alternatives. In so doing, they could maximize their OEM customer's access to technological and performance capabilities and create a significant marketing advantage.

Increasing volumes with several major OEMs meant increasing volumes purchased from suppliers, thereby allowing Solectron to negotiate preferential ramp-up, quality, technology, and pricing capabilities that could be passed on to OEMs (which would otherwise be unavailable to them). Furthermore, Solectron began shipping finished products directly to distribution points and, in some cases, resellers. This growth has been accompanied by major global expansion, involving the acquisition of some of its major customers' outsourced facilities. Solectron has manufacturing sites in Milpitas, Fremont, and Newark, California; Penang and Johor, Malaysia; Charlotte, North Carolina (formerly IBM); Bordeaux, France (formerly IBM); Tokyo, Japan; Everett, Washington (formerly Hewlett-Packard); Dunfermline, Scotland (formerly Philips); Boeblingen, Germany (formerly Hewlett-Packard); Westborough, Massachusetts; Austin, Texas (formerly Texas Instruments); Guadalajara, Mexico; Norrkoping, Sweden (formerly Ericsson); São Paulo, Brazil (formerly Ericsson); and Suzhou, China.

Today, that vision is being pushed even further, with OEMs focusing on simple product definition and marketing. Even the design of printed circuit boards and systems is increasingly being outsourced to Solectron, which has developed the internal capability to provide the needed services. OEMs can now approach companies like Solectron and state, "Here is what I want my computer to look like, what I want it to do, and what I want it to cost—how it works is up to you!" This evolution has allowed Solectron to increase its leverage with preferred suppliers. Solectron can offer the supplier a greater chance of being "designed in" to the OEM's product, without requiring a sales pitch on the part of the supplier. However, this means that suppliers must be able to offer "black box" designs, which offer integrated solutions that can be integrated by Solectron designers.

To achieve this capability, Solectron has both developed internal resources and purchased two major design and prototype houses, Force Computers and Fine Pitch Technology, enabling it to meet these additional customer requirements. Further, it is seeking to ship products directly to distributors and resellers, and perform traditional channel and warehouse activities such as build-to-order and configure-to-order systems assembly. In doing so, Solectron can effectively minimize the total cost of acquisition, which is a function of information, logistics capability, early design engagement, and supply-base management. In this respect, its role will be much like that of a "bandleader" who orchestrates the designs of multiple suppliers into new products required by major OEMs and fulfills orders through multiple distribution channels with minimal cycle times and inventory, in order to reduce total cost with a focus on delivering value in the market. Its core competence has thereby changed from a focus on manufacturing and logistics two years ago (in a low margin business) to manufacturing, logistics, new-product integration, and end-customer value.

STRATEGIC CHALLENGES

A new set of strategic challenges has emerged with this change, especially concerning how the company must manage its new role in this web of multiple supply chain relationships. Its role in value creation has shifted dramatically, and the blurring of core competencies across customers and suppliers continues to take place. Solectron must now work closely with suppliers' engineers in their R&D facilities to ensure leading-edge technology. This growth has not occurred without growing pains. Says one industry analyst: "When you grow as fast as Solectron through acquisition, there are major issues to address, such as integrating information systems, coordinating JIT deliveries, and other automated supply systems and maintaining high quality levels." The company's chief financial officer admits that

> We face the typical issues that any company encounters with the additional complexity of integrating several acquisitions at the same time. Fine Pitch is very entrepreneurial. . . . TI is more compatible with our existing business . . . and Force is much more engineering intensive than our core business. With each of these acquisitions we have to spend a lot of time looking for commonalities. On the IS front, we have a hodgepodge of systems that we have to link up. It's not the most efficient approach but it's a problem that has a technical solution. Regarding quality, that is more of a people-related issue.

These challenges have occurred as the company rapidly acquired new divisions over the last several years in response to demands made by its customer base. Unlike some of the disastrous acquisitions made by major companies in the last two decades, however, these acquisitions made sense. Each acquisition was analyzed thoroughly and was ultimately approved based on the following criteria:

- Creates new or expands existing customer and supplier relationships;
- Adds unique capabilities to Solectron's value chain, such as design for manufacturability or order fulfillment;
- Creates a presence in a new, attractive market;
- Adds capable people to the company and integrates them into the core business; and
- Provides low labor cost.

In conjunction with this evolution, Solectron has developed a materials vision that includes the following objectives:

- Create value via supply chain design and management;
- Be the supplier of choice;
- Be the customer of choice for suppliers;
- Be the employer of choice for top materials professionals; and
- Develop processes that are consistent, repeatable, and scaleable.

Solectron's organization today is centered around two major functional processes, which reflect its two major channels shown in Figure 5-5-1: sourcing and order fulfillment. Each of these will be discussed in detail.

SOURCING

The sourcing function includes supply-base management, controlling total cost, creating and exchanging long-term value, and creating value partnerships with suppliers. The latter point emphasizes Solectron's objective of becoming an agent for its preferred suppliers, seeking to have them "designed in" to the next generation of products for OEMs in exchange for preferential pricing, technology, and so forth. The sourcing function has evolved over time, as shown in Figure 5-5-2. In the early 1980s, supply management between customers and suppliers was primarily transactional in nature. Over the 1990s, customers developed strategic supply-base management initiatives that focused on optimizing the supply base, measuring supplier performance, developing relationships with key suppliers, and improving quality and delivery performance. In the future, executives at Solectron believe that elements of both prior periods will be retained, but a new type of relationship with suppliers will need to evolve, focusing on total supply chain performance beyond customer-supplier linkages.

This evolution is driven by the nature of the computer industry. A supplier in this industry has several channels available to choose from in doing business with OEMs, with its primary objective being to get its product into the OEM's final product (see Figure 5-5-3). It can do so through a parts distributor, directly through the OEM's purchasing function, or via competing contract manufacturers such as SCI Systems, Solectron, D2D, Flextronics International, and so on. The challenge to Solectron becomes how to ensure that its channel provides the lowest total cost of acquisition for both suppliers and customers, thereby creating the greatest value. The lowest total cost of acquisition is a function of improved access to information, logistics excellence, early design involvement, and responsiveness. The challenge comes in replicating the capability shown in

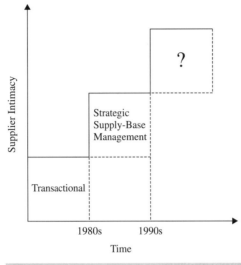

FIGURE 5-5-2 Supply-Base Management Evolution

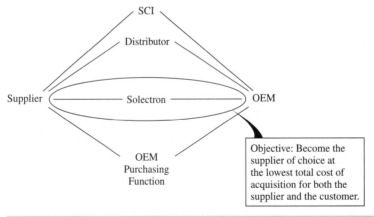

FIGURE 5-5-3 Channel Relationships Available to Suppliers

Figure 5-5-3 across multiple commodities and suppliers, in order to become the channel of choice for all major products provided by suppliers. (Solectron currently has 50 preferred suppliers.) In the past, supplier quality was not as much an issue, because the choice of suppliers was dictated by OEMs. Because Solectron is increasingly being challenged to work directly with suppliers, it has become more involved in quality audits and performance measurement. However, quality has not been a major problem because most suppliers that Solectron is engaged with today are top global suppliers, and in this industry, quality is a critical prerequisite for entry. OEMs today require suppliers with global capabilities because they must be able to ship to manufacturing locations all over the world. In some cases, Solectron has helped develop smaller regional suppliers into global suppliers (see Plant Operations section).

To facilitate relationships with suppliers, Solectron holds a number of supplier councils every year. These include supplier value partnership councils, cross-functional councils on system integration, and materials councils, which help develop better relationships with suppliers and manufacturing.

Solectron employs a set of materials measures that are consistent with the theme of supply chain excellence. The primary measures of supplier performance include:

- Reliability
- Fulfillment lead time
- Mean time between failure (quality)
- Commodity allocation
- Inventory risk reduction
- Lowest price

A major challenge in becoming the channel of choice for suppliers is that Solectron's strongest competition is the in-house procurement functions within the OEMs. However, as the industry evolves, Solectron believes that more OEMs will outsource procurement, despite internal resistance to this change. Solectron has a history of being a low overhead organization, which has permitted it to perform sourcing processes more efficiently than many of the larger OEMs. Furthermore, because Solectron is purchasing multiple families of standard components across multiple customer relationships, its aggregate volumes purchased in many cases surpass the amounts purchased by any single OEM. Its position expressed to OEMs is that "We have the infrastructure—your only concern should be that our expertise is best-in-class."

ORDER FULFILLMENT

The order-fulfillment function focuses on those activities included in the right-hand section of Figure 5-5-3, namely plant management, OEM relationships, distribution, configuration of products to customer orders, tying into OEMs customer order systems to identify configurations, and postmanufacturing support.

Solectron utilizes a unique customer satisfaction index, which reflects its emphasis on customer service. Customers are polled often on the level of quality, delivery, communication, and service being provided by Solectron, using a standard A, B, C scoring system. These scores are translated into numerical percentages and are used to evaluate personnel and business unit performance.

A number of ongoing challenges emerge in managing the order-fulfillment process. Because contract manufacturing is such a competitive industry, Solectron has had to overcome the perception by major OEM customers that it is a "sweatshop stuffing parts," rather than a high-technology company. Second, the rapidly changing nature of the industry means that it must constantly seek new and innovative ways of maintaining flexibility. A major initiative in this area is designing products and sourcing from suppliers using an approach that considers supply chain order fulfillment for products with extremely short product life cycles. Product life cycles tend to ramp-up exceedingly quickly at an exponential rate but shrink to almost nothing overnight. Some of the major "design for supply chain" criteria that must be planned for in selecting suppliers to fulfill orders include the following:

- Increased flexibility
- Increased ramp-up capability
- 30% upside capacity capability for suppliers of major components

- Ability to forecast
- Ability to adopt processes to product specifications
- Two-week delivery
- 50% ramp time to full production from prototype

These demanding criteria are necessary in order to respond to quickly changing product and customer requirements driven by some of the shortest product life cycles in the industry (in some cases, less than 3 months!). Because customer forecasting is unreliable and is unlikely to get better, quick response and flexibility is simply a way of life for the materials group. Moreover, anticipating customer demand and communicating that demand to its 50 preferred suppliers will become more important as OEMs adapt to using contract manufacturers as business partners. For instance, on Friday Solectron may request 50,000 units of product A from a supplier for delivery on Monday, then call back on Monday and not only ask it to retake the 50,000 units, but deliver 25,000 units of product B instead! This type of flexibility is rapidly becoming a requirement for doing business in this industry.

On the fulfillment end, Solectron is willing to "shut down" production of a product assembly line for a customer overnight, if necessary. Because it maintains low inventory in the pipeline, it reduces the cost to customers who do not have to worry about inventory obsolescence, supplier bidding, and the like. This is a major benefit to customers.

INVENTORY PLANNING— "DESIGN FOR THE SUPPLY CHAIN"

Managing supply chain inventories is one of the most daunting tasks at Solectron. Because the company deals with so many different market segments (computers, networking, work stations, etc.), each major sector/customer has a dedicated customer supply chain manager who is tasked with serving its product needs. Each industry sector has different life cycles, cost constraints, and market windows. Some customers must bring new products to market faster, whereas others emphasize cost reductions, so the constraints between customers are continually evolving. This makes the role of inventory planning even more complex and involves a significant amount of speculative planning and risk management.

The major requirement for successful inventory management in this industry is a capability to rapidly change upside and downside flexibility in the form of excess inventory and capacity and fulfillment speed, and trade this off against the risk of obsolete inventory or unused capacity. For instance, a single customer can ask for a different product configuration involving a complete mix change overnight, which Solectron must immediately respond to. To achieve this capability, Solectron is also pursuing a strategy of increasing standardization through a *design for supply chain strategy*.

A good example of this strategy is in the purchase and integration of capacitors. Due to its large customer base, Solectron is the fifth largest purchaser of capacitors in the world. Thus, the issue is not how many capacitors it will purchase, but rather how it will allocate the capacitors it does purchase to customers. Therefore, when negotiating with suppliers, Solectron commodity managers do not negotiate at the part number level, but at the *capacity* level. That is, they essentially purchase a supplier's capacity without specifying what exact part numbers will be produced, because of the variation in mix.

This situation is illustrated in Figure 5-5-4, which shows the role that technology plays in achieving a delicate balance between customization and cost. In many new applications, customers want a capacitor that is relatively inexpensive but that must be suited for very specific applications in the field. To accomplish this task, Solectron uses Field Programmable Gate Arrays (FPGA), which are standardized but can be configured in the field to specific applications by changing the "gate arrays" on the board.

In some cases, customers in networking, servers, and other areas may decide that FPGA's function will stabilize and be used for a longer period. At this point, an Application Specific Integrated Circuit (ASIC) is introduced, which has no gates but instead has a frozen design customized for a specific application. The ASIC is cheaper than an FPGA and can be mass-produced in large quantities. On the other end of the scale, application-specific crystals and PCBs can be produced for a broad range of uses as capacitors and programmable logic devices.

The set of technologies shown in Figure 5-5-4 is constantly changing as new technologies enter the field, meaning that Solectron must monitor the technology horizon to avoid inventory obsolescence. Technology drives demand management, lead time, price, and inventories. To manage individual components would be impossible, so Pareto analysis is used to drive risk management, in terms of weighing off missed shipments versus excessive inventory exposure. Risk can be reduced by using technologies such as FPGA, especially early in the product design cycle. Risks can also be reduced by providing the right information to customers on emerging technologies and for suppliers to consider in their designs.

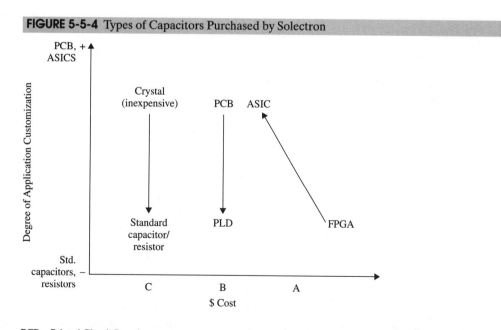

FIGURE 5-5-4 Types of Capacitors Purchased by Solectron

PCB—Printed Circuit Board
PLD—Programmable Logic Device
ASIC—Application Specific Integrated Circuit
FPGA—Field Programmable Gate Arrays

HUMAN RESOURCES

The nature of its business has also led Solectron to seek talented people that possess the following important skills:

- Technological function experience
- Willingness to tolerate ambiguity
- Decisiveness
- Communication skills
- Assertiveness
- Decision-making and problem-solving capabilities
- Commitment to tasks
- Good interaction skills

As the company continues to grow, supply chain managers must become more involved up front with engineers to offer competitive pricing or different supply-base recommendations from "cradle to grave." Customer supply chain management teams work with customer designers very early in the concurrent engineering stage to influence which supplies are to be used, because the largest proportion of total cost is incurred in design. The team works with the customer through the life of the product, focusing on reducing cost, creating upside flexibility, and managing risk for the customer's bill of materials. The company also focuses on strategic materials on a global level and has worldwide commodity teams with representatives of different locations to source and manage parts used by multiple Solectron sites. The teams meet or interact frequently to handle negotiations and to meet with suppliers to discuss market changes and Solectron's needs. Solectron also holds a twice-a-year worldwide materials council. At this council, people who run materials functions all over the world meet during a three-day session to review current positions and future directions.

WORLD WIDE MATERIALS SYSTEM

A major enabler as this strategy unfolds is the creation of an integrated information system across suppliers, OEMs, and distributors. The focus of Solectron's strategy is the development of its World Wide Materials System (WWMS). This system is being developed using a Baan template, which seeks to integrate its 7 different MRP systems across 13 different locations worldwide. The system will essentially bridge multiple information systems into a single data repository, using a data warehouse management approach. Managers will be able to generate spending reports on any part numbers, customers, and so on.

The implementation of this system has recently focused on coding part numbers according to standard manufacturer codes. This is difficult because the computer industry has technologies in different stages of maturity and evolution. Prior to this system, a commodity manager could do a Pareto analysis of only the top purchased part numbers in a commodity classification by site. The new system will allow the manager to roll in all of the items purchased by part number and by supplier, to uncover opportunities for leveraging, JIT delivery, and the like. This information system will allow commodity managers to better manage the process of supplier performance alignment, measurement, commodity team analysis, and supplier negotiation and reviews.

On the order-fulfillment end, the system will allow for regional contract management for various commodities, demand, open order, and inventory visibility, common part codes from customers, worldwide availability for part selection, and supplier selection for different components by site. Distribution centers selling products from OEM manufacturers need to meet customer requirements and will be provided access to quality and price data, based on an information system linked to all warehouses. By selecting computer configurations, any distribution center can order from any supplier, worldwide, for any part that Solectron currently purchases, using global contracts. To serve its numerous worldwide sites, Solectron's system will permit worldwide demand aggregation, worldwide site pricing visibility, and worldwide inventory and excess inventory visibility. A future role for this integrated system is for Solectron to have access to warehouse demand information. Customers will have access to recommended parts, technologies, prices, availability, and future price reductions on any particular type of component offered by suppliers. Thus, distributors should be able to configure their requirements according to supplier preferences and pricing, which is then assembled and delivered by Solectron. Solectron has been able to develop a pricing index, which enables it to avoid confidentiality issues between competing suppliers. This will create a significant competitive advantage, as customers currently have no access to this supply chain information. Other benefits of this system include negotiating leverage, global visibility, and alignment with preferred suppliers.

PLANT OPERATIONS

Unlike many heavy manufacturing industries, electronic and computer manufacturing plants are in a constant state of flux, with production lines in various stages being assembled, ramped-up, and disassembled. Because product life cycles are so short, production lines at Solectron may exist for only a few months (or even weeks!) before the product is discontinued.

A visit to the High Velocity Systems Division in Milpitas reflected this environment. The "high-velocity" designation reflects the fact that high-asset velocity is critical for successfully manufacturing its products (personal computers (PCs), printers, and other computer peripherals). In most cases, parts received on the receiving dock are shipped as part of finished products within 24 to 48 hours. All of these products have demands that escalate ("ramp-up") very quickly, have very low margins, and have very short life cycles. All of the lines employ equipment that is on carts or on wheels, which can be easily moved around. On one line, workers assembled a set of brand-name computers, which in turn was being manufactured for another major OEM that sold the computers to the brand-name sellers. On another line, workers packaged a cable, board, and instructions into boxes, which were shipped to a distributor selling peripherals. On yet another line, a new type of trackball for a mouse was being assembled and packaged. Workers are cross-trained on different lines to minimize boredom caused by repetitiveness and to improve workforce flexibility. Solectron employs workers from diverse international backgrounds, who go through quality training when they begin their employment.

The most interesting line on the floor was a printer line. Solectron had worked with designers from the OEM company on the design of the printer and was currently taking the working prototypes on the production line "up to ramp" (e.g., up to full production). Once the line got up to 80,000 units from 30,000 units with no major bugs or production flaws, the line was scheduled to be broken down, packaged, and shipped intact to Guadalajara, Mexico, where it would be set up again and put into full production! This was being done to take advantage of lower labor costs in this region. A dedicated supplier engineer was employed by Solectron to interface with suppliers of components, and engineers from the OEM were carefully watching the line and working to improve processes.

One of the most interesting sites in this facility was a supplier's production line. Puget Plastics, a small minority-owned supplier from Alaska, had been subleasing space in the facility for just over a month and was in full production of a plastic cover for one of the printer lines. The supplier was considered a "strategic partner"; employees for the supplier were busily feeding raw resin into supplier-owned injection machines, which heated the plastic, injected it into molds, and pressed out the printer covers. The covers were then carried over to the printer assembly line in an adjoining building.

The development of this strategic partnering arrangement took over a year to implement. The supplier was originally identified by the OEM customer, who was paying a significant amount to transport the printer covers to its manufacturing sites. At the end of 1996, the supplier was approached to discuss the possibility of an alliance. The negotiations proceeded through a formal analysis of investments and costs, as well as potential long-term leveraging possibilities (including expanding the supplier's operations to the Guadalajara plant). A series of meetings and visits ensued, including a visit by Solectron's North American president to Puget's facilities. His objective was to ensure that the companies were aligned both operationally and philosophically up through the senior executive level. Although the supplier was not as mature and well developed as others, it was felt that with some guidance on the part of Solectron it could emerge as a global strategic supplier. In the next few months, Puget was aided by Solectron in developing a strategic supplier agreement on improvement of capabilities, support, systems capabilities, and so on. Both parties were very receptive to this process, which culminated in the current production line being set up in Milpitas. Puget is now currently being considered for a number of other projects within Solectron.

TOTAL SUPPLY CHAIN COST MODEL

One of the major drivers underlining Solectron's competitive strategy is its total supply chain cost model. Steve Ng, Solectron's senior vice president and chief materials officer, discussed four major challenges associated with deploying supply chain management strategies at Solectron:

1. Where is the value created in the supply chain and who controls the value? Furthermore, if one controls the value, where should one invest next to improve value? Such decisions cannot be left up to people with tactical thinking, although execution of strategies can occur at a lower level.
2. How can we get the ear of top management at our customers, so that they understand our supply chain management strategy? Unless the customer understands the benefits of the strategy and its execution, it is very difficult to execute it down the line.
3. The U.S. environment is still operating in a "partnership" mode. The next major challenge will involve *cross-enterprise decision making,* in which decisions are made to optimize value parties across multiple organizations in the supply chain. Whereas the Japanese *keiretsus* have operated in this mode to some extent, U.S. companies are very unfamiliar with this type of competitive environment.
4. How can we simplify our supply chain strategy and capture it in a quantitative model, so that all supply chain decisions flow down from this model?

The last challenge is being addressed by a new "total supply chain cost" model currently being developed by Solectron. The model is containing to evolve but will be used as a basis for making supply chain decisions in the future. The elements of the model are shown in Figure 5-5-5. The model expands decision making from a simple "buying price" perspective to one that emphasizes total supply chain cost improvements and joint competitive advantages that accrue from doing so, as materials and information pass from the supplier, to Solectron, and on to the customer. This is reflected in the bottom-line selling price to the customer. Note that in Figure 5-5-5, the speculation returns and speculation cost reflect the fact that grow margins can be increased through greater responsiveness, achieved by positioning inventory, capacity, and so forth, strategically throughout the supply chain.

Until now, Solectron has deployed its supply chain strategy primarily on the principle of entrepreneurship. People have believed in the strategy and have followed it vigorously. Now, however, the total supply chain cost model will help balance this sense of

FIGURE 5-5-5 Total Supply Chain Cost Model

Total supply chain cost =	BUY PRICE	
	+ Supplier performance cost	• Supplier quality • Delivery performance
	+ Cost of acquisition	• Document control • Component engineering • Planning • Sourcing • Tactical buying • Freight/dusty • Receiving • Internal quality assurance • Warehouse cost • Production control • Kitting/kanban • Manufacturing accounting
	+ Out of sync planning	• Delays between MRP runs • Changes amplfied by MRP (bull ship effect)
	− Speculation returns (ability to meet upside demands)	• Driver: profit margins
	+ Speculation cost	• Buffer cost (inventory, capacity) • Fulfillment speed requirement costs • Upside flexibility cost (e.g., +30% in a given week or month) • Excess inventory • Mark-downcd inventory
	+ Manufacturing cost	• Labor, etc.
	+ Selling cost	• Sales, general, and administrative expenses
	+ Distribution cost	• Transportation cost
	+ Profit	
= SELLING PRICE		

entrepreneurship with the need for global integration by providing a structured framework for decision making. However, this structure may need to be customized somewhat for the customers. The model will help Solectron to understand customer requirements about what needs to be delivered, the variables and constraints to doing so, and how to optimize direct material cost, cost of acquisition, plant-to-plant and plant-to-volume flexibility, and help minimize excessive exposure to obsolescence due to engineering change orders. The model can also be used in "what if" analysis to help set customer expectations, especially about product introduction time to volume, margins, and liability to exposure.

On the supply end, the structure will help to organize "value partnerships" with key strategic suppliers. Such partnerships will virtually eliminate the need for negotiation and pricing, as the total cost model will be the basis for making all supply chain decisions, with an objective of maximizing return on assets and cash flow as the primary driver for the nature of the relationship. Each supplier relationship should increase price and value, reduce cost, and remove uncertainties preventing the increase of market share.

The total supply chain cost model, therefore, acts as an important bridging mechanism between customers and suppliers. Customers may often make extraordinary demands that require major investments in upside capability (lead time, cost, inventory, etc.). This requirement is used as a baseline for creating innovative solutions by working backward with the supply-base management group. To create these solutions, Solectron must be able to leverage its preferred suppliers to create solutions. It can then go back to the customer and offer potential solutions that might arise by considering a different set of suppliers, technologies, and the like. The total cost model thus serves as the integrating mechanism for driving supply chain relationships backward and forward in the chain. Although such demands are often unique from the suppliers' perspective, suppliers are also rewarded with demand generation and are presented with business they did not even anticipate!

Solectron is also actively involved in end-of-life systems and strategies, including repair and refurbishment, end-of-life production, remanufacturing, and installing new parts and networking cards. This is still in the early stages, but managers envision having a network of distribution points to better serve customers.

CONCLUSIONS

One of the capabilities that distinguishes Solectron from other major competitors in the contract manufacturing industry is its focus on supply-chain optimization to create value for both its customers and its own bottom line. The company has made strategic investments in expanding its range of capabilities and services offered, which help it to wring cost out of the product process, beginning at design and continuing through manufacturing and distribution. Solectron is able to offer customized services to meet its customers' unique needs, yet still maintain core common processes (such as its Malcolm Baldridge Quality standards and customers feedback process) in order to show the "same face" to customers worldwide. As the company moves forward with these strategies, it will surely need to continue its entrepreneurial spirit, but also to invest in the common infrastructure needed to keep pace with the dynamics of the information systems and computer industries. Maintaining the appropriate balance between this structure and the multiplicity of market needs will perhaps be the greater challenge for Solectron as it charts its growth toward $10 billion and several dozen operations worldwide. ■

C H A P T E R

Future Challenges in Supply Chain Management

The practices described in this book are considered "leading edge" in many organizations in that they have only begun to be deployed within the last several years. Even the cases described in the last chapter represent the organization's initial attempts at supply chain management and are in the process of being improved today. One manager interviewed in the course of writing this book emphasized that functional capabilities (new-product development, manufacturing, technology, marketing) are enablers for success, but are no longer sources of competitive advantages, because they can all be replicated in time. However, this manager and many others believe that truly integrated supply chain management does provide a means to achieve a definitive competitive advantage.

The very nature of supply chain management is unique. Because of the incredible complexity and scale involved in managing the flow of goods and information between multiple entities in the supply chain, there exists a broad and ever-changing set of priorities that must be managed at any given moment. As supply chain strategies evolve, managers will encounter new and challenging situations every day. Some of these challenging situations are internal and involve getting people to adopt the new way of thinking. Other challenges relate to government regulation and how to comply with a multitude of rules and regulations as goods traverse international borders. Finally, there also exist challenges set forth by customers, whose needs and requirements change rapidly and continue to escalate. These changes will require a level of responsiveness never before encountered in the business world. As one major CEO succinctly stated: "Doing what we've always done will no longer sustain us. Our future success will be directly proportional to our ability to recognize changes occurring in our markets and respond positively to them."

This chapter explores some of the challenges facing supply chain managers and identifies a set of future strategies to address these challenges. These include the following:

- Sharing risks in interorganizational relationships,
- Managing the global supply chain,

- The "greening" of the supply chain,
- Design for supply chain management, and
- Intelligent information systems.

We will discuss each of these challenges separately, then conclude with some predictions on where supply chains are likely to go from here.

Sharing Risks in Interorganizational Relationships

As noted in chapter 4, trust is a very fragile element binding organizations in a supply chain. Clearly, the concept of collaboration and joint competitiveness is often more appealing than "going it alone." However, as demands on supply chains continue to escalate, the relationships between organizations will be tested. In any supply chain structure, a number of risks exist that must somehow be managed between participating companies.

CONFIDENTIALITY

In order to function, companies in a supply chain will need to know more about one another than ever before. To manage the flow of information and materials, organizations will need to share both strategic-level information (regarding corporate and business unit strategies, process investments, market intelligence, etc.), as well as operational-level information (number of orders, promotions, forecasts, pricing, etc.). For example, knowing when a competitor will be advertising a promotion in newspapers can be considered a strategic advantage (albeit, a short-term one). Suppliers and customers who leak such information to competitors are potentially reducing the impact of the promotion. However, demand generation strategies such as promotions are useless unless the required products can be provided. This requires that all supply chain partners have advance notice, in order to prepare their own processes and channels for the upcoming increase in sales.

This double-edged sword was encountered by a manufacturer of durable goods interviewed while writing this book. A retail promotion for a new product was very successful and exceeded all expectations. In fact, demand for the product was so high that its manufacturing function was unable to produce enough units to meet the retailers' requirements. Retailers became extremely upset about the manufacturer's inability to meet demand for the product. Upon further investigation, it was discovered that the bottleneck resource was a small Asian supplier of a relatively easy-to-produce part. The part had been sourced from this supplier based on its low costs and on the assumption that its production was sufficient to meet forecasted demand (i.e., as long as demand remained stable). However, because the supplier had not been informed of the upcoming promotion, it simply did not have enough capacity to produce the part. As a result, the company decided to begin internal manufacture of the part, which further delayed shipment of the product.

Individuals making major decisions, such as product volume, mix, capacity, and shipping dates, in the supply chain are bounded by the information available to them and attempt to make rational decisions in light of this information. On the downside, such information is often highly confidential and, if revealed to competitors, can potentially undermine major strategic marketing and product strategies. As companies become more and more dependent on their supply chain members, they will have to find new and innovative ways to manage the risks associated with sharing proprietary and sensitive information with supply chain members.

RESEARCH AND DEVELOPMENT

As supply chain partners work together, sharing new-product information will become increasingly important. Moreover, suppliers will bring with them proprietary technologies to be used in their customers' products, whereas customers may also jointly develop new products with suppliers and share with them their new-product configurations and architectures. Control over technology will continue to be a major issue as this process moves forward. Supply chain partners will have to reach an understanding over who controls the technology, what is fair regarding shared ownership, and determine an appropriate division of return on investment for the technology.

In the computer industry, technology ownership is becoming an increasingly important issue as manufacturers and suppliers collaborate in building new products that often have product life cycles of less than six months. In one major company, all of the technology ownership issues are decided *early in the relationship.* All suppliers are required to sign a standard contractual agreement *prior* to the start of all design work with the buying company. This contract outlines the general nature of the relationship between the company and the supplier and establishes a protocol for issues such as nondisclosure of confidential information and patent rights for inventions related to the design activity. Such a contract is required before any business takes place with a supplier, and serves to define the underlying expectations for the future relationship.

Technology ownership and splitting market share will become even more important because of the increasing trend toward consumer direct marketing being driven by technologies such as the World Wide Web. It is estimated that by 2005, over 20 percent of product sales will be directly from manufacturer to consumers, thereby eliminating distributors and retailers. As this trend unfolds, there will undoubtedly be conflicts regarding market access, market share, and risk/cost/benefit sharing between the parties involved.

INCREASED SERVICE EXPECTATIONS

Most companies today are focusing primarily on the elements of a business transaction that take place at a single point in the supply chain. However, future challenges will involve how to manage both the pretransaction and posttransaction elements. Because of increasing customer expectations, companies must find ways to determine customer needs, even before customers themselves know what their requirements will be! Such information might be developed by reviewing customers' preferred configurations and product designs, which leads to improved planning of processes prior to the actual transaction. Posttransaction service will also become increasingly critical for supply chain members. After the transaction has occurred, companies in a supply chain will need to identify methods of guaranteeing that customers will return to them for future business. Companies must find innovative ways to provide ongoing service to customers so that they can offer integrative solutions to their problems for a given future planning horizon.

LEVERAGE

Power bases in supply chains have shifted from manufacturers in the early 1980s to large distributors and retailers such as Wal-Mart and Best Buy in the 1990s. As companies continue to merge and acquire one another, power bases will continue to shift up and down the supply chain. This positive tension is in general a good thing, but the specter of too much control residing with a single supply chain member is a constant threat to organizations. How can a less powerful supply chain member achieve a competitive advantage in the face of this power imbalance?

MASS CUSTOMIZATION

The previous issue will become even more complex when companies begin to "partition" their markets. In the future, organizations may belong in a "collage" of different supply chains, with each one focusing on a specific mix of end customers. This shift will also be determined by the aging of the "baby boomers" and may increasingly focus less on durable products and more on nondurable products and services. Customers will also continue to demand increasingly "mass-customized" products. This means that although aggregate demand forecasts may remain relatively stable, the number of different products will continue to increase, resulting in a fragmented array of customer options. Further, the forecasts for the product mix, demand at different locations, and volumes required will become increasingly difficult to develop and manage. Inventories may accumulate at one location, whereas another is starved for product and is turning away unhappy customers. How are companies to organize themselves to manage mass-customized markets in an integrated supply chain environment?

SHARED RESPONSIBILITY

As supply chain structures begin to evolve, increasing investments in distribution centers, information systems, training, transportation carriers, and new technology will be required to integrate members. The payoff on such investments is not always evident, yet managers are constantly evaluated on detailed financial measures, which in turn drive analysts' responses on Wall Street. One of the most closely monitored ratios lately has been a company's return on managed capital and economic value added, which measures the return achieved given a company's existing level of debt and asset base. To justify supply chain investments, managers will need to determine who takes on the risk of the investment, and who is entitled to the reward if and when it pays off. There will be no easy solutions in determining these financial arrangements. Such interorganizational issues will continue to pose a challenge to supply chain managers.

Managing the Global Supply Chain

Trade is increasingly taking place within blocs, such as the European Union, the North American Free Trade Area, and other regional groups. These blocs are established to promote regional development, which often leads to tariff and nontariff barriers to imports from outside of the bloc. Global companies wishing to supply markets within these blocs will eventually have to set up production inside the bloc if they wish to serve their markets with significant volume. The result accelerates a phenomenon already taking place that emphasizes the growth of intraregional economies and trade, at the expense of trade from outside of these blocs.[1] Table 6-1 shows the increasing growth of world trade in different regions of the world. In particular, growth in China, Asia Pacific, central and eastern Russia, and Latin America has escalated in the last few years.

Another important trend in this regard is that the bulk of international trade takes place in materials and intermediate components. Global corporations will ship semimanufactured products between their own facilities or from suppliers to assembly plants and distribution centers. The trend toward global supply chains has been fueled by needs for centralized research and development, the development of homogeneous markets and global products and global market segments for many products, the need for economies of scale in specific industries, wage differentials between advanced countries and other less developed countries, and political efforts to maintain low tariff barriers. Global networks have also been further aided by lower transportation and communication costs, the explosion of the World Wide Web and Internet, and the expansion of services that connect remote parts of the world with each other and with major markets. Finally, the development of organizational capacity to manage complex supply chains has improved.

TABLE 6-1 Growth in the Value of World Merchandise Trade by Region, 1990–1994 (billion dollars and percentage)

Exports *Value* *1994*	*Exports Annual Change*				*Imports* *Value* *1994*	*Imports Annual Change*		
	1990–1994	*1993*	*1994*			*1990–1994*	*1993*	*1994*
4090	5	−1	13	**World**[a]	4,210	5	−1	13
680	7	5	11	North America[b]	845	7	9	14
185	6	6	16	Latin America	220	15	9	16
1795	2	−7	13	Western Europe	1,795	1	−10	12
1525	3	−7	13	European Union (12)	1,525	2	−11	12
245	2	−8	16	EFTA	225	−0	−11	16
120	3	7	17	Central/Eastern Europe and the former USSR	115	0	8	11
55	4	−2	21	Central and Eastern Europe	65	9	9	13
90	−3	−7	2	Africa	100	1	−4	3
120	−2	−2	−0	Middle East	120	5	−4	-3
1105	11	7	15	Asia[a]	1,020	10	8	16
395	8	7	10	Japan	275	4	4	14
120	18	8	32	China	115	21	29	11
420	12	9	18	Six East Asian traders[a,c]	450	13	8	20

[a] Excluding Hong Kong re-exports and imports for re-export.
[b] Canada and the United States.
[c] Chinese Taipei, Hong Kong, Republic of Korea, Malaysia, Singapore, and Thailand.
Source: World Trade Organization (http://www.unicc.org/wto).

[1] Philip B. Schary and Tage Skjott-Larsen, *Managing the Global Supply Chain* (Copenhagen: Handelshojskolens Forlag, 1995).

A number of important issues will have to be addressed in the coming decade with respect to global supply chains:

- What are the critical success factors for managing the global supply chain?
- In a global context, how does crossing international borders influence management decisions in the supply chain?
- How can management organize this process to serve the needs of global corporations?
- Is it even possible to manage a task of this size and scope?

Economic structures will have a major effect on how global supply chains are designed and developed, including both technical separation in production and distribution and in the production process and ownership of functions. A supply chain design will also be impacted by risk, trade restrictions, and long lead times. For instance, transportation systems required to manage supply chains in European markets are very unique. The movement toward a single market has led to an impending set of bottlenecks that will occur in the already strained transportation infrastructure. This structure is being challenged by the deregulation of the transport market and the liberalization on cabotage (i.e., carrying goods in domestic commerce by a foreign carrier). (These trends are currently being disputed and resisted by the German trucking industry.) A number of other significant transportation barriers exist in Europe, including the problems associated with nationally owned rail networks, water transport, and the new types of transport operators that may emerge in the coming years. In the next decade, we may witness the emergence of pan-European companies, megacarriers, subcontractors, and niche carriers, all seeking to fill different market needs within the European Union.

In other regions of the globe, the infrastructure to deploy an integrated supply chain presents even a greater set of challenges. Emerging markets such as China, India, Latin America, Southeast Asia, Africa, and central Europe have incredibly large numbers of consumers with rapidly rising spending power. A visitor to any of these countries will be bewildered by the number of global corporations attempting to form joint ventures, build plants and distribution centers, and establish market channels in an effort to "get a piece of the action" found in these rapidly growing markets. However, the infrastructure within many of these countries is not adequately developed for these changes. Legal constraints exist that prevent many common supply chain systems from being deployed. Shipments may be held in customs for interminable periods for any number of reasons. Corruption and bribery are commonplace in many countries, yet organizations must uphold their ethical policies in the face of these demands. Infrastructure is often primitive. Highway systems are inadequate in scope, and roads are often in poor repair. In other cases, transportation may be nearly impossible at certain times of the year due to adverse weather conditions, such as monsoon rains. Telecommunication systems are often unreliable. In some cases, workers may be unfamiliar with the technology and may even unknowingly destroy equipment due to lack of proper training. Negotiation in such countries with potential alliance members can also be challenging, as domestic nationals may place little trust in Western managers and present extravagant requirements for doing business. Governments may also be unstable, resulting in constantly changing leadership with varying levels of support for the foreign corporations doing business in their country. Finally, rapidly fluctuating currency markets and economies can change a fair economic proposal into a major financial loss in a relatively short period. In the face of these problems, developing global suppliers, managing global operations, and shipping to global customers becomes an increasingly complex process fraught with uncertainty and risk. Corporations will need to develop personnel with foreign language, negotiation, and problem-solving skills, who are willing to be assigned to these areas. These individuals may be faced with a daunting set of challenging problems and will need to be flexible, open to change, and skilled at developing key relationships with new supply chain members.

The "Greening" of the Supply Chain[2]

The roots of environmentalism can be traced to the period during World War II when severe material shortages occurred worldwide. As a result of these shortages, people were forced to become creative and reuse or recycle many different materials. More recently, in response to heightened government regulation and increasing public awareness of the effects of industrial production on the environment, many organizations are now undertaking massive initiatives to restructure their supply chain processes and products to minimize their environmental impact. A number of manufacturing firms have already begun to develop environmentally friendly practices. Hewlett-Packard has made "green" part of its top-level corporate mission, along with time-based competition and cost reduction, and has reduced releases of toxic chemicals 71 percent.[3] Dow Chemical and General Motors have already established functions that are specifically responsible for waste and recycling management. Xerox has developed a feedback loop, which includes the "reverse logistics" process involving the removal of old equipment from its customers' facilities, the removal of good parts from these old products, and the disposition of scrap parts into recycling efforts (see Figure 6-1). International Paper is investing in large-scale ink-removal processes to tap into the growing market for recycled paper.[4] All of these firms have come to realize that *recycling reduces energy requirements, reduces gaseous and solid pollutants, and conserves raw materials.*[5] As a result of adopting environmentally friendly supply chain practices, these firms have also become more competitive and have improved their financial performance.

In undertaking initiatives to implement "environmentally friendly practices" that have an impact on the level of waste produced, manufacturing organizations are adopting a variety of both short- and long-run strategies. Ideally, environmentally friendly practices begin at the product design stage. That is, design engineers should consider the recycling content of products before production begins and consult with supply chain managers in determining the availability of such materials. This trend has already begun in European countries such as Germany, in which manufacturers are held responsible for the total cost of recycling or disposal of all materials used in their product (including packaging). This has led to radical redesigns of German products such as automobiles, food packaging, and shipping materials in order to increase their recyclable content.[6] In the future, there will be more and more products produced entirely of recyclable materials, and organizations will have to make all supply chain decisions within the context of environmental concerns.

---

[2] Adapted from S. Melnyk and R. Handfield, "Greenspeak," *Purchasing Today,* July 1996, pp. 32–36.

[3] Faye Rice, "Who Scores Best on the Environment?" *Fortune,* July 26, 1993, pp. 59–60.

[4] "How Green Is Green Paper?" *Business Week,* November 1, 1993, pp. 60–61.

[5] U.S. Environmental Protection Agency, *Report to Congress on Resource Recover,* April 1973. See also *Phoenix Quarterly,* Institute of Scrap and Iron, Fall 1980, p. 10.

[6] Francis Cairncross, "Waste and the Environment," *The Economist,* May 29, 1993, pp. 50–65.

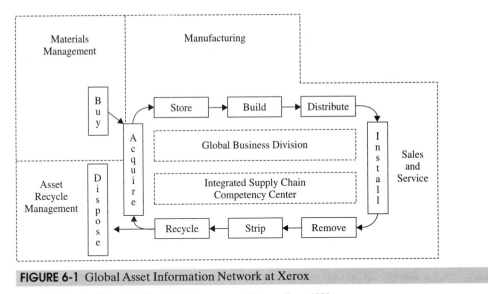

FIGURE 6-1 Global Asset Information Network at Xerox

Source: F. Hewitt, Council of Logistics Management, Proceedings, 1993.

Until companies reach this level of environmental awareness, many organizations must take interim steps that will have an immediate effect on waste reductions. There are several reasons for this necessary expediency. First, government regulations are becoming increasingly harsh on polluters. The Clean Air Act of 1990 imposes large fines on producers of ozone-depleting substances and foul-smelling gases, and the Clinton administration is introducing laws regarding recycling content in industrial materials.[7] Second, the number of states willing to open new landfill sites is shrinking rapidly, while the available landfills are filling up rapidly. Third, critical shortages of different types of raw materials, especially minerals, are forcing firms to increase their recycling efforts for these critical commodities. Fourth, manufacturers are seeking to become leaner and more cost effective, and greater pressure is being put on supply chain managers to seek cost reductions in material procurement, transportation, and disposition.

Within the context of these corporate initiatives, supply chain managers will play an increasingly important role in implementing environmentally friendly practices. The supply chain is central to this issue for several reasons. To begin with, supply chain managers are the primary agents of change in making decisions about the procurement and disposition of materials and are responsible for the entire flow of materials throughout the supply chain. Design decisions, cost control, manufacturing planning and control, and supply-base strategy all have a major effect on the environmental performance of an organization.

To understand the impact of the supply chain, consider that the total cost of production is the sum of the costs of labor, materials, and overhead *minus* any return from the successful sale of all kinds of surplus materials. Disposition of surplus materials, including (1) scrap and waste, (2) surplus, obsolete, or damaged stock, and (3) surplus, obsolete, or damaged equipment, is, therefore, important not only to the environmental

---

[7] "How Green Is Green Paper?"

movement in North America but also to the profit maximization objective of North American firms. This fact is frequently overlooked by supply chain managers, who often hold diverse views on environmental issues, ranging from those who are active environmentalists, are merely sympathetic to the cause, or view it as a radical conspiracy against big business.

In integrating "green" approaches into the purchasing function, two generic types of orientations are generally adopted by organizations: *proactive* versus *reactive* supply chain approaches (see Figure 6-2).[8]

FIGURE 6-2 Environmentally Friendly Supply Chain Practices

Materials Function	*Proactive*	*Reactive*
Supplier Selection and Evaluation	• Disclose and label material composition • Consider long-term costs of doing business with supplier • Reusable packaging and shipping materials • Use suppliers who can show evidence of sustainable and well-managed sources of raw materials • Require supplier participation on industry-wide environmental panels and organizations • Environmental risk assessment • Sustainable resource management	• Environmental issues not included as an evaluation criterion • Dispose of packaging materials • Sole reliance on EPA regulations
Surplus and Scrap Disposition	• Careful analysis of material impacts *prior* to use in new products • Reclaim hazardous materials	• "After the fact" remedial actions to solve environmental disposition problems • Dump hazardous waste, and use nonspecialists to take care of the problem
Carrier Selection and Transportation of Hazardous Materials	• Environmental audits of major carriers • Extra protection on rail cars and trucks • Reduction of dumping extra leftover hazardous material	• Relatively little attention paid to transportation selection, except when a spill occurs
Product Design, Packaging, and Labeling	• "Cradle to grave" life cycle analysis of materials used at the design stage • Remanufacture • Recycle corrugated • Standardized, reusable containers • Label plastic parts for later reuse	• End-of-life strategies not part of design process • Dump products at end of life • No recycling • Nonreusable containers • No plastic labeling

[8] Melnyk and Handfield, "Greenspeak."

Reactive approaches refer to policies aimed at meeting the minimum set of actions required to comply with government regulations or customer requirements regarding environmental concerns. This includes such actions as the proper disposal of toxic waste, meeting emissions requirements, meeting recycling content requirements,[9] and maintaining adequate facilities to meet Environmental Protection Agency inspection criteria. In such cases, avoidance policies aspire to meet the minimum penalty associated with the failure to satisfy a set of "floors" dictated by customers and governments. Clearly, these "floors" differ according to industries, but the strategic equivalent is the same across industries.

Reactive approaches often rely solely on public relations ploys as a means to address the public's environmental concerns. These activities often involve token "feel good" measures, such as recycling Styrofoam cups in the office, rather than a full-fledged commitment to zero emissions. In other cases, reactive strategies are "end-of-pipe" strategies, in that they fail to address the source of the problem and merely attempt to minimize the effects of toxic elements in the air and water after they have already been produced. Such approaches are often considered as "add-ons" to corporate strategy, as opposed to a real commitment to improvement.

In contrast to reactive policies, proactive policies are maximization-oriented. They set about to reduce costs or maximize profits using waste reduction in a variety of programs designed to benefit both the environment and the firm's financial performance. With regard to the supply chain, four specific areas were identified as potential candidates for such programs:

1. Supplier selection and evaluation,
2. Surplus and scrap disposition,
3. Carrier selection and transportation of hazardous materials, and
4. Product design, packaging, and labeling.

During visits with a number of firms, these different policies were discussed with environmental engineers and purchasing and logistics managers. Clearly, the relative importance of these areas will vary according to the industry. However, in order to have a significant impact on corporate environmental initiatives, supply chain managers must become aware of the opportunities for proactive versus reactive policies within each of these areas, which are now described.

SUPPLIER SELECTION AND EVALUATION

There is a great deal of work that documents the various criteria used in the supplier selection process as well as ongoing supplier performance measurement systems, which generally assess quality, cost, service, and delivery.[10] However, many leading-edge companies are now considering the supplier's environmental record as a key determinant of performance. The suppliers' environmental practices relating to their sources of raw materials, disposal methods for scrap and surplus, how they reduce surplus packaging, their actions to reduce fuel usage, and whether they are using environmentally friendly practices to lower their cost of materials should all be addressed.

---

[9] "How Green Is Green Paper?"

[10] Lisa Ellram, "The Supplier Selection Decision in Strategic Partnerships," *International Journal of Purchasing and Materials Management,* Fall 1990, pp. 8–14.

An example of an industry where environmental considerations are considered to be very important can be seen in the office furniture industry.[11] At one major furniture manufacturer, environmental concerns are key components of the company's supplier selection and material disposition strategies. For instance, this company participates in a number of joint initiatives with suppliers and customers to solve environmental problems and to better manage environment-related processes. In this manner, the company is helping establish the industry-wide environmental standards and practices.

One of the most important supplier selection initiatives at this furniture company is in its wood procurement policies. Oftentimes, the nations with tropical forests are developing countries. Many of these countries have allowed indiscriminate commercial logging and often the destruction of entire ecosystems. To prevent contributing to this problem, the company has made several environmentally-driven sourcing decisions. To begin with, designers have eliminated all rosewood from their patented lounge chair. Although tropical woods are still an important part of their product line, the company *only* purchases tropical woods from suppliers who can document that they are responsible foresters. This means that supply chain managers work with their suppliers to develop and use management practices that consider environmental, economic, political, and social issues to ensure long-term viability of the forest. They also work with organizations such as the Tropical Forest Foundation and the International Tropical Timber Organization, and have participated in the renegotiation of the Tropical Timber Agreement.

The environmental aspect of supplier evaluation is also very important in the chemical industry. At Dow Corning of Midland, Michigan, a big part of supply chain management involves assessing the environmental policies and practices of suppliers (primarily other major chemical companies). Some of the evaluation criteria that address environmental issues include:

- Are the supplier's costs higher than those of competitors, potentially signifying that it has had to pay environmental cleanup fines in the past?
- Is the supplier in danger of being shut down by the government because of environmental violations?
- Is it a healthy company, and what is its employee exposure and safety records?

A key element of evaluation involves understanding and assessing the environmental risk associated with the particular chemical being purchased. Environmental risk is assessed by analysis of the quality of the item. Different purity levels will result in different waste considerations. For example, limestone has a low risk, but titanium dioxide has a very high risk. Dow looks for suppliers who are green according to industry standards.

SURPLUS AND SCRAP DISPOSITION

Companies must also find ways to reduce scrap and waste, and thereby send less material to landfills. This is becoming more important because of the limited number of landfills, which is due to the fact that people are increasingly protesting the opening of new landfills with an attitude of "not in my back yard" (NIMBY)!

A good example of an organization's efforts to manage portentially hazardous waste materials can be seen in an automotive company's policies about procurement of

---

[11] See R. Handfield, S. Walton, L. Seegers, and S. Melnyk, "The Green Value Chain: Practices from the Furniture Industry," *Journal of Operations Management* 15, no. 4 (1997), 293–316.

indirect materials for the plant. If a process engineer or maintenance person elects to bring a new material into the plant, such as an adhesive or paint, the engineer must first file a Material Safety Data Sheet ("MSDS") with the plant's environmental engineer. The environmental engineer serves as a contact person to ensure that the emissions standards are being met, and the material must be approved by a Hazardous Materials Approval Committee. This committee is composed of a cross-functional team of employees that may work with the new hazardous materials, the fire marshal, and other employees who complete the reports that must be filed with the EPA and other regulatory agencies. If the composition of the material is unknown, the implementation process is delayed until the suppliers disclose any and all ingredients for materials that require an MSDS. Even in cases when the supplier has refused to provide this information on the grounds that the material composition is proprietary, the company will refuse to introduce the new material into the plant until its environmental effects are fully known. The supplier will simply not be allowed to do business with the company under these conditions! Hence, the plant environmental engineer plays a key role as a liaison and information support person to aid purchasing and plant employees who are encountering potentially hazardous environmental situations.

In the furniture industry, many companies are seeking to reduce scrap and hazardous waste disposal through a number of mechanisms. Hazardous liquids used in the manufacturing processes are reclaimed, and scrap materials such as steel, cardboard, polyfoam, and fabric are recycled whenever possible. At one company, waste is handled by trained specialists, and in cases when it contracts the disposal of hazardous solids, it is very active in its relationship with the contractor.

Another company has sought to eliminate hazardous wastes at the design stage and has worked closely with external sources in implementing environmental initiatives. In the manufacturing area, the company has worked to be an industry leader in water-based transfer processes for coatings and has sought to limit the amount of formaldehyde emitted by its adhesives. It has also worked on the wood yield rates within its processes by employing computer-controlled cutting systems and computer-based cutting pattern systems. It is also diligent in working with state environmental and safety agencies, has a high-level representative who serves on the federal solid waste board, and has played an active role in the development of various federal environmental regulations and guidelines.

CARRIER SELECTION AND TRANSPORTATION OF HAZARDOUS MATERIALS

The transportation of materials in the supply chain is an important factor to monitor. Dow Chemical considers environmental concerns as a critical feature of its supply chain transportation policies.[12] As a member of the Chemical Manufacturers Association, Dow is a participant in the "Responsible Care" program initiative. Responsible Care involves a dedication to act responsibly regarding the community's concerns about chemicals, including their manufacture, transportation, use, safe disposal, health and safety issues, prompt reporting of problems or regulatory violations, and counseling of customers. This initiative was initially driven by the Valdez principles. The Valdez principles were devel-

---

[12] Melnyk and Handfield, "Greenspeak."

oped as a result of the Exxon *Valdez* oil spill in Alaska. It is interesting to note that the Valdez principles were at first perceived as too difficult to meet, especially by the top environmental executive representation on the board of directors—this requirement has now been espoused by Dow.

Carrier selection is a critical consideration in the purchase of raw materials. Dow carefully analyzes its supplier's capabilities regarding distribution, safety, incidents, health records, and adherence to Responsible Care. Generally, only suppliers who are signatories to Responsible Care will be considered. If not, they are viewed on an exception basis—will the supplier subscribe in the future? Dow specifies sources and routings and then relies on the supplier to comply. The supplier will be allowed to move the product if it is considered safe. Otherwise, Dow will control product transportation and arrange distribution. Dow has its own group of contract carriers to carry out this function.

As a leader in transportation safety, Dow Chemical has designed special railcars for carrying hazardous chemicals to prevent the likelihood of a spill. The cars have extra-thick steel armor to prevent punctures from releasing toxic liquids and gases in the event of a derailment. In addition, special couplings have been designed to reduce the likelihood that they would puncture the tanks. Finally, Dow designed a special tank that would reduce the amount of material left over in the tank after pumping it out. Normally, this leftover material would be thrown out when the tank is cleaned. In this manner, Dow helped to set the standard for railcars determined by the Chemical Manufacturers Association (CMA). Although these precautionary measures cost more, the cost of litigation, cleanup of a spill or accident, and loss of customer goodwill would far surpass the extra investment.

PRODUCT DESIGN, PACKAGING, AND LABELING

Companies that are truly leading edge in creating a green supply chain use techniques such as life-cycle analysis, which identifies all of the potential environmental effects of using a given material in a product from "cradle to grave." Although this requires a significant development effort, it can measurably improve environmental performance for a product throughout its life cycle. Many companies are now seeking ways to reuse and recycle products after they have reached the end of their useful life. This requires a number of innovative approaches, including closer cooperation with customers in the supply chain.

One furniture manufacturer visited by the authors has created a database for environmental programs that are currently active within the firm. This database helps its sales force answer specific environmentally oriented customer questions. In addition, the company produces and distributes numerous brochures, white papers, and videos about the handling of environmental issues. These actions are a function of the company's founder, who had strong philosophical beliefs about the role of business in the community and believed that organizations should act as "stewards" for the environment. These beliefs filtered down throughout the organization over the years and eventually became a key part of the company's mission statement.

A separate and very profitable division of this company focuses on remanufactured furniture. The company acquires used furniture, sends it to the remanufacturing division. This division recycles materials that can no longer be used and refurbishes the furniture, which it sells in secondary markets. In addition, the company is recycling metal chair arms because it offered a new feature, adjustable chair arms. When customers buy these new arms, they can arrange for pickup of the old arms by the dealer. This reverse logistics service has been well received by the company's customers, and salespeople even claim that it has helped to win orders over their competitors in some cases.

Packaging is another important element to be managed in greening the supply chain. Corrugated packaging is being used more extensively because it is easier to recycle. Standardized, reusable shipping containers are also replacing disposable ones—in fact, such containers can be used as a good "kanban" (signal) to indicate the need for a JIT delivery between buyers and suppliers. For instance, the same furniture company mentioned previously uses molded plastic trays that accommodate a fixed number of parts, which can be stacked easily and then stretch-wrapped. As pieces are removed, workers simply pile up the trays for return to the supplier. The packaging tray is lightweight and easy to handle and is composed of plastic material that would otherwise be destined for a landfill. These packages also help promote productivity—the labor required to handle the packaging has been reduced by 40 percent.

This same company is now requiring its suppliers to label the chemical composition of plastic items. This is so future recyclers will know the exact content of the different types of plastic found in the parts. One of the major problems associated with recycling plastic is that there are so many different variations that it becomes difficult to determine the appropriate process to use for recycling. By documenting the material composition, future recycling efforts can be significantly improved.

These examples illustrate the importance of environmental considerations being integrated into supply chain decisions. All of the companies discussed here believe that they have an obligation to the public at large to make environmentally responsible decisions throughout their supply chains. This goes beyond simply being a "good corporate citizen"; this means taking a leadership role on key environmental issues. Many companies are also finding that such policies are not only good business decisions from a public relations perspective but also good business decisions from a profitability perspective![13]

Design for Supply Chain Management

Supply chain members will increasingly need to improve coordination not only in the area of demand replenishment but also in the area of demand generation through joint development of new products. By joining forces and sharing design information and technology trends, significant synergies can be achieved to create new products that can quickly capture market share. An equally important benefit of this collaboration is the increased standardization and simplification of product designs that can lead to a "design for supply chain" approach. This approach is likely to become more frequently used in the future.

Design for supply chain extends the concept of "design for manufacturability," which refers to the process of simplifying product designs to allow easier manufacture and assembly, to the broader scope of the entire flow of material across different supply chain entities. A product structure defines the set of component modules or elements for a product or a family of products. It influences both production and distribution

[13] M. Porter, and C. van der Linde, "Green *and* Competitive," *Harvard Business Review* 73, no. 5 (1995), 120–134.

processes for a number of reasons. First, production flexibility and responsiveness are improved when components are interchangeable, and distribution complexity is minimized when standard components reduce inventory requirements.

An important attribute associated with a product's design is the actual complexity of the design, with respect to the number of standard parts and components that go into the final product. Such attributes can have a significant impact on manufacturing and overall supply chain performance. For example, simulation studies have found that product structures with fewer end items, more intermediate items, and fewer levels in the bill of materials are associated with lower inventories and higher customer service.[14] Several firms have found that reducing the number of parts in a product helped avoid quality problems occurring later in manufacturing, which also led to lower direct labor and overhead costs associated with receiving, scheduling, purchasing, storing, and moving parts throughout the supply chain.[15]

Design complexity affects performance both in the new-product development cycle and throughout the demand-fulfillment cycle. By effectively reducing design complexity in the initial product development stage, fewer engineering change notices (ECNs), fewer quality problems, and fewer new processes to develop and implement can result in shorter lead times. For instance, John Deere & Company used multifunctional design teams consisting of product and manufacturing engineers, marketing, manufacturing management, and outside suppliers to reduce the number of parts used by 30 percent and the number of operations by 45 percent, resulting in lead-time reductions of 75 percent in its product lines.[16] Design complexity is reduced through the increased use of existing and standard components, integration of suppliers early in the product development process, reduction in the number of options for the product, simplification of the assembly process, use of design reviews, and knowledge and understanding of existing manufacturing capabilities by design teams. Value engineering activities can also be built into the design process with the objective of reducing the cost and complexity of a product while retaining the original specifications to the highest degree possible. Value engineering involves creating a catalog of internally produced parts, reviewing the catalog while the design is still in a formative stage, and providing a cost function for parts. In so doing, existing parts are used more often and part proliferation is avoided.

In recent years, technology has also enabled companies to offer innovative solutions to the dilemma of mass-producing standard items that are easier to manage from a supply chain perspective but can still be customized to customer's specific needs (see the Solectron case in chapter 5). For instance, in the electronics industry, field programmable gate array (FPGA) integrated circuits can be mass-produced, yet configured by distributors in the field to a customer's specific application in its computer network. This avoids having to produce an application specific integrated circuit (ASIC), which would cost much more because of the small batch run. New research in product technology will continue to drive design for supply chain improvements in the future in the electronics and other industries as well.

---

[14] L. Krajewski, B. King, L. Ritzman, and D. Wong, "Kanban, MRP and Shaping the Manufacturing Environment," *Management Science* 33 (1987), 39–57.

[15] R. Walleigh, "Product Design for Low-Cost Manufacturing," *Journal of Business Strategy* 4 (1989), 37–42.

[16] J. Kirik, "New Product Design at John Deere," *Proceedings of the 1989 American Production and Inventory Control Society Just-in-Time Conference* (Falls Church, VA: APICS, 1989).

Designs for supply chain processes have resulted in major improvements in supply chain performance. For example, a major manufacturer of personal computers (PCs) decreased the number of final assembly parts from 160 to 25, leading to fewer suppliers in the chain (i.e., reduced from 600 to 50), shortened manufacturing lead times (4.00 hours to 1.25 hours of labor), and fewer steps in the process (allowing the workforce to be reduced from 633 employees to 291).[17] Another strategy used at Western Data was the development of a set of design rules that helped reduce complexity, such as limiting the number of exotic or unique components, avoiding electrical cables and other flimsy parts, designing modular products with fewer items, and designing for ease of assembly.[18]

As product designs become more complex and less manufacturable, there is generally an increase in the number of possible options and configurations of the product, as well as an increase in the number of nonstandard parts. On the other hand, using fewer options and more standard parts results in products that are less complex and more adaptable to changes in product mix and volume, leading to more predictable planning and forecasting throughout the supply chain.[19]

In many industries, complexity is a difficult property to manage and in fact may be a function of several external factors. A good example is the fiber-optic cable industry, where the number of possible end items numbers in the hundreds due to the range of options available, even though the actual product consists of about 25 parts. In several fiber-optic cable firms visited by the authors, only 40 percent to 50 percent of the parts were standard. The fiber-optic cable industry is currently in the growth stage of the product life cycle, meaning no international standards exist that establish fixed guidelines for product standardization. To help manage the proliferation of possible product combinations, organizations are having to modularize their products at lower levels in the bill of materials. A product family can be designed as a product group with standardized components that can be assembled into a broader range of final products. The vast number of possible combinations can effectively create "mushroom products"—an analogy of the fact that few components "mushroom" into many possible end combinations.[20] Components can be held in inventory and assembled after the order arrives. This stage of production at the last possible moment is an application of postponement and can be performed at the factory or distribution center, or even within the distribution channel. Product structure of this type can compress the time between order and shipment because part of the production process has been undertaken in advance in anticipation of actual orders.

A good example of this strategy is an office furniture manufacturer that builds standardized furniture ahead of schedule (e.g., desktops in different colors, fabrics, partitions, etc.) and stores them in approximate quantities based on forecasts. This company provides a wide array of colors and stains for its products to meet the broad range of customer tastes found in the market. Major customers are demanding 24-hour turnaround on customized orders. When an order arrives, the parts are assembled according to the specific order and shipped within the 24-hour time frame.

---

[17] R. Walleigh, "Product Design for Manufacturing Success," *Proceedings of the 1989 American Production and Inventory Control Society Just-in-Time Conference* (Falls Church, VA: APICS, 1989).

[18] K. Crow, "Role of Product Design in JIT/TQC," *Proceedings of the 1989 American Production and Inventory Control Society Just-in-Time Conference* (Falls Church, VA: APICS, 1989).

[19] Henry Stoll, "Design for Life-Cycle Manufacturing," in *Managing the Design-Manufacturing Process,* ed. John E. Ettlie and Henry W. Stoll (New York: McGraw-Hill, 1990), pp. 79–113.

[20] H. Mather, "Design for Logistics (DFL)—The Next Challenge for Designers," *Production and Inventory Control* 25 (Fourth Quarter 1992), 7–10.

Another good example is Phillips Consumer Electronics, which uses a concept called diversity planning in product development. When the company centralized production of television sets within Europe in a few plants, establishing common components became a major challenge because of the differences in technical broadcast systems within the European countries, as well as with U.S. standards. The solution was to overdesign a standard integrated circuit to encompass all standards, even though only one is actually used in a given model. The standard component enables leveraging of purchases for cost savings and allows production of more than one model on the same production line, which simplifies scheduling and increases flexibility.[21] This is a situation where the company is utilizing a key component within the end product that may be more costly than the country-specific model but that results in a lower total cost when viewed from an integrated supply chain perspective.

Xerox Corporation has standardized the design and product structure of new copier machines to create products that can be introduced rapidly to world markets.[22] The initial step involved assigning joint design teams for each new product line from the parent company and its joint venture partners, Fuji-Xerox and Rank Xerox, combining different functional and geographic areas into single teams. Core products were developed with universal power supplies, and in some cases with dual language instructions, and a capacity for later design variations in order to match local market needs. These machines could be further adapted to local markets through specific adaptation kits.

Another related factor affecting product complexity is whether or not a dominant design has evolved over time. In newly developing markets, a number of product designs frequently are competing to become the industry standard.[23] In the telecommunications industry, for example, thousands of different options are required on telephone switches, and there is no way to reduce these specific customer demands.

Nowhere is this more important than in industries with short product life cycles. For instance, one company interviewed manufacturers' products with life cycles ranging from six months to two years. The company faces the engineering challenge of developing products that meet customers' requirements for higher performance (e.g., speed and capacity) and yet also consume the same or less energy and space than existing products. These products must also provide improved quality and shorter development time, all while meeting market-driven cost targets. The basic technology of these products has not changed dramatically since they were first introduced nearly 40 years ago. However, the more demanding performance requirements have driven technological improvements in the materials, components, and subassemblies used within the product. The most significant technological advances for these products have been and will continue to be made in the components and subassemblies that create functionality for the basic technology. In seeking to develop products that are easier to manage from a supply chain perspective, supply chain partners with this company have pushed for product standards. Customers, manufacturers, and suppliers have formed an industry group that meets every quarter to review proposals and share opinions on emerging

[21] J. Boorsma, "Diversity Planning," *Logistics News (Philips Consumer Electronics)* 102 (January 1991), 2.

[22] M. E. McGrath and R. W. Hoole, "Manufacturing's New Economies of Scale," *Harvard Business Review* 70 (May–June 1992), 94–102.

[23] David Teece, "Profiting from Technological Innovation: Implications for Integration, Collaboration, Licensing and Public Policy," *Research Policy* 15 (1986), 285–330.

product standards. Over 250 companies are involved in the effort. Two acceptable standards have been adopted as a result of these efforts.

This industry collaboration is beneficial for all parties involved. Customers may better manage new-product introductions as the standards help them plan their product designs. Suppliers are able to identify technology requirements early on, which allows them to invest in the capabilities and capacity requirements needed to meet challenging project goals. Furthermore, suppliers may influence or develop standards relevant to their products and processes.

Other important design issues to consider are those elements of the design that may facilitate movement of the product through its supply chain channels.[24] An increasing number of shipments are now taking place via intermodal transportation, which utilizes some combination of sea, air, trucking, or rail modes. Products are increasingly being stored in "containers," which allows easier storage on carriers and facilitates movement between the different transportation modes. Design decisions can have a major impact on the ease with which products can be stored, assembled, shipped, broken down, and delivered to customers. Supply chain transportation experts should participate early in the design cycle to ensure that these issues are addressed in the design process. Designing products requires adopting a supply chain perspective that includes the entire process required to move the product to customers, including transportation, storage, and material-handling considerations. Some of the critical factors that need to be addressed include the following:

- *Design considerations.* The characteristics of the product that make it transportable, with ease of handling and stowability.
- *Packaging.* The degree of protection needed for product fragility, climatic conditions, dimensional considerations to fit unitized loads such as warehouse pallets, and labeling identification for automated bar-code scanning.
- *Monetary density.* This is the monetary value per unit of weight, such as dollars per kilogram, and is normally inherent in the nature of the product. It determines the mode of transport and the costs of storage. High-value products are less sensitive to transport rates but are more sensitive to inventory holding costs.
- *Physical density.* This is the ratio of cubic volume to weight. The ratio determines the costs of transportation and storage. Products with high volume-to-weight ratios are costly both to transport and store. Such products are best produced in local domestic locations in order to reduce transportation and storage costs.

Product design affects the costs of handling and shipping. One company producing and shipping electronic equipment incurred higher than necessary transportation costs because it failed in the design stage to consider whether the product could be shipped as a disassembled unit with less damage and at lower transportation cost. Another company developed products that were too large for the conveyor sorting system for the customer's preferred carrier. Although such details may seem minor at the design stage, they become significant later when the product begins moving through the various supply chain channels.[25]

---

[24] Schary and Skjott-Larsen, *Managing the Global Supply Chain.*
[25] Ibid.

A good example of design for supply chain is IKEA, an international furniture retailer.[26] Its furniture has high physical density and low damage potential, making it easier to ship. IKEA builds furniture that customers assemble themselves and specifically designs its products for ease of shipping and handling by both carriers and the final customer. Products are shipped as complete kits of components, to be held on store shelves and carried home by customers for final assembly. The cost savings come from both labor savings in final assembly and more efficient shipping as a result of higher physical density and low damage in transit.

Another excellent example of design for supply chain management was realized by Hewlett-Packard (HP).[27] HP manufactures printers for worldwide distribution at its Vancouver (Washington) division. The printers have a few country-specific components, such as the power supply and owner's manual. The U.S. factory produced the printer to meet worldwide demand forecasts, but often by the time they reached the international distribution centers, demand had changed, and the DCs had no flexibility to respond to changing demand patterns. This resulted in inventory imbalances, with simultaneous inventory stockpiles and backlogs (e.g., too many "Spanish" printers while being out-of-stock in Germany).

To address this situation, a project team studied the problem and analyzed the potential savings realized if the distribution center performed the final localization step (customized the printer for the local country) instead of the factories doing it. This concept is known as "demand for localization." This required input from engineering, manufacturing, and distribution. Engineering had to redesign the product so that the power supply module could be plugged in externally instead of being internal to the product. Buy-in from manufacturing was imperative because the tasks performed by the factories and DCs would change. Distribution also had to support the change, because it would now be responsible for procuring parts, power supply modules, and manuals, performing final localization operations, and ensuring quality. As a result of the change, both cost and service was improved, and HP now designs all of its new products to be localized at the DCs.

Intelligent Information Systems

As many authors have done, we have emphasized in this book the need for integration of the different supply chain information systems into a single system that spans multiple functions and processes. Without an integrated system for communication between partners in the supply chain, decision making is hampered severely. A number of integrated systems are currently being offered by SAP, BAN, Oracle, and other companies. Although these systems offer a single integrated system for capturing transaction information, making sense out of the resulting flow of information may result in "information overload."

Nowhere has this trend become more prevalent than in the recent proliferation of the World Wide Web in the last few years. The Web is essentially a tool that "sits" on top of the Internet and provides a user-friendly graphical interface for searching out information on

---

[26] Ibid.

[27] Hau L. Lee and Corey Billington, "The Evolution of Supply-Chain-Management Models and Practice at Hewlett Packard," *Interfaces* 25, no. 5 (September–October 1995), 42–63.

people, products, services, companies, and just about any area of interest possible. Although this technology is fascinating, it is important to note that the Web *requires human interaction:* It does not work on its own. Generally speaking, companies in an integrated supply chain do not want their users "signing on" to a supplier's or customer's Web site every time they want to conduct a transaction. This would be an excessively tedious and time-consuming process. Instead, the Web should be used as a search engine to get information on new products and services, or for exceptions when a very specific communication with a supplier or customer is required. Although the Internet can also be used as a "highway structure" for data, the Web itself is not a medium for conducting transactions. Instead, companies require application-specific systems that can handle all of the many daily transactions between supply chain members.

Because of the volume of transactions that occur within a single supply chain, the complexity of managing the material and information flows that occur can be daunting. A major challenge facing companies with integrated supply chain information systems is how to process and utilize the information available to users within the chain. To deal with this situation, companies are beginning to introduce new types of "intelligent" decision support systems. Such systems offer a three-tiered vehicle that allows:

- Better planning and decision making via intelligent decision support tools;
- Network systems with intelligent communications support; and
- Enterprise systems that offer intelligent operations response.

One of the major weaknesses of traditional supply chains is the lack of collaborative planning between supply chain partners. Moreover, some tactical demand requirements may be shared, but there is little collaboration in developing forecasting and replenishment strategies. The result is that decisions are made sequentially, with no joint planning, and predictably, these decisions are often mismatched and suboptimal. Sequential decision making does not account for possible variances in the system, which can sometimes be planned for using simulation and "what if?" analysis.

Traditional information systems also tend to focus on static forecasts. Decisions are made on the basis of "what will be based on what was." A more dynamic form of forecasting is known as *demand planning,* in which decisions are made on the basis of "what might be based on what is." These systems use real-time information to create different simulated scenarios. All relevant information is linked to these scenarios, including current demand distributions, probabilities of major customer preferences, existing inventory levels, supply chain performance measures, existing capacity at different levels in the supply chain, and corresponding predicted lead times. With these "most likely" decision support scenarios in place, users can make decisions that enable end-to-end optimization throughout the supply chain.

What makes these systems so important is the instability caused by inaccurate forecasts. An often-cited forecasting rule is "Sherman's Law of Forecasting Accuracy," which states that "Forecast accuracy improves in direct correlation to its distance from usefulness." This requires further explanation. Generally speaking, many aggregate forecasts are correct. For example, the total amount of beer consumed in the United States is fairly stable. A domestic beer producer, therefore, has an accurate estimate of how many gallons of beer will be produced and sold in aggregate next year. However, aggregate forecasts propagate huge errors based on units of measurement. If you were to ask that beer producer how many kegs versus six packs, bottles versus cans, and light versus regular brands are required at different locations in the United States, you would probably get a blank stare! Moreover, the mix of products and volumes is more critical than the overall aggregate level of beer produced but is almost impossible to predict. A customer whose current requirements call for a six-pack of a given company's bottled light beer is not likely to buy a keg of the company's brown ale if the six-pack is not available. Instead, the customer will probably buy an available competing brand.

Intelligent decision support systems allow users to model variations in product mix, volume, and demand simultaneously prior to execution of decisions. Such models consider costs, constraints, business objectives, customer segmentation, and other variables to make the best decisions based on simulated trials. Such systems also offer graphical environments for easy interpretation of results, so users do not have to possess detailed knowledge of mixed integer programs, algorithms, and the like. The interface also allows collaborative replenishment strategies, as information on inventory and demand levels at stocking points is pulled from the information systems of other channel members. The simulation models then create a simulated "confidence zone" with an optimal flow of product to meet the plan (see Figure 6-3). This zone creates a tolerance to the optimal flow based on risks associated with variability, cost, customer response, capacity, schedule deviations, and so on. Over time, users can monitor actual flows, planned flows, and gaps between the two. In this manner, users can compensate for location-by-location variability and prevent it from affecting the aggregate forecast and production levels, which in most cases are fairly stable and are not causing the problems. In so doing, supply chain members can maximize their gross margins at the fastest rate of return on capital employed, via an integrating mechanism between the physical world and information networks.

Supply chain information systems will need to provide a single point of contact for customer service, order fulfillment, shipment, and invoicing. Although this statement appears obvious, the challenges associated with developing such a system are significant.

When Things Go Wrong

Although the supply chain management concepts presented in this book are intuitively appealing and fairly straightforward, readers should nevertheless be aware of the challenges associated with adopting an integrated supply chain management approach. Change of this magnitude is not easy. Information and inventory systems do not manage supply chains; people do. Reengineering a supply chain requires every individual in

FIGURE 6-3 Simulated Optimal Product Flows

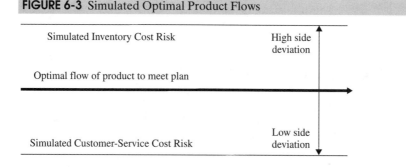

every functional area to be aware of the vision and goal that lie beyond all of the changes taking place around them. For this reason, it is absolutely critical that ongoing training, feedback, and communication take place with all people involved within every enterprise in the supply chain. The length of time to fully develop the levels of trust, training, and comfort for people within the supply chain will vary considerably company by company, so there is no magical formula for making this work. The experience of one company can serve to illustrate what happens when the change process is "short-circuited."

A major building products distributor decided to implement a new supply chain information system that would link the organization with its major customers and suppliers. This company sold a commodity product with relatively little demand or mix variance and had an established customer base that it had developed over thirty-five years. It identified an external consulting company to implement the new information system and, after assessing its capabilities, decided that there was a good potential fit. A five-year contract worth $25 million a year was signed with the consulting company, which would work in the building products distributor's five major warehouse locations across the United States. The new warehouse management system was anticipated to provide major benefits, including a 40 percent reduction in headcount (286 people) as a result of improved administrative processes. The new systems were to be put in place by consulting personnel, who would work side by side with the building products distributor's employees.

At first, managers in the warehouses believed that the system would make their jobs easier. However, when the consultants showed up, most of them were relatively young and inexperienced and possessed a somewhat "high and mighty" attitude. Among the experienced managers, the new visitors quickly became known as the "kids with laptops." As the consultants' air of superiority continued, managers who had been with the company for over thirty years began to "retreat into their shells" and in some cases took early retirement. As a result, replacements were transferred in who had been in dissimilar operations and who had no prior knowledge of the products or customers being served.

Thirty days prior to "flipping the switch" on the new system, things were in a state of chaos. The system itself was still not running, so there were no test data available to evaluate the feasibility or effectiveness of the system. Because there was no system, there was no employee training! Employees had no idea of how the system would work, or even what the computer screens would look like! Nevertheless, final employee headcount reduction (layoff) plans had already been implemented, and affected employees had been given their thirty-day notice. The level of concern at the facilities was running extremely high, but assurances were made that everything would work according to plan.

Five days prior to flipping the switch, the systems issues were finally resolved. Limited volumes of product flows were being tested through the system, and some initial testing was begun. The system appeared to work adequately, and employee training was initiated. At that time, a major customer notified the building products distributor that business had suddenly picked up, and that they would see a major volume spike in the next few days.

Had you been a decision maker in this scenario, what would you have done?

The answer to this question is clear, given the outcome. Fifteen days after system roll-out, all of the information systems had failed. In fact, incoming orders from customers had been input into the system and could not be retrieved, so there was no way of knowing what to ship to whom! Customers were not on-line and could not place any further orders. No contingency planning had taken place, because all of the attention had been focused on resolving the systems issues. The 40 percent headcount reduction did not take place, because these employees were still needed to run the system. Major customers who had loyally purchased only from this company for thirty-five years were actively trying to cancel their orders as quickly as possible and were placing these orders with a major competitor. Employees who had no adequate training were idle, and the entire business was essentially at a standstill. The CEO surveyed the ruins of the business and quietly stated that the business was almost in bankruptcy and his career and reputation ruined.

In this case, the system should not have been implemented until all individuals within the organization were comfortable with the new system or at least aware of the changes that were going to occur in the near future. Supply chain integration is a process that cannot be rushed, and the changes required throughout the process are significant. Once established, failure is not acceptable. Managers who enter the process must carry it through and devote appropriate levels of time, resources, and effort to making it work.

Summary

As mentioned in the first chapter, markets are more and more difficult to predict, and customer needs are an increasingly difficult target to hit. As supply chain management moves from the realm of concept to reality, new ways of doing business will continue to evolve. As these changes occur, organizations will have to respond, while maintaining a focus on the long-term vision of an integrated supply chain. Although no clear formulas exist for achieving this vision, we hope that the frameworks, cases, and examples discussed in this book can help readers to learn from the experience of others.

Index

A

Activity ratios, 77
Actra Business Systems, 30
Adversarial supply chain strategies, 11
Adverse selection, 87
Affect-based trust ("goodwill"), 86–87
Aghajanian, Mike, 22
Algorithms, scheduling, 37
Alignment, 73
Alliance development model, 69–83
  alliance conceptualization, 69, 70–71
  alliance confirmation, 69, 80–82
  alliance implementation/continuity, 69–70, 82–83
  alliance pursuance, 69, 71–80
  vertical components of, 69, 70
Alliances, strategic, 68–69, 95, 96–99
Ambiguous goals and objectives, 56
American Arbitration Association, 91
American Production and Inventory Control
    Society (APICS), 36
Anticipatory-scheduling, 130
Application processing node, 20
Application Specific Integrated Circuit (ASIC),
    147, 167
Arbitration, 90–91
Asgekar, Vinay, 53
Assessment of supply chain partner, 73–80
Assets, performance measures addressing, 65
Asymmetric investment, 87
Attributes, 27
Automation, 52
  cycle-time reduction by, 98, 132, 133–134
  of sales/order-processing, 100, 104–105
Automotive industry, surplus and scrap disposition
    in, 163–164
Available-to-promise, 38

B

"Balanced scorecard" approach to performance
    measurement, 63–64
*Balanced Scorecard: Translating Strategy into
    Action, The* (Kaplan and Norton), 63
Bar coding and scanning, 32
Barrett, Stephanie S., 19, 20
Barriers to alliance, 71, 82

Base Rate, Carrier Select, and Match Pay (software),
    29
Batching, 55
Benchmarking, 45, 132
Benevolence, affect-based trust and, 86
Biochemicals, case study involving, 123–136
  action team initiatives, 126–134
  cycle-time reduction workshop, 124–126
  project overview, 123–126
Blocked scheduling, 37
Bowersox, Donald J., 16
Bribery in emerging markets, 158
Bristol-Myers Squibb, 18
Bulk stock inventory
  with express shipment of reorders, 129
  with standard shipment of reorders, 127–129
Bullwhip effect, 17–18, 31–32
Business Document Gateway (software), 30
Business sense, 85
Business systems planning (BSP), 24, 25

C

Campbell's Soup, 32, 100
Carrier selection, environmental considerations in,
    161, 164–165
Challenges facing supply chain managers, 12. *See
    also* Future challenges and strategies
Chemical Manufacturers Association (CMA), 164,
    165
Clean Air Act of 1990, 76, 160
Clinton Administration, 160
Closs, David J., 16
"Co-destiny" relationships, 10
Collaboration. *See also* Interorganizational
    relationships
  dispute prevention in, 92
  on standards, industry, 169–170
Co-location, cycle-time reduction with, 99
Communication
  electronic data interchange (EDI), 31–32, 103
  for information requirements determination,
    22–23
  long cycle time due to poor, 56
  relationship management and, 9–11
Company profile information, 74

Compaq Computer, 50
Competence, trust and, 85–86
Competition, time-based. *See* Time-based
    competition
Competitive advantage, logistics as source of, 46
Competitive environment, 7–9
Competitor relationships between SCM members,
    43
Complete inventory, 107, 114, 115
Complexity, design, 167–168
Computer hardware and software company, case
    study of, 100–106
Computer industry. *See also* Information systems
    and technology
    channel relationships available to suppliers in,
        143–144
    proliferation of new technology, 6
Computer supplies, case study on consumable,
    94–99
Confidentiality, 154–155
Conflict management in interorganizational
    relationships, 12
Conflict resolution, 89–93
Consolidated distribution strategy of Daisytek,
    96–97, 98
Contacts across supply chain, establishing, 44
Continuous replenishment program (CRP), 32
Contract manufacturing in supply chain, 140–142
Contracts
    alliance confirmation through written, 80
    resolving contract disputes, 89–93
Controls
    cost/benefit analysis for, 56
    evaluating, 78
    excessive, 55–56
Con-Way Transportation Services, 35
Cook, Sarah, 45
Cooperation, limited, 57
Coordination, limited, 56
Corruption in emerging markets, 158
Cost/benefit analysis for controls, 56
Costs
    costs categories for international supply chain, 48
    of handling and shipping, product design and, 170
    performance measures addressing, 65
    total supply chain cost model, 150–152
Cost structure, evaluating, 75
Council of Logistics Management (CLM), 36, 46, 49
Councils, supply chain, 11, 144–145
Critical success factors (CSF), 24–25, 61
Cross-enterprise decision making, 150
Cross-functional perspective, 23–24
Cultural differences, international supply chains
    and, 48–49
Currency markets, fluctuating, 158
Customer order-fulfillment process. *See also* Order-
    processing system
    modeling, 126–131
    proactive approach to customer order
        information, 97
    worksheet, 60

Customer, power of, 11
Customer-oriented performance measurement, 62,
    65
Customer service, importance of, 16
Customization, mass, 7, 156, 167
Customs clearance, reducing time for, 131–132
Cycle time, 8–9, 54–61
    causes of long, 54–57
Cycle-time reduction, 57–61
    case studies of
        biochemical division, 123–136
        Daisytek's distribution strategy and, 98–99
        Insight Direct, 100–106
    continuous improvement efforts for, 60–61
    critical success factors in, 61
    key principles of, 130, 132, 133–134
    opportunities for, 57–61
    points of leverage for, 124–126
Cycle-time reduction team (CTRT), 58–60
Cycle-time reduction workshop, 124–126

D

Daisytek International, Inc., case study of, 94–99
Database, user definable, 38
Data capture, 7
Data interchange, 7
Data warehouse, 33
Debt ratios, 77
Decentralized distribution of Daisytek, 95–96
Decision support systems (DSS), 36–38, 172–173
Delivery time reduction, 8–9
Demand for localization, 171
Demand management, 38
Demand planning, 172
DeRoulet, David G., 49
Design capability, evaluating, 76
Design complexity, 167–168
Design for manufacturability, 166
Design for supply chain management, 145–146,
    166–171
Design for supply chain strategy, 146–147
Direct shipment process, 129–130
Dispute prevention, 92
Disputes, resolving contract, 89–93
Distribution at Daisytek International, 95–99
Distribution magazine, 29
Distribution management, 4
Distribution network, 4
Diversity planning in product development, 169
"Dock to stock" delivery systems, 9
Dow Chemical Company, 50–51, 159, 164–165
Dow Corning, 163
Downstream supply chain, external, 4

E

Effectiveness standards for alliance, expected, 80–81
Electronic commerce, 6, 29–31
Electronic data interchange (EDI), 31–32, 103
Electronic funds transfers (EFT), 7

Electronic scanning, 32
Eliminating, cycle-time reduction by, 130, 132, 133–134
Emerging markets, infrastructure in, 158–159
Emotion, dispute resolution mechanism and level of, 92
End-customer perspective on performance measurement, 65
Ends/means (E/M) analysis, 25, 26
Enterprise Transportation Management, 35
Entity-attribute analysis, 27
Environmentalism, 159–166
Environmental regulation compliance, evaluating, 76
European Community (EC), 48, 158
Evaluation of potential partner, 73–80
Excessive controls, 55–56
Expectations, increased service, 155
Expert system rules of DSS, 37
External logistics service providers, 47–48
External supply chains, 3–4, 42–43

F

"Fairness," perception of, 87
FedEx, 32, 96–99
Feedback systems, 82–83, 90
Fiber-optic cable industry, design complexity in, 168
Field Programmable Gate Arrays (FPGA), 147, 167
Financial capability/stability, evaluating, 76–78
Financial ratios, assessment using, 77–78
Flowcharts. *See* Process map (flowchart)
Forecasting, inaccurate, 172–173
Forms, poorly designed, 56
Fuji-Xerox, 169
Furniture industry, environmental considerations in, 163, 164
Future challenges and strategies, 153–175
  design for supply chain management, 166–171
  global supply chain management, 156–159
  "greening" of supply chain, 159–166
  intelligent information systems, 171–173
  problems in reengineering supply chain, 173–175
  risk sharing in interorganizational relationships, 154–156

G

Gagliardi, Gary, 52
General Electric (GE), 30–31, 32
General Motors, 159
Gertz, David, 46
Global inventory management, 6
Global Procurement and Supply Chain Benchmarking Initiative, 35
Global sourcing, 7
Global supply chain, 48–49, 156–159
Goals
  alliance, types of, 72
  ambiguous, 56
  compatible, of SCM members, 43

Good customers, 11
Goodwill, 86–87
Government regulations, 48, 76
Graphical user interface (GUI), 38
"Greening" of supply chain, 159–166
  carrier selection and transportation of hazardous materials, 161, 164–165
  proactive vs. reactive approaches to, 161–162
  product design, packaging, and labeling, 159, 161, 165–166
  supplier selection and evaluation, 161, 162–163
  surplus and scrap disposition, 160–161, 163–164
Grow to Be Great: Breaking the Downsizing Cycle (Gertz), 46
Gustin, Craig M., 51

H

Hardware, 28
Harrington, H. James, 58
Hazardous materials, transportation of, 161, 164–165
Heap, David, 94–95
Hewlett-Packard (HP), 49, 159, 171
Highway systems in emerging markets, 158. *See also* Transportation

I

IKEA, 171
Incentive costs and subsidies for international supply chain, 48
Incentives on special orders, 109–110
Industry collaboration on standards, 169–170
"Information overload," 171
Information sharing, 17, 19, 56, 81. *See also* Interorganizational information system (IOIS)
Information systems and technology, 6–7, 14–39
  applications, 28–38
    bar coding and scanning, 32
    data warehouse, 33
    decision support systems, 36–38
    electronic commerce, 6, 29–31
    electronic data interchange (EDI), 31–32, 103
    Internet, 6, 30, 33–34
    Intranet, 6, 34–35
  importance of, 14–19
  intelligent, 171–173
  interorganizational. *See* Interorganizational information system (IOIS)
  as key enabler for reengineering, 51–52
  problems in implementation of, 12
  Solectron's World Wide Materials System, 148–149
  World Wide Web, 6, 30, 33, 35–36, 171–172
Information systems capability, evaluating, 78
Information technology (IT), 15
Infrastructure
  in emerging markets, 158–159
  information technology, 16

Insight Direct, case study of, 100–106
Insights into current organizational practices, gaining, 44
Intangible costs, 48
Integrated supply chain approach, 5. *See also* Information systems and technology; Inventory management; Relationship management
challenges in implementation of, 12
Integrating network node, 20
Intelligent information systems, 171–173
Intercompany information access, 7
Intermodal transportation, 170
Internal functions, 2
Internal supply chains, 2–3, 42
International Paper, 159
International supply chains, 48–49, 156–159
Internet, 6, 30, 33–34
Interorganizational information system (IOIS), 19–28
defined, 19
EDI as useful component of, 133
information categories, 27, 28
information requirements determination for, 21–28
background information, 21–22
methods, 24–26
overview of, 22–24
prototype review, 27–28
translation to information systems prototype, 26–27
levels of participation, 20, 21
order-processing system in, 102–105
Interorganizational relationships
benefits of, 43–44
conflict management in, 12
risk sharing in, 154–156
Interpersonal competence, 85
Interviewing techniques, structured, 24–26
Intranet, 6, 34–35
Intraorganizational processes, 16
Inventory decision model, 110–112
Inventory management, 7–9. *See also* Retail inventory strategies, case study on
automation and, 52
complete inventory, 107, 114, 115
design for supply chain strategy, 146–147
global, 6
no-inventory approach, 107, 116
Pareto approach, 107, 109, 115, 116, 122–123
problems in implementation of, 12
vendor-managed inventory, 32
Investment, shared responsibility of, 156
IOIS. *See* Interorganizational information system (IOIS)

J

John Deere & Company, 167
Johnson Controls, 8
Joint application design (JAD), 24
Joint problem solving, 82

Joint projects between supply chain members, 44
"Just-in-case" approach to retail inventory, 109
Just-in-time (JIT) deliveries, 7, 50

K

Kallock, Roger W., 49
Kaplan, Robert S., 63
Konsynski, Benn, 20
KPMG Peat Marwick study (1995), 51–52

L

Labeling, product, 161, 165–166
Landfill availability, 160, 163
Layton, Mark C., 99
Legal alternatives to resolve disputes, 89–90
Legal constraints in emerging markets, 158
Leverage, 156
Life-cycle analysis, 165
Limited cooperation, 57
Limited coordination, 56
Linear programming capabilities of DSS, 37
Liquidity ratios, 77
Localization, demand for, 171
Logistics, 46
of international supply chain, 48–49
reengineering, 46–53
reverse, 4, 159, 166
role of third-party logistics service providers, 47–48
as source of competitive advantage, 46
total logistics management, 6
Logistics managers, responsibilities of, 4
"Logistics Renaissance," 1
Logitility Planning Solutions (software), 29
Longer-term relationship potential, evaluating, 79–80
Loyalty, 88–89

M

Management capability, evaluating, 74
Manufacturing costs for international supply chain, 48
Maquiladora operations, U.S.-Mexican, 61–62
Market share, splitting, 155
Mass customization, 7, 156, 167
Material-handling, product design and, 170
Material management, 10
Materials flow management, 40–66
lack of synchronization, 56
performance measurement, 61–65
reengineering logistics, 46–53
time and, importance of, 8–9, 53–61
understanding supply chains and, 41–45
Materials managers, responsibilities of, 3
Mediation, 91
Merle Norman, 52
Metasys Inc., 35
Minitrial, 91
Monetary density, 170

Monte Carlo computer simulation, 107
Moral hazard, 87
Movement costs for international supply chain, 48
Multiparticipant exchange node, 20
Multisite/multistage scheduling, 37–38

N

Nabisco, Inc., 32, 52
National Association of Purchasing Management (NAPM), 36
National Industrial Transportation League, 35
Negotiation of contract disputes, 90
Network control node, 20
Ng, Steve, 150
Nishimura, Koichi, 141
No-inventory approach, 107, 116
Non-value-added activities, 55
Norton, David P., 63

O

Objective performance information, 44–45
Objective performance measurement system, 11
Objectives, ambiguous, 56
Office furniture industry, environmental considerations in, 163
Openness with other party, goodwill and, 86
Operating standards, joint, 81
Operational component of alliance development model, 69, 70
Opportunities for cycle-time reduction, 57–61
Oracle Web Applications Server, 35
Order-change notices, 6
Order-processing system, 2
    EDI used in, 132–134
    at Insight Direct, case study on, 100–106
    in interorganizational information system, 102–105
    modeling order-fulfillment process, 126–131
Organizational dynamics, supply chain, 18–19
Original equipment manufacturers (OEMs), case study of contract manufacturer for, 138–152
Osram, Inc., 17
Outsourcing of logistics activities, 47–48
Overhead costs for international supply chain, 48

P

Packaging, 161, 165–166, 170
Parallel vs. serial operations, 55
Pareto inventory approach, 107, 109, 115, 116, 122–123
Partnership, 132. *See also* Alliance development model
    defined, 47
    third-party, 47–48
    trust in, developing, 67, 83–89
    value, 152
Performance information, objective, 44–45
Performance measurement, 11, 60, 61–65, 81, 132
    "balanced scorecard" approach to, 63–64

mutual agreement of partners about, 81
objective, 11
of process cycle time, 60
Personnel capabilities, evaluating, 75
Phillips Consumer Electronics, 169
Physical density, 170
Planters LifeSaver unit of Nabisco, Inc., 52
Point-of-sale data, 7
Points of leverage, 124–126
Portfolio approach to information requirements determination, 22
Power, organizational dynamics and, 18–19
Power bases in supply chains, shifting, 156
"Principles of Cycle Time Reduction: You Can Have Your Cake and Eat It Too" (Wetherbe), 59
Privacy of information in Internet, 34
Proactive approach
    to customer order information, 97
    to "green" supply chain, 161–162
Problem awareness, 71
Problem solving, joint, 82
Procedures, poorly designed, 56
Process capability, evaluating, 75–76
Process component of alliance development model, 69, 70
Process map (flowchart), 42, 43, 58, 124, 125, 135–136
Procter & Gamble (P&G), 16, 17, 19, 32
Product design, environmental considerations in, 159, 161, 165–166
Product development, diversity planning in, 169
Product group with standardized components, 168–169
Production scheduling, 2, 78
Productivity, EDI and, 31
Product life cycles, industry standards for short, 169–170
Profitability ratios, 77
Promotion, confidentiality of, 154
Prototype, information systems, 26–28
Prototyping, cycle-time reduction by, 130
Puget Plastics, 150
Purchase order (PO) processing, excessive control of, 55
Purchasing managers, responsibilities of, 3

Q

Quaker Oats, 32

R

Rank Xerox, 169
Raw material shortages, 160
Reactive "green" supply chain approach, 161–162
Recovery, recycling, or reuse of products, 4, 159, 165–166
Reengineering
    key enablers for supply chain, 51–52
    logistics, 46–53
    problems in supply chain, 173–175

Regional trade blocs, 156–158
Regulations, government, 48, 76
Relationship management, 9–11, 67–93
    alliance development model, 69–83
    challenges in implementing, 12
    conflict resolution and, 89–93
    trust, developing, 67, 83–89
Reliability, trust and, 84–85
Remote I/O node, 20
Rent-a-judge, 91–92
Repair network, 4
Repeating process activities, 55
Research and development (R&D), 77, 155
Responsibility, shared, 156
Responsiveness, mutual agreement about, 81
Retailers, shift of power to, 18–19
Retail inventory strategies, case study on, 106–123
    complete inventory, 107, 114, 115
    inventory decision model, 110–112
    no-inventory approach, 107, 116
    Pareto inventory approach, 107, 109, 115, 116, 122–123
    simulation model on, 107, 112–114, 137
    special orders, improving acceptance rate on, 109–110, 116, 118
    total cost analysis of, 118–122
    traditional approach, 109
Reverse logistics, 4, 159, 166
Risk
    in interorganizational relationships, sharing of, 154–156
    organizational dynamics and, 18–19
    vulnerability and, 87, 88
Rockwell Semiconductor Systems, 53
Rummler-Brache Process Improvement Approach, 50–51

S

Scanning, electronic, 32
Scheduling, 2, 37–38
Scrap disposition, 160–161, 163–164
Security problems on Internet, 34
Sensitivity to long-term costs, 48
Serial vs. parallel operations, 55
Service expectations, increased, 155
Shared responsibility, 156
"Sherman's Law of Forecasting Accuracy," 172–173
Shipping and handling, product design and cost of, 170
Simulation models, 107, 112–114, 137
Software applications, 28–29
Solectron, case study of, 138–152
    background, 138–140
    contract manufacturing in supply chain, 140–142
    human resources, 148
    inventory planning, 146–147
    order fulfillment function, 145–146
    plant operations, 149–150
    sourcing function, 143–145
    strategic challenges, 142–143
    total supply chain cost model and, 150–152

World Wide Materials System (WWMS), 148–149
Sourcing, global, 7
Sourcing function, 143–145
Southern Motor Carrier, 36
Special orders, improving acceptance rate on, 109–110, 116, 118
Specific competence, 85
SQL interface of DSS, 37
Standards
    expected effectiveness, 80–81
    industry collaboration on, 169–170
Storage, product design and, 170
Strategic alliances, 68–69. See also Alliance development model
    Daisytek-FedEx, 95, 96–99
    of Solectron, 149–150
Strategic component of alliance development model, 69, 70
Structured interviewing techniques, 24–26
Structured query language (SQL), 37
Supplier councils, 144–145
Supplier network, 2, 3
Supplier selection and evaluation, environmental considerations in, 161, 162–163
Supplier sourcing strategies, policies, and techniques, evaluating, 79
Supply chain, 32
    basics of, 41–42
    external, 3–4, 42–43
    internal, 2–3, 42
    international, 48–49, 156–159
Supply-Chain Council, 36, 53
Supply chain councils, 11
Supply chain management, 32
    information systems and, 6–7, 14–39
    inventory management and, 7–9
Supply Chain Operations Reference Model (SCOR), 52–53
Supply chain partner node, 20
Supply Chain Planning (software), 29
Supply chain relationships. See Relationship management
Supply process worksheet, 59
Surplus materials disposition, 160–161, 163–164
"Switching" behavior, 117
Synchronization in materials movement, lack of, 56

T

Technological capability, evaluating, 75–76
Technologies. See also Information systems and technology
    mass customization and, 167
    mutual agreement about adoption of, 81
    as supply chain "enablers," 6–7
Technology ownership issue, 155
Telecommunications, 6, 158
Third-party partnership, 47–48
3M, 17
Time, performance measures addressing, 65
Time-based competition, 8–9, 53–61. See also Cycle time

Time pressures for dispute resolution, 92
Toshiba, 52
Total cost analysis of retail inventory strategies, 118–122
Total logistics management, 6
Total quality management philosophy, evaluating, 75
Total supply chain cost model, 75, 150–152
Trade blocs, regional, 156–158
Training, lack of/ineffective, 57
Transportation
    barriers to, 158
    global visibility into resources, 6
    of hazardous materials, 161, 164–165
    intermodal, 170
    product design and, 170
Transportation Consumer Protection Council, 36
Transportation Network Optimization (software), 29
Trial and error, prototype to allow for, 26–28
Trusting relationship, developing, 67, 83–89
    affect-based trust ("goodwill") and, 86–87
    competence and, 85–86
    loyalty and, 88–89
    reliability and, 84–85
    vulnerability and, 87–88

U

U.S. Department of Defense, 34
U.S.-Mexican maquiladora operations, 61–62
Universal Product Code (UPC), 32

Upscale men's shoes, case study on, 106–123
Upstream external supply chain, 3
User definable database, 38

V

Valdez principles, 164–165
Value engineering, 167
Value partnership, 152
Vendor-managed inventory (VMI), 32
Venkatraman, N., 28
Vulnerability, trust and, 87–88

W

Waiting, long cycle time caused by, 54–55
Wal-Mart, 16, 19, 32
Web, the. *See* World Wide Web (the Web)
Web sites, examples of, 35–36
Western Data, 168
Wetherbe, James C., 59
Whirlpool, Inc., 49
White, Monte, 95
World Wide Materials System (WWMS), 148–149
World Wide Web (the Web), 6, 30, 33, 35–36, 171–172
Written contracts, alliance confirmation through, 80

X

Xerox Corporation, 159, 169